Herbert Aptheker on Race and Democracy

Herbert Aptheker on Race and Democracy

A READER

Edited by Eric Foner
and Manning Marable

UNIVERSITY OF ILLINOIS PRESS
Urbana and Chicago

Manufactured in the United States of America
∞ This book is printed on acid-free paper.
C 5 4 3 2 1

Library of Congress Cataloging-in-Publication Data
Aptheker, Herbert, 1915–2003.
Herbert Aptheker on race and democracy : a reader / Herbert Aptheker ; edited by Eric Foner and Manning Marable.
p. cm.
Includes bibliographical references and index.
ISBN-13: 978-0-252-03029-1 (cloth : alk. paper)
ISBN-10: 0-252-03029-X (cloth : alk. paper)
1. African Americans—History. 2. African Americans—Politics and government.
3. United States—Race relations.
I. Foner, Eric. II. Marable, Manning, 1950– III. Title.
E185.A615 2006
973'.0496073—dc22 2006036184

Contents

Foreword

BETTINA APTHEKER

In September 1999, my father was invited to Columbia University for a series of lectures and to be honored by his colleagues in the Departments of History and Ethnic Studies. Herbert always enjoyed his visits to Columbia because it held a special place in his heart, and because he regretted that he was not able to be part of its history faculty as a consequence of the anti-Communist purges of the 1950s. He never regretted his political choices, of course, but he did miss Columbia. From this point of view, the invitation was especially kind. An informal gathering of old friends in a private home was also arranged. It was only a few months after the death of my mother, Fay P. Aptheker, and Herbert was devastated. My parents had been together for sixty-two years.

It was on this visit that the idea for an Aptheker reader was first proposed, and Eric Foner and Manning Marable graciously undertook the project. My father was thrilled. Although in failing health, he actively participated in the selection process of the essays to be included, and vigorously added his corrections, even as his handwriting gradually deteriorated. It should be noted that he loved everything he ever wrote and so a decision to delete one or another piece from this volume inevitably met with a bewildered query as to its failures. We assured him that it was largely a matter of space. After all, I explained, we can't reprint *everything!* Then he would smile sheepishly, and say, "Oh, of course, darling. Of course," very purposefully and as though it were a matter of no great importance. We regret that he died before this publication could be completed.

In addition to the editorial work of Eric and Manning, I would like to acknowledge the prodigious labors of Paul L. Kranz, who was among Herbert's closest friends. Paul met my father when he was a law student at Boalt Hall at the University of California, Berkeley, in the late 1970s where Herbert taught a course on racism and the law. Paul provided all the technical assistance that made this publication possible. I also wish to thank Clayborne Carson, director of the Martin Luther King Jr. Papers Project, Stanford University; Herbert Shapiro, professor emeritus, Department of History, University of Cincinnati; and Richard Wentworth, our editor at the University of Illinois Press.

Preface

ERIC FONER AND
MANNING MARABLE

Herbert Aptheker, who died in 2003 at the age of eighty-seven, enjoyed a long and controversial career as a scholar and political activist. *Herbert Aptheker on Race and Democracy* focuses on his pathbreaking historical scholarship. Although Aptheker's historical writings covered a wide range of subjects, we have chosen to focus on the area closest to his heart, and in which he helped to revolutionize the study of the American past—African American history.

The selections that follow include articles well known to scholars, which have done much to shape our understanding of such issues as the nature of the abolitionist movement and the experience of Reconstruction, and more obscure pieces of which even specialists may not be aware. With a few exceptions, they originally appeared in scholarly or political journals, or in books of essays now out of print. All are reproduced in their entirety, except for the excerpts from *American Negro Slave Revolts,* Aptheker's first, and in some ways most influential, book, and *The Negro in America,* a lengthy pamphlet in which Aptheker analyzed some of the shortcomings of Gunnar Myrdal's 1944 report on American race relations, *An American Dilemma.* Taken together, the writings in this volume offer an introduction to a scholarly career that lasted six decades and that had an enduring impact on our understanding of American history.

There is no need in this preface to offer a detailed account of Aptheker's career or a discussion of his influence on scholars, students, and all those seeking illumination on the African American struggle for substantive freedom in this country. We have included three pieces that provide information about Aptheker—a survey of his career by Herbert Shapiro, an appreciation by Clayborne Carson, and the transcript of a recent discussion of Aptheker's impact and legacy involving the two editors and Jesse Lemisch. But it is worth reiterating what these contributions make clear—that while barred from academic employment for most of his life because of political views, Aptheker helped to transform the way we view the American past. It is difficult, but important, to recall that ideas central to Aptheker's scholarship—that slaves engaged in persistent acts of resistance, that slavery was the fundamental cause of the Civil War, that African Americans played a major role in the abolitionist movement, that Reconstruction was a heroic struggle for interracial democracy—were radical and widely dismissed by established historians when he first advanced them. Today, as a glance at any U.S. history textbook will reveal, they have been fully assimilated into the scholarly mainstream. Other insights in Aptheker's works, including the complex interconnections of race and class in shaping the boundaries of American freedom and the importance not only of racism in the nation's past but of interracial efforts to combat it, have yet to be fully assimilated by historians.

We hope that by bringing together in a single volume some of Aptheker's most important writings, as well as appreciations of his career, this volume will remind those already familiar with his work of his enormous contribution to American scholarship and will introduce younger readers to one of the most important historians of his generation.

INTRODUCTION

A Biographical Sketch

HERBERT SHAPIRO

Herbert Aptheker was born in 1915, in Brooklyn, New York, the son of Rebecca (Korman) and Benjamin Aptheker. He was educated in the city's public schools and completed his undergraduate and graduate education at Columbia University. Among the faculty he recalled being influenced by while an undergraduate was economist Addison T. Cutler, who from time to time contributed articles to the Marxist-oriented magazine, the *New Masses*. Aptheker's master's thesis, completed in 1937, was titled "Nat Turner's Revolt: The Environment, the Events, the Effects." His doctoral dissertation, a study of slave revolts in the United States, was published by Columbia University Press in 1943. Beginning with his first publications in the mid-1930s, Aptheker followed a path that led to a position of prominence in American historical scholarship. In innumerable essays, reviews, and introductions to books by others, and in a series of volumes, perhaps most notably his *American Negro Slave Revolts* (1943), *A Documentary History of the Negro People in the United States* (1951, 1969, 1973, 1974, 1990, 1993, 1994), and the three-volume work, *The Selected Correspondence of W. E. B. Du Bois* (1973–78), Aptheker has illuminated the centrality of African American history in the experience of the United States. Writing with passion and eloquence, he marshaled the evidence refuting the racism permeating much of what previously had been written about American history. Drawing upon painstaking research and carefully defining what constituted a revolt, he set forth the thesis that, within a general pattern of resistance to bondage, the existence of at least 250 slave revolts was characteristic of American slavery. He defined his standard for determining the existence of a revolt or conspiracy—the involvement of at least ten slaves, freedom as the avowed aim, and contemporary references marking the incident as an uprising or plot. Taking into account that some number of rebellions probably escaped his notice and that slaveholders were not always anxious to publicize news of such events, it is likely that more than 250 such incidents occurred.

Following publication of *American Negro Slave Revolts,* the drift of critical responses to the book was markedly favorable. Kenneth Stampp, whose own benchmark study of slavery, *The Peculiar Institution* (1956), was largely consistent with Aptheker's findings, wrote that a scholar who called attention to the uglier aspects of slavery was open to the accusation of heresy and Aptheker was indeed such a heretic. But Stampp wrote that Aptheker had carefully studied the documents and "cut through the mystical beauties of the slave system and exposed harsh facts." The sociologist E. Franklin Frazier observed that Aptheker had proved that revolts were more numerous than previous scholarship had recognized.

Believing, as he did, that Marxism provided a scientific method of analysis that, used creatively, could most effectively uncover the workings of society, he rooted his work in the reality of class as fundamental to the making of history. Where others saw North American racism as essentially conditioned by the negative mental images seventeenth-century Englishmen formed of Africans, Aptheker viewed it as stemming from the white planters' need for a profitable labor system.

While Aptheker's work in African American history formed the core of his scholarship, he probed widely into a number of other historical themes, into other social science disciplines, and into issues of American public policy, as expressed at home and in foreign policy. Committed to the Marxist idea that it is necessary not only to study the world but to change it, he was the paradigmatic scholar-activist. In the 1930s, he worked in the South for the Food and Tobacco Workers Union and the Abolish Peonage Committee. Two months following the United States' entry into World War II in December 1941, Aptheker joined the army, serving as an artillery officer in the European theater, rising to the rank of major. His army training was done at the army installation at Livingston, Louisiana, and at camps in Texas and North Carolina. Already in 1939 he had joined the Communist Party, an association that lasted through the long years of the cold war and McCarthyite repression. When asked by one university president in the course of an interview for a regular faculty position whether he belonged to the Communist Party, Aptheker answered yes and then added that he was proud of such membership. After 1991, Aptheker was affiliated with the socialist-oriented Committees of Correspondence.

Aptheker married Fay P. Aptheker, with whom he lived and worked for sixty-two years, until her death in June 1999. She read, commented upon, and edited all of his work, typed many of his manuscripts, and was particularly instrumental in the research for his *Documentary History,* going into southern black communities and libraries when it was too dangerous for him to do so. They had one child, Bettina, born in 1944.

Although he was awarded a Guggenheim Foundation fellowship in 1946 to further the research leading to the *Documentary History,* Aptheker's political stance denied him a faculty position. From the late 1940s to the mid-'50s, he regularly taught courses at the Jefferson School of Social Science, a New York City adult education facility supported by the Communist Party. He testified as an expert witness on the meaning of Marxist-Leninist ideas at a number of court cases brought against Communists. In 1951, Aptheker testified as a defense witness at the Pittsburgh trial of Steve Nelson, charged under the 1919 Pennsylvania Sedition Act with attempting to overthrow the state and federal governments by force and violence. Nelson recalls that Aptheker was "wonderful" in discussing the history of the United States and that this testimony "captivated jurors and audience alike."

Aptheker was an unflagging participant in the epochal struggles for peace that followed the onset of the cold war. Highlights of his peace activism were his participation in an international conference against nuclear weapons held in Japan and his role at the August 1965 World Peace Congress held in Helsinki, where he vigorously urged condemnation of the interventionist American war in Vietnam. During the Christmas season of 1965 Aptheker traveled to North Vietnam with Yale historian Staughton Lynd and Students for a Democratic Society leader Tom Hayden, observing firsthand the devastation caused by the war and returning home to correct the campaign of official misinformation about what was happening. Following the trip, Aptheker stressed the need for unity in the antiwar movement, writing, "Whatever prevented unity in the struggle against slavery was helpful to the slave owners. Whatever prevents unity now in the struggle to stop the *killing in Vietnam* is helpful only to the 'crack-pot realists' and the 'stone-age' generals." Lynd also saw the trip as a step towards unity on the Left and as exemplifying the words of C. Wright Mills: "We must become internationalists again. For us, today, this means that we, personally, must attempt to get in touch with our opposite numbers in all countries of the world—above all, those in the Sino-Soviet zone of nations. With them we should make our own separate peace."

Along with W. E. B. Du Bois, Shirley Graham Du Bois, and Paul Robeson, Aptheker became a symbol in the struggle to reverse the U.S. State Department's insistence it could deny critics of cold war policies their right to travel abroad. In this case, *Aptheker v. Rusk* (1964), the Supreme Court overturned the government's denial of a vital citizenship right.

Aptheker communicated his thought as a historian and as a critic of public policy through the medium of the printed page but also by means of the many speeches and scholarly papers presented from the public platform. To put it plainly, he was a presence to reckon with and those who heard him lecture are unlikely to forget the experience. The list of the college and university campuses at which he has spoken is long. I have a vivid recollection of a talk on the occasion of Negro History Week that Aptheker delivered to a student audience at New York City's Queens College during February 1948. He devoted much of his remarks to a powerful refutation of the racist views of slavery set forth by U. B. Phillips, views that even then exerted much influence upon American historical scholarship. Aptheker eagerly and effectively took up the challenge of the debate. In December 1949, he debated historian Arthur M. Schlesinger Jr. at Harvard University; and that same year he debated labor historian Henry David at Queens College on the question, "Should Liberals and Communists Cooperate?" Within months, as the cold war intensified, debate on such a topic became most unlikely.

In several instances Aptheker's academic freedom, his right of participation in the free expression of ideas, was denied. After all, philosopher Sidney Hook had written that it was perfectly proper to exclude Communists from teaching positions, because Communist affiliation, he claimed, meant inability to search for the truth. The American Association of Universities likewise held it was appropriate to exclude Communists from the academy. On March 9, 1966, in a public atmosphere shaped by then–media commentator Jesse Helms, Aptheker was banned from speaking on the campus of the University of North Carolina, Chapel Hill, and instead addressed an audience of some two thousand students off campus. That evening he presented a prepared address to a standing-room-only audience at Chapel Hill's Community Church. At Ohio State University, prohibited from speaking at a campus gathering, he sat on the platform while a student read excerpts from some of his writings.

In the mid-1970s, Aptheker was invited by Yale University's Davenport College seminar committee to propose a one-semester seminar course. Such courses for some years had been a regular feature of Yale's undergraduate program, and a wide variety of public personalities had participated. Aptheker proposed to offer a course on W. E. B. Du Bois. Aptheker's appointment as a visiting lecturer required sponsorship by an academic department, but Yale's history department refused such sponsorship, with the eminent C. Vann Woodward stating that Aptheker did not meet the university's academic standards. Eventually, the course was given under sponsorship of the political science department, but—given his widely recognized stature as an authority on Du Bois—hanging over this controversy was the sense that it was Aptheker's politics, rather than his scholarly record, that had come into question.

With all his varied activities, the center of Aptheker's life's work was scholarship. Beside his focus on slave revolts he studied other manifestations of resistance, such as the formation of maroon settlements of runaway slaves within the boundaries of the slave states. More recently, in 1999, historians John Hope Franklin and Loren Schweninger carried this work forward, studying the phenomenon of maroons (or "outlying slaves," as they termed them) and concluding that such persons struck terror into the hearts of slaveholders.

A repeated theme in Aptheker's work is insistence that whites have not been monolithic regarding slavery and racism. This theme is explicated in his article, published in 1939, "Class Conflicts in the South, 1850–1860." He effectively made the case that secession in 1860 was forcibly imposed upon the South by the most militant slaveholders. Aptheker also called attention to the fact that during the Civil War significant numbers of Southern whites served in the Union Army.

Aptheker's *Documentary History of the Negro People in the United States,* the first volume of which appeared in 1951, has become a standard reference work in African American history. W. E. B. Du Bois contributed a preface to this volume, writing, "It is a dream come true to have the history of the Negro in America pursued in scientific documentary form. . . . At long last we have this work which rescues from oblivion and loss, the very words and thoughts of scores of American Negroes who lived slavery, serfdom, and quasi-freedom in the United States of America from the seventeenth to the twentieth century." He further added: "Historical scholarship has done all too little of this sort of research." Such neglect had profound significance: "We have the record of kings and gentlemen ad nauseum and in stupid detail; but of the common run of human beings, and particularly of the half or wholly submerged working group, the world has saved all too little of authentic record and tried to forget or ignore even the little saved." Du Bois hailed Aptheker's work "as a milestone on the road to Truth."

In his introduction to the volume, Aptheker explained that he attempted within the limitation of half a million words "to present the essence of the first three hundred years of the history of the American Negro people." He set out his understanding of what history is. "It is," he wrote, "what the masses endure, how they resist, how they struggle that forms the body of true history." He noted what had hitherto been the dominant approach of historians to the history of African Americans: "A Jim Crow society breeds and needs a Jim Crow historiography. The dominant historiography in the United States either omits the Negro people or presents them as a people without a past, as a people who have been docile, passive, parasitic, imitative. This picture is a lie. The Negro people, the most oppressed of all people in the United States, have been militant, active, creative, productive." He went on to emphasize that all the world's oppressed peoples shared a common understanding of and resistance to their subordination.

Aptheker's words exhibit a passion about the struggle of black people that was not previously found among white scholars. The 450 documents Aptheker reproduces sustain his view of the role black people have played in American history. The first volume begins with the Revolutionary Era and carries this history through the early years of the twentieth century. Subsequent volumes have documented the record up to the assassination of Martin Luther King Jr.

The impact made by the *Documentary History* is illustrated by historian Sterling Stuckey's recollection that when he was a high school history teacher in Chicago in 1962 and ordered copies of the book for his students, a number of the students had him order copies for their parents. He ascribed this to the intellectual excitement the book evoked and to the context of the early '60s, "when African American self-hatred was such that Negro history was not generally appreciated in public schools, to say nothing of universities and colleges." During 1964, in the course of a boycott by African American students of Chicago pubic schools, the *Documentary History* was used as a text in Freedom Schools housed in black churches on the city's south side. Stuckey writes that the students in the Freedom Schools "were among the first anywhere to be exposed to history from the bottom up." Stuckey's experience was not unique; historian John Bracey also has noted that in the 1960s, students at Howard University were excited by the volume.

An issue that has occupied the attention of scholars is the nature of the

American abolitionist movement. Numerous historians have noted the contribution abolitionists made to the advance of democracy in the United States. Among them have been Louis Filler, Benjamin Quarles, Gilbert H. Barnes, Dwight L. Dumond, Philip S. Foner, David Blight, Gerda Lerner, Darlene Clark Hine, Rosalyn Terborg Penn, Bettina Aptheker, and Jean F. Yellin. A significant contribution to the discussion has been Aptheker's book *Abolitionism: A Revolutionary Movement* (1989). His work emphasizes the dynamic role abolitionists played in bringing about the end of the slave system, the interracial nature of the movement, and the strivings of abolitionists to overcome racism.

A feature of Aptheker's scholarly life was his close relationship with W. E. B. Du Bois. Acknowledging that he thought of Du Bois as something of a father figure, he was chosen by Du Bois to serve as his literary executor and retained custody of Du Bois's papers until arrangements were made for their deposit at the University of Massachusetts. Aptheker selected the letters comprising the three volumes of Du Bois's correspondence. During the 1970s and '80s, he edited a multivolume collection of Du Bois's published works.

Aptheker played a significant role in the historical controversy of the 1960s surrounding William Styron's *The Confessions of Nat Turner.* Three decades prior to publication of Styron's book, Aptheker had written his master's thesis at Columbia University on the Nat Turner rebellion. As historian Mark Solomon has written, Aptheker's essay demonstrated his grasp of the interrelated nature of events. Aptheker carefully portrayed the context in which the rebellion took place. He found in the deeds of Turner and his followers "further examples of the woefully long, and indeed endless, role of human beings willing to resort to open struggle in order to get something precious to them—peace, prosperity, liberty, or in a word, a greater amount of happiness." In beginning work on his novel, Styron consulted Aptheker, but the finished product moved in quite a different direction than Aptheker's study. Styron portrayed an isolated event that had its roots in the aberrant, repressed personality structure of slaves. The novelist's view of Nat Turner was shaped by Stanley Elkins's thesis that under the weight of the masters' rule, slaves had become infantilized, that the Sambo image was not merely a stereotype but rather reflected the reality of slave personality structure. In a 1963 review of a new edition of *American Negro Slave Revolts,* Styron dismissed the book, writing of "many millions of slaves, reduced to the status of children, illiterate, tranquilized, totally defenseless, ciphers and ants." This distorted personality generated sexual frustration, particularly regarding white women, and this frustration would find outlet in senseless violence. Aptheker challenged Styron's notion concerning slaves, pointing out that the generalization about infantilization was unsupported by historical evidence. Aptheker wrote: "The fictional image of the Dunning school was *The Clansmen;* the fictional image of the Phillips school was *Gone With the Wind;* the fictional image of the Elkins school is William Styron's *The Confessions of Nat Turner.*" Later, in 1983, Aptheker commented: "Deny the existence of resistance and one negates the dynamic, the soul, the reality of that history."

In 1992, Aptheker published *Anti-Racism in U.S. History: The First Two Hundred Years,* a book carrying forward his conviction that racism is not some immutable characteristic of white people. To be sure, racism has deeply marked American history, but Aptheker argued that there has been also a tradition of antiracism found among significant numbers of white people. He put forward the following generalizations: "(1) anti-racism is more common among so-called lower classes than among the so-called upper class; (2) anti-racism especially appears among white people who have had significant experiences with people of African origin; and (3) anti-racism seems to be more common among women than men." There were those whites in the abolitionist movement who sought to rid themselves and the society within which they lived of racism. In later years there have been activists in the labor, radical, and civil rights movements who recognized that racism is the enemy of democracy, corrupting our society at home and this nation's relationships with the rest of the world.

In this volume the editors have brought together a selection of his essays, writings that exemplify the nature of Aptheker's approach to intellectual inquiry. His writing is straightforward and lucid, with nothing of the convoluted or the obscure about it. Readers will interpret these articles for themselves, and facilitating such discussion is the roundtable exchange between historians Eric Foner, Manning Marable, and Jesse Lemisch published in this volume.

As is true of all scholarly work, Aptheker's writings are subject to reconsideration on the basis of further thought and new evidence. But what he has given us is marked by an uncompromising intellectual integrity. We are in his debt for what he did to enrich American intellectual life. Herbert Aptheker died on March 17, 2003, in Mountain View, California.

An Appreciation

CLAYBORNE CARSON

Prepared for memorial service on March 29, 2003

I first met Herbert at a Stanford conference honoring his work that was held during the late 1970s, about the time he came to live in San Jose. It was not long after he had weathered a controversy—yet another among the many that marked his life—this time at Yale, where students had invited him to teach a course on W. E. B. Du Bois over the objections of some faculty members of Yale's history department. The historians were wary enough to avoid arguing that Herbert was insufficiently knowledgeable about Du Bois, and insisted instead that Herbert's political views had tainted his scholarship. The students prevailed, salvaging Yale's reputation more than Herbert's. I later learned that Herbert was forced to hold his class in an isolated room, with enrollment limited to fifteen—although far many more attended his lectures.

I did not get to know Herbert well at that first meeting but was pleased to learn that he had come to the Bay Area. I had been an admirer of his writings long before then. He had been one of the few historians to have made much of an impression on me during my undergraduate years, when I spent more time protesting than going to class. Like many other politically active black students of my generation, I knew Herbert as one of the pioneers in the field of African American history. I had obtained his little book on the Nat Turner revolt, and his first major study, *American Negro Slave Revolts,* based on his doctoral dissertation at Columbia, was among the first books that suggested what could happen when serious scholarship was combined with a commitment to social justice. One of the demands of the Black Power era was that black people should write our own history, but, during the years before many of us were skilled enough to do so, Herbert demonstrated that history could be carefully researched and documented and still move forward the struggle for freedom. I also had a copy of the first volume of his *Documentary History of the Negro People in the United States,* a book that I have consulted over the years more than any other single work in my library. The *Documentary History* had already placed a crucial weapon in the hands of the black intellectuals who had responded to William Styron's libelous novel, *The Confessions of Nat Turner,* because one of the documents included in Herbert's edition was Nat Turner's actual confession, dictated shortly before he was executed for leading a slave revolt in Virginia. In 1971, during my first year as an acting assistant professor at UCLA, I used Herbert's books and articles in a seminar I led on slave resistance.

I knew even then that Herbert was white and that he was a member of the Communist Party. These labels, I must admit, were not incidental to me during the heyday of Black Power. I had entered the 1960s believing that Communists were too radical and ended the decade seeing them as insufficiently so. Like many other Black Power enthusiasts seeking to define blackness, I initially resisted the notion that we had much to learn from white Reds. Only as the Black Power movement began to falter in the face of repression and internal ideological conflicts did I begin to examine it critically and especially to study its historical roots. I read the works of Delany, Douglass, Du Bois, Aptheker, and many others and began to realize that it mattered less that Herbert was white than that all of them had contributed to the great freedom struggles of their time. No black radical of my generation was unaffected by cold war anticommunism, but many of us came to see Communists from the perspective of our own freedom struggle. We knew who stood with us, who was on the side of justice when it required great risk to be so. If the Communist Party was the god that failed, it was because we expected so much more from it than from gods that did not have such ambitious goals. We did not romanticize the Communist Party, but we also did not romanticize the Republican Party of Lincoln or the Democratic Party of Roosevelt, Truman, Kennedy, and Johnson.

Herbert's critics saw him and the Communist Party through the lens of cold war anticommunism, but I and many other black radicals saw him and the Communist Party through a different lens. We appreciated that he contributed significantly to two of the great movements of the twentieth century—anticapitalism on the one hand and the related causes of anticolonialism and antiracism on the other. Herbert believed strongly that both movements were worth supporting. Capitalism survived him, but the battles in which he invested most of his heart and mind turned out better for him. He fought valiantly in the victorious campaign against Nazism, although his sacrifice was not rewarded with the recognition of a grateful nation or with the military pension he had earned. He also fought valiantly in the victorious campaign against the southern Jim Crow system and witnessed the success of his intellectual assault upon the racist portrayal of African Americans in historical scholarship. His sacrifices on behalf of these causes were never rewarded with a tenured academic position.

It was the black historians of my generation who reaped the rewards. That is why a few of us—Manning Marable for one—who have achieved academic success in the post–Jim Crow world that Herbert helped to create have used our positions to accord him some of the recognition he deserved. We saw him as one of us. Is it possible for a person to be a white black red or a white black historian? Why not? Herbert was our twentieth-century academic John Brown. I, for one, would not want to be part of any group that would not welcome Herbert as a member.

All of this is a way of saying that I came to know Herbert through his scholarship and his politics. I suppose there are other ways to know Herbert. He could be charming, especially to women, and gracious and considerate. He could talk knowledgeably about sports. As Herbert became an acquaintance, I learned about these aspects of his life. I learned that he was a wonderful husband who had the good fortune to have married a very understanding and supportive woman. He was a concerned father and a loyal friend. But I saw him first of all in his role as a politically engaged scholar whose political convictions made him a superb documentary editor and historian of the African American experience. I wanted to know what he knew and wanted to know what he had experienced, because he linked me to my own roots as an African American. He knew Du Bois, after all, and Carter G. Woodson and so many other major African American figures. Of the scholars I have known, only two others—John Hope Franklin and St. Clair Drake—elicited from me the awe and admiration I held for Herbert.

We saw each other occasionally during the 1980s, but it was only after I became editor of Martin Luther King's papers that I began to establish a closer friendship with him. I valued his opinion, as a pioneer in the field of documentary editing, about the work I had unexpectedly begun to do. He had the role with respect to Du Bois's papers that I had with respect to King's, but he had the enormous advantage of having known Du Bois for many years, while I merely saw King from a distance.

I began inviting Herbert to lecture in my class on the modern African

American freedom struggle. Students loved to attend his lectures, and he loved to lecture to them. He was a gifted teacher, able to talk engagingly about his own experiences and about the ways in which memory and history had merged in his life. I learned quickly that Herbert's heart was in his teaching and that for him one of the worst consequences of his cold war ostracism was that it kept him away from regular contact with students.

As I came to know Herbert, I also came to know Fay. Indeed, he often told me that he was eager to accept my invitations to lecture but needed to talk to Fay before deciding whether my modest honorarium was sufficient. He trusted her to protect him from exploitation, especially from an institution as rich as Stanford, but she offered advice with an understanding that monetary payment was only part of the calculation. Those of us who loved him also came to love her and to love the very public way they loved each other. I will always treasure the dinners that Susan and I and other King Project staff members shared with the Apthekers—often at their favorite restaurant, the Good Earth. Since her passing, there has hardly been a conversation with Herbert that did not include a reference to Fay and how much he missed her.

During the past decade he has worked closely with the King Papers Project, offering valuable comments on our volumes. His praise was generous and greatly welcomed, and his criticisms were sharply worded and always appreciated. It was this work that brought him to the project on a regular basis during the past decade. From the start, he worked well with my youthful editorial staff, for they had not yet produced a volume, while he had produced so many. He would come in once a week to work diligently in our library, at least until he had to move to Mountain View to receive nursing care. Student researchers in the King Project who had listened to him in my classes would occasionally take opportunities to talk with him, and he would welcome their interruptions. "Speak up, I can't hear so well," I can still hear him say. Even as his health declined during the past few months, he asked about lecturing in my class. He also insisted on reviewing the manuscript for the introduction to our latest volume and promptly returned his handwritten comments.

During the past two years I began working with him on a project to bring the *Documentary History* up to date. He had ended the seventh volume of his edition with King's assassination, and he was able to work toward the completion of the edition by making use of resources created to carry on King's legacy. As much as I complain that we have too few resources, especially given Stanford's enormous wealth, I appreciate our good fortune to have resources at all. I often wonder what Herbert might have accomplished if he had had the King Project's resources available to him throughout his career—or if Du Bois or Woodson had had such resources. His last project will be completed, and the edition that we agreed to rename *The Documentary History of African Americans* will, I am sure, become a memorial to Herbert's lifetime of dedication to the field of African American history.

His visits to the project led to an expanding network of relations between Herbert and members of the King Project staff. Sometimes he would forget names, but he would never fail to ask me about my wife and coworker Susan or about how he wanted to be certain that the person driving him to the project was assistant editor Tenisha Armstrong or associate administrator Regina Covington. He loved to see them, and I sometimes feared that he would be disappointed on days when I was to be his driver. We loved his occasional crankiness because we loved him and valued his selfless contribution to our work. For a long time, Herbert Aptheker was a constant item on the agenda of our weekly staff meetings. All of us who were able to see him during his last few days felt fortunate that we were able to express our final appreciation. We will miss him because he became one of us.

We have decided that the library of the King Papers Project, where Herbert often studied during his final years, where so many of his books are on the shelves, where he shared many happy moments with the many King Project staff members and student researchers who loved him, and where we celebrated his eighty-seventh birthday last summer, will become the Herbert Aptheker Memorial Library. It will remain a place touched by his spirit.

1

Negro History: Its Lessons for Our Time

Atop the dome of our Capitol building in Washington stands the Goddess of Freedom. It was cast in 1859—by Negro slaves. When patriots gave battle to the forces of Great Britain in our Revolutionary War, Negro and white fought side by side. Emblazoned on their banners was the slogan, "Liberty or Death"—but within the United States, then being so painfully born, lived less than three million people, and of these, over half a million were Negro slaves. This contradiction has pervaded American life from its beginning to the present moment. Its existence does not mean that there is not passionate devotion to the principles of the Declaration of Independence—freedom, equality, brotherhood, the sovereignty of the people, and their capacity and duty to build a full and noble life. There *is* such devotion and the Declaration of Independence is an American document, is, indeed, our country's birth certificate. But such contradiction does mean that the devotion has been partial, that the promise of the Declaration has not been made real. Therefore millions of Negro Americans have suffered veritable crucifixion for centuries, and this in turn has cost the whole people much of their own freedom and treasure and blood. This contradiction did not simply come into being; it has been created and maintained by the ruling classes which have dominated the economics, politics, and culture of our country. Racism is the creation of capitalism; it was not present in ancient and medieval life and thought. The conquest of the darker peoples of the world and, first of all, those in Africa—the robbery of their resources and the enslavement of their labor power—was of primary consequence in the early development and in the growth of capitalism, just as their super-exploitation has been of such fundamental importance to the existence of imperialism.

It is the merchant capitalists, the slave owners, the monopoly capitalists, who breed and need racism, because racism serves as a justification for and a bulwark of the enslavement or near-enslavement of colored peoples, which has been so vital to their interests.

One of the areas in which racism has been most apparent in our own country, and that with which we are here directly concerned, is history writing. A Jim Crow society produces a Jim Crow historiography. After the security of their property, any exploiting ruling class guards most jealously the history of its country. This is because history, far from being "dead," is quick and powerful with life. For the present is made up of the past, and the future consists of both of them. Controlling, then, what is written and taught and believed about the past, becomes very important in terms of dominating the present and shaping the future.

Jim Crow Historiography

American history writing and teaching has been predominantly white supremacist. It has conveyed a picture of the Negro people as being docile and imitative, stupid and parasitic—children, primitives, buffoons. It has done this in two ways: by sins of omission and of commission. To illustrate this truth, but a few examples, characteristic of the body of literature as a whole, may be offered.

As to sins of omission:

These sometimes reach ludicrous depths of stark ignorance. Thus, there is the not-unsympathetic biography of the militant abolitionist and Civil War Congressional leader, Thaddeus Stevens, by Thomas F. Woodley, published in 1934. The author quotes a reference by Stevens to the magnificent Negro leader, Frederick Douglass, in which the congressman stated his belief that Douglass was perhaps the outstanding orator then living in the United States. For the convenience of his reader, Mr. Woodley identifies the Negro involved, as "Stevens' barber"!

More often what one has is sheer blindness. A leading publisher—one of the most enlightened and distinguished—Alfred A. Knopf, of New York, for instance, issued in 1942 a history of Georgia—*Georgia: Unfinished State* by Hal Steed—which closes with these words:

"*I would not say that the Anglo-Saxon is superior to other races, but that this race makes up nearly a hundred per cent of the population in the South augurs well for unity—unity in political beliefs, in religion, in social problems.*"

Happy we are over what Mr. Steed "would not say." But is it not unfortunate that his modesty led him to confine his shattering finding to the last page of his pedestrian book? Will it not come as a great shock to the ten million Negro people of the South to learn that they are, after all, Anglo-Saxons—not to speak of the hundreds of thousands of others in the South who had hitherto thought of themselves as of Mexican or Russian or German or French or Spanish descent?

It is usual to find, even among books produced by quite liberal-minded authors, a complete ignoring of the Negro. Thus, Charles A. Madison's *Critics and Crusaders* (1947) studies eighteen militant figures from Garrison to John Reed, but all are white; Daniel Aaron discusses perhaps a dozen *Men of Good Hope* (1951) from Emerson to Brooks Adams and again every one of them is white.

Henry Steele Commager, one of the most learned and courageous scholars in the United States, produced a volume of some 1,200 oversize, double-column pages, entitled *Documents of American History* (4th edition, 1948), and in it there is not a single word produced *by* a Negro himself. Again, Professors Allan Nevins and Henry Steele Commager pooled their enormous erudition and produced another 1200–page documentary textbook, *The Heritage of America* (revised edition, 1951), and once again not a word in the volume comes from a Negro; even the documents illustrating slavery, the underground railroad, abolitionist movement, the Civil War, and Reconstruction are all chosen, without exception, from the works of white people,

Sins of commission mark all the "standard" history works. From George Bancroft to Charles Beard, the Negro is presented explicitly as an inferior and particularly docile species of humanity, not to speak of the obscene chauvinism permeating the works of the still-authoritative delineator of what slavery was and of what it meant to be a slave—the late Ulrich Bonnell Phillips.

Characteristic are the comments in the *Encyclopedia Britannica* (14th edition). Here the reader is told that following Reconstruction the disfranchisement of the Negro "has aroused little protest [from him] while it has tended to improve the government." How diligently the anonymous author of this "study" must have searched for evidences of protest from the Negro people! And that their disfranchisement improved the government is manifest from the sterling careers of the statesmen dominant since that "purification" such as Ben Tillman, Tom Watson, Hoke Smith, Eugene Cox, Huey Long, Martin Dies, Theodore Bilbo, John Rankin, James Eastland, and other Bourbon pillars of decency, progress, democracy, and brotherhood.

We may close this painful catalogue with a quotation from W. E. Woodward's *Meet General Grant,* a best-seller and Literary Guild selection a generation ago. This scholar told his scores of thousands of readers: "Negroes are the only people in the history of the world, so far as I know, that ever became free without any effort of their own."

Of course, Mr. Woodward had a saving phrase in that sentence—"so far as I know." But I fear—given the nature of American history writing and teaching—that very few of Woodward's readers were intellectually equipped to especially observe those most important five words and mentally to add, "How very little you know, ignorant and bigoted Mr. Woodward!"

Note, in considering these sins of omission and commission, that their result is not only a complete distortion of the truth concerning the past of the Negro people, but also a false rendering of American history in general. Of course, the ruling class proceeds uncontested in nothing, and while this country produced John C. Calhoun, it also produced John Brown. It is instructive that the first named—an arch-exponent of slavery—was an honored Senator and is memorialized in a dozen eulogistic biographies, while the second—an arch-enemy of slavery—died on the gallows as a traitor and is presented to most of our youth as an insane monster. Nevertheless, it is equally instructive that the cause for which Brown gave his life did triumph and that the institution to which Calhoun dedicated his talents was destroyed shortly after he himself died.

Battlers for a Scientific History

The fact is that, as the ruling class and its servitors bolster Negro oppression by racist ideology, so do the opponents of that class and the fighters for Negro freedom combat that ideology, and not least in the field of history.

The pioneers in this regard have been, of course, Negroes themselves. The effort to present a true picture of Negro history goes back to the pre–Civil War days when Negro abolitionists like Frederick Douglass, William C. Nell, William Wells Brown, James McCune Smith, and others published highly useful studies. Their white comrades in the movement also participated, notably Wendell Phillips, Harriet Beecher Stowe, James Mott, and Joshua Coffin.

The post–Civil War period saw further contributions, again especially from Negro authors like George Washington Williams, William T. Alexander, Edward A. Johnson, and others. But the flowering of this effort comes as a part of the Negro people's mounting struggles against American imperialism with the beginnings of the present century. Of decisive significance were the founders of scientific Negro historiography, the late Dr. Carter G. Woodson (who established the Association for the Study of Negro Life and History in 1915), and the dean of American scholars, Dr. W. E. B. Du Bois, whose promethean talents have made him outstanding in half a dozen intellectual fields but whose first published work (1896) and whose main area of concentration has always been in history. During the past generation perhaps a score of excellently trained younger Negro scholars have come forward and have made and continue to make indispensable contributions towards a truthful re-creation of the American Negro's past.

Again, some white people have been of assistance. This has been notably true of such among them who are Marxist in their thinking. Much of these contributions, as well as others with, of course, notable additions of his own penetrating analysis, have gone into William Z. Foster's recent work, *The Negro People in American History* (1954).

In addition, there have been clear signs of the beginnings of correction penetrating into the sanctums of the academies and universities of the land, with such white professors as Melville J. Herskovits, Harvey Wish, Helen T. Catterall, Elizabeth Donnan, George B. Tindall, C. Vann Woodward, and others making important contributions.

The fact remains, however, that the American social order is white supremacist, and its dominant history writing and teaching remains intensely racist. Battle has been given, advances have been made, but the greater part has yet to be won. The winning is very much worthwhile, because it serves the cause of truth and of freedom. Indeed, the lessons to be derived from the truth about Negro history are many and are of transcendent consequence for our country at this time.

Let us briefly consider what these lessons are.

The Truth About Negro History

The first great lesson has already been indicated to some degree—the truth about Negro history is a smashing blow against white supremacist ideology. For an important component of that ideology is the insistence that the Negro people do not, in fact, have a history; that is, it is held that things happened to them, that their status was involved in past occurrences, but it is maintained that they themselves did not *do* anything. But the great fact is that the heart of Negro history is the Negro's own incessant and heroic struggle for freedom. History shows the Negro people to have be active, not passive; creative, not parasitic; militant, not docile; ingenious, not stupid. It is a history that is filled with nobility and drama, with self-sacrifice and vindication. It is as stirring as that of the history of any people in the world. It is a history which gives the lie, in irrefutable and throbbing form, to every chauvinist stereotype and slander that greed and tyranny have concocted.

The truth about Negro history is of great consequence also to the Negro people themselves. The sins of omission and distortion naturally have had very much less effect upon the Negro people than upon the whites, and, knowing themselves and knowing American society, they understand the lying character of the depiction of themselves that remains dominant here. Nevertheless, it is true that the systematic campaign of the rulers to hide and to distort the truth about Negro history, to keep it out of textbooks and out of teaching outlines, etc., has made it difficult for many of the Negro people themselves *to* get the *facts* about their own past. This has been meant to weaken them, of course, and it has weakened them, for a sense of continuity and a fully grounded feeling of pride in the accomplishments of one's own people is a basic component of every people's strength and confidence. This is a central reason why the study and the propagation of Negro history comes into being and continues as an organic part of the Negro liberation movement. In this sense, recapturing the inspiring truth about the *Negro* past arms and strengthens the Negro people for the great struggles still before them.

Only Struggle Brings Progress

Another basic lesson shines through the *history* of the Negro people. It was expressed in a single sentence by the magnificent Frederick Douglass, speaking in 1857: "The whole history of the progress of human liberty shows that all concessions yet made to her august claims have been born of earnest struggle."

Oppressors and exploiters try in every possible way to hide that fact. They detest nothing so much as an informed and aroused multitude, one which knows *its* enemy, understands its needs and knows that it gets only what it is strong enough to win. The masses have been freely given nothing; only to the degree that the masses are involved exactly to that degree will their advance be meaningful and lasting.

Successful struggle has at least two prerequisites: the enemy must be known; one's own strength, including all possible allies, must be effectively mobilized. Negro history, characterized as it is by the relative nakedness of the oppression its subjects have undergone, reveals *with* particular clarity whom the enemy has been and is.

Surely, in the days of slavery the enemy was the slave owner. He ruled the system that existed on the basis of Negro enslavement; he held slaves because they were basic to his profit, to his power, to his "way of life." The enemy was the slave-owning class and the basic demand had to be—and was—the immediate emancipation of the slaves.

In our own day, in the day of the monopoly capitalist as the ruler, it is his system which is the enemy. It is his class which dominates the social order. So basic an aspect of that order as discrimination and segregation, practiced in every walk of life and in every part of the country against the Negro people, exists and is maintained because the ruling class wants it that way. That class finds the Jim Crow system of immense benefit to itself directly and indirectly in an economic and political sense. It has been a central divisive instrument among the natural opponents of that class; it has been the single most debilitating force eating away at the ideological, cultural, and moral nature of these natural opponents.

The enemy today is the Jim Crow system and the basic demand is, and has to be, the immediate abolition of segregation and discrimination from every facet of American life.

The Negro People's Allies

Negro history has much to say, too, as to allies and the need for unity. First of all, it is a fact that when enslaved the Negro people alone could never have freed themselves. Let it be remembered that in the history of humanity all people have at some time been enslaved, but there has been but one example of an enslaved people freeing itself and doing this alone. That single example is highly instructive of the reasons for the rule to which it is the only exception.

It was only the Negro people of Haiti who, though enslaved, rose up in revolt and forced their own emancipation and thereby also created their own nation. But those people numbered some ninety percent of the total population of their country, and of the remaining ten percent, about half was made up of mulatto slave owners, who themselves wavered when it came to putting down the bid of the Negro masses. Moreover, the metropolitan power, France, was in the midst of a great revolution when the Haitian masses rebelled, and the left of the French revolutionary movement was urging the emancipation of all slaves. When the Napoleonic reaction set in, the French state had its hands full with wars in Europe and so could turn but a fraction of its power against the Haitians. Even so, it took those heroic people about thirteen years of armed struggle before they did consolidate their freedom and their independence.

In the United States, the slaves never amounted to more than twenty percent of the whole population and never more than about thirty-five percent of the entire Southern population. With the enslaving power right in the territorial limits holding the slaves (not, as in the case of France, over 3000 miles away), and with the slaves so heavily outnumbered by white non-slaves, it was simply impossible in a physical sense for slavery to be abolished through the struggles and efforts of the Negro masses *alone.*

In the successful movement to abolish slavery, the Negro masses (four million slaves; half a million free) played an absolutely decisive role. They were the pioneers; they were the most principled and the most militant; they were the most eloquent and persuasive; they knew best the nature of slavery and the slave owner. And they led in the battle against racism, within and without the abolitionist movement, because they were fighting for unity between Negro and white. The Negro abolitionists knew that without much unity the movement could not succeed; with it, the movement could not fail.

The Need for Unity

But observe that the need for unity was mutual. It was not simply a matter of the unity being needed by the Negro people in order to achieve *their* freedom. Had that been the case, the unity would never have been established, for it would have been benevolence and not an alliance. Unity, to be real and fraternal rather than fake and paternalistic, must be based upon a common need; it must have an objective base in a common enemy and a common minimum program. So, specifically in the movement for the elimination of slavery, the unity was needed by the Negro people in order for them to win freedom, and the unity was needed by the vast majority of white people because the enslavement of the Negro was colliding more and more with their own pressing needs and aspirations.

The slave owners, in possessing the millions of slaves and the best land of the South—and the crops raised by those slaves on that land—thereby not only owned the Negro people; they also thereby dominated the government of the United States. That dominance meant no protective tariffs for straining industry; it meant no homestead act for millions of eager poor in the East and the West; it meant no vast internal improvements (bridges, roads, canals, railroads) at federal expense to knit together the farmers of the West and the factories of the East; it meant no national currency and banking act to bind together in effective financial form a developing national market for the growing bourgeoisie. It meant, on the contrary, a continued aggressive foreign policy in the service of the voraciously expansionistic plantation system, with occasional unpleasant and sorely unhealthy wars (as against Mexico) thrown in; it meant the continued threat of the loss of hundreds of millions of acres of public lands to the monster of slavery; it meant continued stultification of thought, perversion of the press; the educational institutions and the church to the demands of the slavocracy; it meant growing attacks upon the Bill of Rights; it meant continued oligarchic domination by perhaps 250,000 slave owners of the seven million non-slaveholding whites in the South itself—in Mississippi and Alabama and Georgia and the Carolinas—against whose every interest the slave owners bore only less harshly than upon the slaves themselves.

It meant finally the death of the Republic itself, for rather than have slavery limited—let alone abolished outright—the slave holders took the path of counter-revolutionary force and violence. That it was unity against the slave owners—which meant in fact and in life, unity against slavery—or it was disunity in the face of that attack, and the existence of slavery at the expense of the destruction of the United States.

So the need for unity was a mutual one; it was a life and death matter to the Negro people and to the vast majority of the white people too. This does not mean that the unity is one of "selfishness" or that it is one in which humanism and decency are not potent ingredients. It does not mean that simple revulsion against human slavery and the atrocity that it—whatever the religious or secular source of such revulsion might be—plays no part in the building of a Negro-white unity. Of course it does.

Unity Has Been Forged in the Past

In the days of slavery it was reason enough, God knows, to fight against the institution "only" because of what that meant in the barest human terms to millions of Negro men, women, and children; and today there is reason enough in the abominations of Jim Crow forced upon sixteen million men, women, and children to make one eager to help wipe it out. But in terms of moving millions into action, it is a fact that existing institutions, having the backing of potent vested interests, can be and are successfully rationalized, no matter how terrible they may appear to others having the benefit of long hindsight. Moreover, all the good will in the world is not as effective in moving masses into action and keeping them organized and active as is an awareness on the part of those masses that their own welfare and their own interests are involved.

Negro history not only teaches unequivocally the *need* for unity. It teaches, also, the possibility of *achieving* such unity. For in the past real unity *was* achieved. To name but the most dramatic instances, the abolitionist movement was a movement of Negro and white; it was a united movement. The crushing of the slave holders' counter-revolution was a united movement, less completely than the advanced abolitionist movement, but still significant unity was achieved.

One of the basically significant features of the great Reconstruction epoch—when an advanced form of bourgeois democracy was brought to most of the South—was the high degree of Negro white unity that was achieved within the South, from its courts and legislatures and colleges to its popular organization. Again, in the stirring days of the Populist movement of the 1890s, great unity of Negro and white was achieved in the South, and again there were Negro representatives in Congress, in the state legislatures, and Negro sheriffs and Negro leaders of the Populist movement itself who labored and organized side by side with white leaders.

Unity has been achieved to a considerable degree in our own day in various movements. The New Deal days saw such unity in the struggles of the unemployed, the battle for the CIO, the farmers' crusades. There is much of it developing today, in the South and in the North, in various peoples' organizations, in churches, in parents' groups, in women's and youth clubs, in the trade-union movement. This unity, based on firmest principles, has reached its high point in the Communist Party where Negro-white unity is the essence of its structure, program, and conduct.

Even where, as in most of these cases, the unity was not perfect and not complete, a significant degree of solidarity *was* achieved, and this is one of the great and heartening lessons of Negro history.

Momentous, also, has been the achievement of unity on the international level. This has deep roots in American history, in the fact, for instance, that among the foreign forces attracted to our great Revolution were not only volunteer fighters from France and Sweden, from Germany and Ireland, but also from Haiti. Similarly, the great abolitionist effort was an international one, with very important support coming from the men and women of England, Ireland, Scotland, and most of continental Europe, especially from France, Germany, and Russia.

Further, the whole struggle against colonialism and imperialism has witnessed the closest unity among peoples of all colors, and today, when that struggle has reached its highest point, that unity is also at a high point. At the historic Bandung Congress, colored peoples representing nearly a billion human beings *in state power* gathered. Though of different political views, they asserted their unanimity in opposition to racism and to colonialism. Moreover, in the Socialist world, comprising today some 950 million people, there is fullest unity among peoples of all colors; there is complete equality. In the Soviet Union, in People's China, and in the People's Democracies of Europe and Asia, racism is treated as criminal and real fraternity prevails.

The Centrality of Negro History

There is also a centrality about the history of the Negro people in the general context of the history of the United States which is one of the most important lessons it teaches. This derives basically from the fact that the enslavement and the super-exploitation of the Negro people have been so important a part of the nature and the strength of the American ruling classes. This special oppression has never been a superficial aspect of the American social order; on the contrary, it has always been and remains a part of the defining nature of that social order.

Hence, throughout American history the position of the Negro people has been a touchstone of general democratic progress, a divining rod for testing the character of any particular movement or organization, and the decisive element in determining outcome. Examples will make clearer my meaning at this point.

At the time of the American Revolution, the failure of the Revolutionists to eliminate slavery almost lost them the war (it did lose them most of the South for much of the war). And that failure grew with the Republic's growth so that less than ninety years after the Revolution it produced a counter-revolution that almost destroyed the nation. During the Civil War itself, as we have seen, emancipation of the Negro slaves was a perquisite for the preservation of the country.

In the history of the labor movement a decisive factor has been the position of the Negro worker. No single thing has cost the white American worker more and nothing has hurt the trade union movement more than boss-inspired white supremacy. The struggle on this front—the effort to forge full solidarity between Negro and white worker—has been, then, of outstanding consequence in the history of the working class itself.

The greatest single force depressing American wages has been the discrimination against the Negro workers. The greatest single force retarding the fullest organization of the American working class has been the boss-made white chauvinism that has kept the white disunited from the Negro. Of central consequence in inhibiting independent political action on the part of the American working class, so indispensable to its well-being, has been the special oppression of the Negro masses and what this has meant in terms of the one-party system of the South. The most powerful and active spokesmen of reaction in the seats of government, and those most responsible for anti-labor laws and administrative procedures, are the Bourbon representatives who owe their illegally-held seats to the disfranchisement of the Negro masses. On every one of these scores, then, the oppression of the Negro people means directly and concretely the worsening of the conditions of the mass of white workers.

In the farmers' protest movements that have intermittently rocked this country, the question of Negro-white unity has been of major importance. This has been overwhelmingly true of the South, of course, but it has been true of the country as a whole. The most significant farmers' movements have been national in scope and so that the position of the millions of Negro tillers of the soil has always been on the historical agenda, if not always on the actual agenda drawn up by major farmers' organizations.

The greatest organized farmers' movement yet to rock this country was that of the post–Civil War generation, of the Greenbackers, and the Alliance and the Populist Party. Its failure to fully break through in the South so far as Negro-white unity is concerned, and especially the failure to hold what unity was built (and it was considerable), was of first importance in the crushing of that movement.

In fact, this rule may be stated as characteristic of American history: every progressive and democratic effort, whether it be for women's rights or the suffrage or social security or civil liberties, or independent political action, or opposition to imperialist war, has forged ahead largely to the degree that it has been able to achieve Negro-white unity. Conversely, every such effort has failed or fallen short largely to the degree that such unity has not been achieved, while the failure to achieve the unity is itself a basic reflection upon the nature of the effort.

The Negro People As Guides to Progress

At this point another consideration arises. The Negro people are most sensitive guides as to the needs of broad democratic and progressive efforts. There is much to be *learned* from the Negro people, for a study of their history will show that they were pioneers in understanding the profoundest needs of all the people. This arises from the fact that they have been the most oppressed and so they are the most sensitive to the problems of all who are ruled.

In every decisive moment of American history the most advanced programs and the most discerning suggestions come from the Negro people and come from them very early. They correctly warned the nation what would be the cost and the result of not excising slavery when the revolution was on; they sensed first every turn in the long struggle against slavery, from the need for political action to destroy it, to the need for transforming the Civil War into a revolutionary rather than a static, "save-the-union-first" effort.

They knew first and best what the failure to uproot the plantation system after the Civil War would cost not only themselves but the South as a whole and the entire nation. They said then that if the land were not distributed to those who tilled it, the Bourbons would return to power in the South, wipe out as much as they could of the results of the Civil War, and remain as a canker spreading reaction throughout the country.

It was a Negro trade union leader, the Baltimore shipbuilder, Isaac Myers, who told the third annual convention of the National Labor Union in 1896 (which then admitted Negro delegates for the first time) that as a worker and as a Negro he was proud that the trade union movement had reached the point of "taking the colored laborer by the hand and telling him that his interest is common with yours, and that he should have an equal chance." It was he and other Negro workers who first clearly comprehended this mutual need for solidarity and tried to wipe out Jim Crow in the labor movement.

Note how clearly the great tribune of the Negro people, Frederick Douglass, speaks on two central questions of our own day: the questions of civil liberties and of loyalty. As to the first: The time is December, 1860; the place Boston. John Brown has but recently been hanged; Lincoln has been elected and is soon to be inaugurated, South Carolina is about to secede. A meeting is assembled to discuss the question: "How shall slavery be abolished?"

This is considered inopportune, if not inflammatory and seditious by all the "respectability" of Boston. Wherefore, as Douglass said, "that meeting was invaded, insulted, captured by a mob of gentlemen, and thereafter broken up and dispersed by the order of the mayor, who refused to protect it, though called upon to do so."

Douglass was present at that invaded meeting. He waited but a few days, and on December 10 organized another meeting in Boston and addressed it with "A Plea for Free Speech." He did this because, as he said, "the time to assert a right is the time when the right itself is called in question, and that the men of all others to assert it are the men to whom the right has been denied."

Then, with marvelous clarity and simplicity, Douglass put the question of civil liberties in its broadest aspects:

> There can be no right of speech where any man, however lifted up, or however humble, however young, or however old, is overawed by force and compelled to suppress their honest sentiments.
>
> Equally clear is the right to hear. To suppress free speech is a double wrong. It violates the rights of the hearer as well as those of the speaker. It is just as criminal to rob a man of his right to speak and hear as it would be to rob him of his money . . . there must be no concessions to the enemy.

The clarity, simplicity, and conviction were natural to Douglass who had been speaking abolitionism in an anti-abolitionist nation for a generation, and had been doing it though he had his head cracked and his arm broken and his character repeatedly besmirched.

The Question of Loyalty

Regularly, Douglass was called traitor to his own land, for he spoke his mind and stood foursquare for freedom and truth, no matter what the cost. He had felt the slave master's lash on his own back many times, and while he spoke, his heart was inflamed with knowledge of the fact that his own mother and brother were then in slavery.

He withstood the hardest test of all; he denounced a war conducted by his own government, while it was being fought, and he did this in the most uncompromising terms. He did it because he believed that that war—against Mexico—was aggressive, robberlike, and unjust. He called it "disgraceful, cruel, and iniquitous." He ascribed it to the slave holders' "grasping ambition, tyrannical usurpation, atrocious aggression." He demanded a halt to such a war, which required of American troops "deeds of atrocious cruelty, lust, and blood." He beseeched the government to "leave off this horrid conflict, abandon their murderous plans, and forsake the way of blood" and the better to accomplish this he urged, "let petitions flood the halls of Congress by the million, asking for the recall of our forces."

When the Negro people were enslaved, their leaders fought against slavery, and in fighting slavery they were fighting against the status quo. Naturally, therefore, they were denounced as "disloyal." But what was the truth of the matter?

When Frederick Douglass said, as he did in 1850, that "the whole framework of the American government is radically at fault," was he being disloyal to the Negro people, to democracy, to the best interests of the vast majority of the American people?

When Charles H. Langston, Negro secretary of the Ohio Anti-Slavery Society, told a U.S. court in 1858, about to jail him for violating the Fugitive Slave Law, "I know that the courts of this country, that the laws of this country, that the governmental machinery of this country are so constituted as to oppress and outrage colored men," was he speaking falsely? Was he being disloyal to the best interests of his people and of his country?

When President Buchanan sent U.S. marshals to Frederick Douglass' home to arrest and question him after John Brown's heroic effort, was Douglass wrong in writing, from Canada: "I have no apology for keeping out of the way of those gentlemanly U.S. marshals . . . I have quite insuperable objections to being caught by the hands of Mr. Buchanan"? Was Douglass disloyal because, as he wrote, he would not "assume the base and detestable character of an informer"? He was disconcerting to the slave holders, but who owes *loyalty* to exploiters and oppressors? Only "base and detestable characters."

When in 1899, Douglass' son, Lewis, carried on the traditions of his father and denounced American imperialism and its annexationist wars, was he displaying loyalty? When he wrote that "whatever this government controls, injustice to dark races prevails," and when he continued, "the people of Cuba, Puerto Rico, Hawaii and Manila know it well as do the wronged Indian and outraged black man in the United States," was he not being truthful, and was he not courageously attacking a policy of conquest and subjugation that meant only death and suffering for thousands of American youth, as well as the peoples of the areas assaulted?

In doing what he did, Lewis Douglass was expressing the keen and principled opposition of the Negro people to colonialism and to imperialism which has marked them ever since and which has characterized the position of their best leaders and spokesmen, from the son of Douglass through Bishop Henry Turner, and, in our own day, Paul Robeson and Dr. W. E. B. Du Bois.

On this whole question of "loyalty" Negro history is splendidly illuminating. It makes clear that the country consists in the first place of its people, and that patriotism is not conformity, let alone jingoism, but that it is devotion to the welfare of the inhabitants of one's country—which in no way conflicts with the welfare of the people of any other country. Once again, Frederick Douglass stated the answer clearly and simply: "I, too, would invoke the spirit of patriotism; *not* in a narrow and restricted sense, but, I trust, with a broad and manly signification . . . not to hide our shame from the world's gaze, but utterly to abolish the cause of that shame . . . *not* to sustain an egregious wrong, but to unite all our energies in the grand effort to remedy that wrong . . ."

Negro History Inspires Confidence

In a period of rising reactionary pressures such as our country has been experiencing for the past decade, there is an acute need to resist moods of defeatism and of despair. In this, too, Negro history is especially helpful, for its study provides a never-ending source of confidence in the staying power of the masses and in the inevitability of their triumph.

Consider: For over three hundred years, American ruling classes have been exhausting their imaginations in their oppression of the Negro people. They [Negroes] have been enslaved, lynched, and Jim Crowed; they have been ghettoed and slandered; they have been hired last and fired first; they have been compelled to work the hardest and they have been paid the least. And yet—with supreme effort—they have endured. They have more than endured.

The ordeal's fire did not consume them, rather, it tempered them. Today the Negro people are more numerous, more fully organized, more militant, more united, and more insistent upon getting immediately full freedom and complete equality than they have ever been in the whole long travail of the past.

With infinite staying power, with salutary humor, with colossal courage, they have held single-mindedly to their goal of freedom, a goal of such consequence to themselves and to all other Americans.

What inspiration is here! See two slaves suspected of plotting for freedom, chained to the stone floor of the Charleston jail in 1822; each is tortured in turn with fire and with knives. One begins to scream intelligibly and the torturers lean forward to get names—it is always names that are wanted—and the other, Peter Poyas, raises himself from a pool of blood and screams: "Die silent, Mingoe, as you shall see me do!"

See, in our day, Dr. T. R. M. Howard of Mississippi publicly defy the terrorists of the White Councils and announce that he will never rest and never silence his voice of protest until Jim Crow is abolished.

See the young Miss Autherine Lucy insisting on her right to a full education and the realization of her desire to be a librarian, despite insult, terror, and lynch mobs.

See the inspiring solidarity and courage of the entire Negro community of Montgomery, Alabama, which persists in its anti-segregation boycott despite intense economic and social pressures and in the face of the mass arrests of scores of leading men and women.

Such courage is produced by the suffering of a people; it is produced by the selflessness and the spirit of comradeship that common suffering evokes. It is a courage born of supreme confidence in the justice of the cause of freedom and in the inevitability of its triumph.

This miracle of resistance and of courage in the face of nearly insuperable obstacles and nearly unendurable pain is a magnificent source of confidence for the struggles in our own time.

And in our own time we are at the supreme moment in Negro history. For we live in the generation that can see the achievement of real freedom by the Negro people. It is this which provokes the desperation of the Eastlands and Talmadges and their bosses in Wall Street.

Negro history teaches us the way and the only way to the achievement of this, its culmination and greatest victory. What is required is boldness in the struggle, unity in the struggle; what is required is an awareness on the part of the vast majority of American white people, and then working class in the first place, that their own happiness and security, their own welfare and peace are bound up with the achievement of the liberation of the Negro people.

2

Maroons within the Present Limits of the United States

An ever-present feature of antebellum Southern life was the existence of camps of runaway Negro slaves, often called *maroons*, when they all but established themselves independently on the frontier. These were seriously annoying, for they were sources of insubordination. They offered havens for fugitives, served as bases for marauding expeditions against nearby plantations, and, at times, supplied the nucleus of leadership for planned uprisings. Some contemporary writers and a few later historians have noticed, in a general and meager way, the existence of this feature of American slavery.[1] It merits, however, detailed treatment.

It appears that notice of these maroon communities was taken only when they were accidentally uncovered or when their activities became so obnoxious or dangerous to the slavocracy that their destruction was felt to be necessary. Evidence of the existence of at least fifty such communities in various places and at various times, from 1672 to 1864, has been found. The mountainous forested or swampy regions of South Carolina, North Carolina, Virginia, Louisiana, Florida, Georgia, Mississippi, and Alabama (in order of importance) appear to have been the favorite haunts for these black Robin Hoods. At times, a settled life rather than a pugnacious and migratory one was aimed at, as is evidenced by the fact that these maroons built homes, maintained families, raised cattle, and pursued agriculture, but this all-but-settled life appears to have been exceptional.

The most noted of such communities was that located in the Dismal Swamp between Virginia and North Carolina.[2] It seems likely that about two thousand Negroes, fugitives, or the descendants of fugitives lived in this area. They carried on a regular, if illegal, trade with white people living on the borders of the swamp. Such settlements may have been more numerous than available evidence would indicate, for their occupants aroused less excitement and less resentment than the guerrilla outlaws.

The activities of maroons in Virginia in 1672 approached a point of rebellion so that a law was passed urging and rewarding the hunting down and killing of these outlaws.[3] An item of November 9, 1691, notices the depredations caused by a slave, Mingoe, from Middlesex county, Virginia, and his unspecified number of followers in Rappahannock county.[4] These Negroes not only took cattle and hogs, but, what was more important, they had recently stolen "two guns, a Carbyne & other things."

In June 1711, the inhabitants of the colony of South Carolina were kept "in great fear and terror" by the activities of "several Negroes [who] keep out, armed, and robbing and plundering and plantations."[5] These men were led by a slave named Sebastian, who was finally tracked down and killed by an Indian hunter. Lieutenant Governor Gooch of Virginia wrote to the Lords of Trade, June 29, 1729, "of some runaway Negroes beginning a settlement in the Mountains & of their being reclaimed by their Master." He assured the Lords that the militia was being trained to "prevent this for the future."[6]

In September 1733, the Governor of South Carolina offered a reward of £20 alive and £10 dead for "several Run away Negroes who are near the Congerees, & have robbed several of the Inhabitants thereabouts." The Notchee Indians offered, in April 1744, to aid the government of South Carolina in maintaining the subordination of its slave population. Three months later, on July 5, 1774, Governor James Glen applied "for the assistance of some Notchee Indians in order to apprehend some runaway Negroes, who had sheltered themselves in the Wood, and being armed, had committed disorders . . ."[7]

The number of runaways in South Carolina in 1765 was exceedingly large. This led to fears of a general rebellion.[8] At least one considerable camp of maroons was destroyed that year by military force. A letter from Charleston of August 16, 1768, told of a battle with a body of maroons, "a numerous collection of outcast mullattoes, mustees, and free negroes."[9]

Governor James Habersham of Georgia learned in December 1771 "that a great number of fugitive Negroes had Committed many Robberies and insults between this town [Savannah] and Ebenezer and that their Numbers (which) were now Considerable might be expected to increase daily."[10] Indian hunters and militiamen were employed to blot out this menace. Yet the same danger was present in Georgia in the summer of 1772. Depredations, piracy, and arson were frequent, and again the militia saw service. A letter from

Edmund Randolph to James Madison of August 30, 1782, discloses somewhat similar trouble in Virginia. At this time it appears that "a notorious robber," a white man, had gathered together a group of about fifty men, Negro and white, and was terrorizing the community.[11]

The British had combated the revolutionists' siege of Savannah with the aid of a numerous body of Negro slaves who served under the inspiration of a promised freedom. The defeat of the British crushed the hopes of these Negroes. They fled with their arms, called themselves soldiers of the King of England, and carried on guerrilla warfare for years along the Savannah River. Militia from Georgia and South Carolina, together with Indian allies, successfully attacked the Negro settlement in May 1786, with resulting heavy casualties.[12] Governor Thomas Pinckney of South Carolina referred in his legislative message of 1787 to the serious depredations of a group of armed fugitive slaves in the southern part of the state.[13]

Chesterfield and Charles City Counties, Virginia, were troubled by maroons in November 1792.[14] At least one white man was killed while tracking them down. Ten of the runaways were finally captured, with the aid of dogs. The neighborhood of Wilmington, North Carolina, was harassed in June and July 1795, by "a number of runaway Negroes, who in the daytime secrete themselves in the swamps and woods . . . at night committed various depredations on the neighboring plantations."[15] They killed at least one white man, an overseer, and severely wounded another. About five of these maroons, including the leader, known as the General of the Swamps, were killed by hunting parties. It was hoped that "these well-timed severities" would "totally break up this nest of miscreants—At all events, this town has nothing to apprehend as the citizens keep a strong and vigilant night guard." Within two weeks of this first report, of July 3, the capture and execution of four more runaways was reported. On July 17 it was believed that only one leader and a "few deluded followers" were still at large.

The existence of a maroon camp in the neighborhood of Elizabeth City, North Carolina, in May 1802, is indicated by the fact that the plots and insubordination uncovered among the servile population at that time were attributed to the agitation of an outlawed Negro, Tom Copper, who "has got a camp in one of the swamps."[16] In March 1811, a runaway community in a swamp in Cabarrus County, North Carolina, was wiped out. These maroons "had bid defiance to any force whatever, and were resolved to stand their ground."[17] In the attack two Negro women were captured, two Negro men killed, and another wounded.

The close proximity of the weakly-governed Spanish territory of East Florida persistently disturbed the equanimity of American slaveholders. Many of the settlers in that region, moreover, were Americans, and they, aided by volunteers from the United States, raised the standard of revolt in 1810, the aim being American annexation.[18] In the correspondence of Lieutenant Colonel Thomas Smith and Major Flournoy, both of the United States Army and both actively on the side of the rebels or "patriots" in the Florida fighting, and of Governor Mitchell of Georgia, there are frequent references to the fleeing of American slaves into Florida, where they helped the Indians in their struggle against the Americans and the "patriots." A few examples may be cited.

Smith told General Pinckney, July 30, 1812, of fresh Indian depredations in Georgia and of the escape of about eighty slaves. He planned to send troops against them, for "The safety of our frontier I conceive requires this course. They have, I am informed, several hundred fugitive slaves from the Carolinas and Georgia at present in their Towns & unless they are checked soon they will be so strengthened by desertions from Georgia & Florida that it will be found troublesome to reduce them." And it was troublesome. In a letter to Governor Mitchell of August 21, 1812, Smith declared, "The blacks assisted by the Indians have become very daring." In September further slave escapes were reported from Georgia. On September 11, a baggage train under Captain Williams and twenty men, going to the support of Colonel Smith, were attacked and routed, Williams himself being killed by Indians and maroons. In January 1813, further escapes were reported, and in February, Smith wrote of battles with Negroes and Indians, and the destruction of a Negro fort. One Georgian participant in this fighting, Colonel Daniel Newnan, declared the maroon allies of the Indians were "their best soldiers."[19]

The refusal of the Senate of the United States, at the moment, to sanction occupation of East Florida, finally led to a lull in the fighting. By 1816, however, the annoyance and danger from runaway slaves against served as justification for American intervention. With Southern complaints ringing in its ears the administration dispatched, in July, United States troops with Indian allies under Colonel Duncan Clinch against the main stronghold of the maroons, the well-stocked Negro fort on Appalachicola Bay.[20] After a siege of ten days a lucky cannon shot totally destroyed the fort and annihilated two hundred and seventy men, women, and children. But forty souls survived.[21]

Another major expedition against a maroon community was carried out in 1816. This occurred near Ashepoo, South Carolina. Governor David R.

Williams' remarks concerning this in his message of December 1816, merit quotation:[22]

> A few runaway Negroes, concealing themselves in the swamps and marshes contiguous to Combahee and Ashepoo rivers, not having been interrupted in their petty plunderings for a long time, formed the nucleus, round which all the all-disposed and audacious near them gathered, until at length their robberies became too serious to be suffered with impunity. Attempts were then made to disperse them, which either from insufficiency of numbers or bad arrangement, served by their failure only to encourage a wanton destruction of property. Their forces now became alarming, not less from its numbers than from its arms and ammunition with which it was supplied. The peculiar situation of the whole of that portion of our coast, rendered access to them difficult, while the numerous creeks and water courses through the marshes around the islands, furnished them easy opportunities to plunder, not only the planters in open day, but the inland coasting trade also without leaving a trace of their movements by which they could be pursued . . . I therefore ordered Major-General Youngblood to take the necessary measures for suppressing them, and authorized him to incur the necessary expenses of such an expedition. This was immediately executed. By a judicious employment of the militia under his command, he either captured or destroyed the whole body.

The *Norfolk Herald* of June 29, 1818, referred to the serious damages occasioned by a group of some thirty runaway slaves, acting together with white men, in Princess Anne County, Virginia.[23] It reported, too, the recent capture of a leader and "an old woman" member of the outlaws. In November of that year maroon activities in Wake County, North Carolina, became serious enough to evoke notice from the local press which advised "the patrol to keep a strict look out."[24] Later an attack upon a store "by a maroon banditti of Negroes" led by "the noted Andey, alias Billy James, better known here by the name of Abaellino," was repulsed by armed citizens. The paper believed that the death of at least one white man, if not more, might accurately be placed at their hands. The *Raleigh Register* of December 18, 1818, printed Governor Branch's proclamation offering $250 reward for the capture of seven specified outlaws and $100 for Billy James alone. There is evidence that, in this same year, maroons were active in Johnston County, in that state, and one expedition against them resulted in the killing of at least one Negro.[25] Expeditions against maroons took place in Williamsburg County, South Carolina, in the summer of 1819.[26] Three slaves were killed, several captured, and one white was wounded. Similar activities occurred in May

1820, in Gates County, North Carolina. A slave outlaw, Harry, whose head had been assessed at $200, was killed by four armed whites. "It is expected that the balance of Harry's company [which had killed at least one white man] will very soon be taken."[27]

Twelve months later there was similar difficulty near Georgetown, South Carolina, resulting in the death of one slaveholder and the capture of three outlaws.[28] The activities of considerable maroon groups in Onslow, Carteret, and Bladen Counties, North Carolina, aided by some free Negroes, assumed the proportions of rebellion in the summer of 1821. There were plans for joint action between these outlaws and the field slaves against the slaveholders. Approximately three hundred members of the militia of the three counties saw service for about twenty-five days in August and September. About twelve of these men were wounded when two companies of militia accidentally fired upon each other. The situation was under control by the middle of September, "although the said militia [sic] did not succeed in apprehending all the runaways & fugitives, they did good by arresting some, and driving others off, and suppressing the spirit of insurrection."[29] A newspaper item of 1824 discloses that the "prime mover" of the trouble mentioned above, Isam, "alias General Jackson," was among those who escaped at the time, for he is there reported as dying from lashes publicly inflicted at Cape Fear, North Carolina.[30]

In the summer of 1822, activity among armed runaway slaves was reported from Jacksonborough (now Jacksonboro) South Carolina.[31] Three were executed on July 19. In August Governor Bennett offered a reward of two hundred dollars for the capture of about twenty maroons in the same region. It is possible that these Negroes had been enlisted in the far-flung conspiracy of Denmark Vesey, uncovered and crushed in June 1822.

The Norfolk Herald of May 12, 1823, contains[32] an unusually full account of maroons under the heading "A Serious Subject." It declares that the citizens of the southern part of Norfolk county, Virginia,

> Have for some time been kept in a state of mind peculiarly harassing and painful, from the too apparent fact that their lives are at the mercy of a band of lurking assassins, against whose designs neither the power of the law, or vigilance, or pe [illegible] strength and intrepidity, can avail. These desperados are [illegible] away Negroes (commonly called outlyers) . . . Their first object is to obtain a gun and ammunition, as well as to procure game [illegible] subsistence as to defend themselves from attack, or accomplish objects of vengeance.

Several men had already been killed by these former slaves, one, a Mr. William Walker, very recently. This aroused great fear. "No individual after this can consider his life safe from the murdering aim of these monsters in human shape. Every one who has haply rendered himself obnoxious to their vengeance, must, indeed, calculate on soon or later falling a victim" to them. Indeed, one slaveholder had received a note from these amazing fellows suggesting it would be healthier for him to remain indoors at night—and he did.

A large body of militia was ordered out to exterminate these outcasts and "thus relieve the neighboring inhabitants from a state of perpetual anxiety and apprehension, than which nothing can be more painful." During the next few weeks there were occasional reports of the killing or capturing of outlaws,[33] culminating June 25 in the capture of the leader himself, Bob Ferebee, who, it was declared, had been an outlaw for six years. He was executed July 25. In October of the same year, runaway Negroes near Pineville, South Carolina, were attacked.[34] Several were captured, and at least two, a woman and a child, were killed. One of the maroons was decapitated and his head stuck on a pole and publicly exposed as "a warning to vicious slaves."

A maroon community consisting of men, women, and children was broken up by a three-day attack made by armed slaveholders of Mobile County, Alabama, in June 1827. The Negroes had been outlaws for years and had lived entirely by plundering neighboring plantations.[35] At the time of the attacks the Negroes were constructing a stockade fort. Had this been finished, it was believed that field slaves, thus informed, would have joined them. Cannon would then have been necessary for their destruction. The maroons made a desperate resistance, "fighting like Spartans." Three were killed, others wounded, and several escaped. Because of the poor arms of the Negroes but one white was slightly wounded.

In November 1827, a Negro woman returned to her master in New Orleans after an absence of sixteen years. She told of a maroon settlement some eight miles north of the city containing about sixty people.[36] A drought prevailed at the moment so it was felt that "the uncommon dryness . . . has made those retreats attainable . . . and we are told there is another camp about the head of the bayou Bienvenu. Policy imperiously calls for a thorough search, and the destruction of all such repairs, wherever found to exist."

In the summer of 1829, "a large gang of runaway negroes, who have infested the Parishes of Christ Church and St. James, [S. C.] for several months, and committed serious depredations on the properties of the planters" was accidentally discovered by a party of deer hunters.[37] One of the Negroes was wounded and four others were captured. Several others escaped, but the Charleston *Mercury* hoped the citizens would "not cease their executions until the evil shall be effectually removed."

Maroons were important factors in causing slave insubordination in Sampson, Bladen, Onslow, Jones, New Hanover, and Dublin Counties, North Carolina, from September through December 1830. Citizens complained that their "slaves are become most uncontrollable. They go and come and when and where they please, and if an attempt is made to correct them they immediately fly to the woods and there continue for months and years Committing grievous depredations on our Cattle, hogs and Sheep."[38] One of these fugitive slaves, Moses, who had been out for two years, was captured in November. From him one elicited the information that an uprising was imminent, that the conspirators "had arms & ammunition secreted, that they had runners or messengers to go between Wilmington, Newbern & Elizabeth City to 'carry word' & report to them, that there was a camp in Dover Swamp of 30 or 40—another about Gastons Island, on Price's Creek, several on Newport River, several near Wilmington."[39] Arms were found in the place named by Moses.

> In possession of a white woman living in a very retired situation—also some meat, hid away & could not be accounted for—a child whom the party [of citizens] found a little way from the house, said that his mamy dressed victuals every day for 4 or 5 runaways, & shewed the spot . . . where the meat was then hid & where it was found—the place or camp in Dover was found, a party of neighbors discovered the camp, burnt 11 houses, and made such discoveries, as convinced them it was a place of rendezvous for numbers (it is supposed they killed several of the Negroes).

Newspaper accounts referred to the wholesale shooting of fugitives. In 1830, the *Roanoke Advertiser* stated: "The inhabitants of Newbern being advised of the assemblage of sixty armed slaves in a swamp in their vicinity, the military were called out, and surrounding the swamp, killed the whole party."[40] A later item dated Wilmington, January 7, 1831, declared, "There has been much shooting of Negroes in this neighborhood recently, in consequence of symptoms of liberty having been discovered among them."[41] It is of interest to note that Richmond papers, on receiving the first reports of Nat Turner's revolt of August 1831, asked concerning the rebels, "Were they connected with the desperadoes who harassed [sic] N. Carolina last year?"[42]

In June 1836, there is mention that a band of runaway Negroes in the Cypress Swamp near New Orleans "had been committing depredations."[43] The next year, in July, was reported the killing of an outlaw slave leader, Squire, near

New Orleans, whose band, it was felt, was responsible for the deaths of several white men.[44] Squire's career had lasted for three years. A guard of soldiers was sent to the swamp for his body, which was exhibited for several days in the public square of the city.

The year 1837 also saw the start of the Florida or Seminole War which was destined to drag on until 1843. This war, "conducted largely as a slave catching enterprise for the benefit of the citizens of Georgia and Florida," was, before its termination, to take an unknown number of Indian and Negro lives together with the lives of fifteen hundred white soldiers and the expenditure of twenty million dollars.[45] The Indians had, at the beginning of hostilities, about sixteen hundred fifty warriors and two hundred fifty Negro fighters. The latter were "the most formidable foe, more blood-thirsty, active, and revengeful, than the Indian."[46]

Armed runaways repulsed an attack near Wilmington, North Carolina, in January 1841, after killing one of the whites. A posse captured three of the Negroes and lodged them in the city jail. One escaped, but two were taken from the prison by some twenty-five whites and lynched.[47] Late in September two companies of militia were dispatched in search of a body of maroons some forty-five miles north of Mobile, Alabama.[48] "It is believed that these fellows have for a long time been in the practice of theft and arson, both in town and country . . . A force from above was scouring down, with bloodhounds &c to meet the Mobile party." A month later, frequent attacks upon white men by runaway Negroes were reported from Terrebonne Parish, Louisiana.[49]

Several armed planters near Hanesville, Mississippi, in February 1844, set an ambush for maroons who had been exceedingly troublesome. Six Negroes, "part of the gang," were trapped, but three escaped. Two were wounded and one was killed.[50] In November 1846, about a dozen armed slaveholders surprised "a considerable gang of runaway Negroes" in St. Landry Parish, Louisiana. The maroons refused to surrender and fled. Two Negroes, a man and a woman, were killed, and two Negro women were "badly wounded." The others escaped.[51]

Joshua R. Giddings referred to the flight in September 1850, of some three hundred former Florida maroons from their abode to present Oklahoma to Mexico.[52] This was accomplished after driving off Creek Indians sent to oppose their exodus. The *Pennsylvania Freeman* of October 30, 1851, citing the *Houston Telegraph* (n.d.), states that fifteen hundred former American slaves were aiding the Comanchee Indians of Mexico in their fighting. Five hundred of these Negroes were from Texas. Giddings also referred to unsuccessful expeditions by slaveholders of Texas in 1853 into Mexico to recover fugitive Negroes, and declared that at the time he was writing (1858), maroons in southern Florida were again causing trouble. F. L. Olmsted gave evidence of maroon troubles in the 1850s in Virginia, Louisiana, and northern Alabama.[53]

A letter of August 25, 1856, to Governor Thomas Bragg of North Carolina, signed by Richard A. Lewis and twenty-one other citizens, informed him of a "very secure retreat for runaway Negroes" in a large swamp between Bladen and Robeson counties.[54] There "for many years past, and at this time, there are several runaways of bad and daring character—destructive to all kinds of Stock and dangerous to all persons living by or near said swamp." Slaveholders attacked these Negroes August 1, 1845, but accomplished nothing and saw one of their own number killed. "The Negroes ran off cursing and swearing and telling them to come on, they were ready for them again." The *Wilmington Journal* of August 14 mentioned that these runaways "had cleared a place for a garden, had cows, &c in the swamp." Mr. Lewis and his friends were "unable to offer sufficient inducement for Negro hunters to come with their dogs unless aided from other sources." The Governor suggested that magistrates be requested to call for the militia, but whether this was done or not is unknown.

A runaway camp was destroyed,[55] and four Negroes, including a woman, captured near Bovina, Mississippi, in March 1857. A similar event, resulting in the wounding of three maroons occurred in October 1859, in Nash County, North Carolina.[56] An "organized camp of white men and Negroes" was held responsible for a servile conspiracy, involving whites, which was uncovered in Talladega County, Alabama, in August 1860.[57]

The years of the Civil War witnessed a considerable accentuation in the struggle of the Negro people against enslavement. This was as true of maroon activity as it was generally. There were reports of depredations committed by "a gang of runaway slaves" acting together with two whites along the Comite River, Louisiana, early in 1861.[58] An expedition was set "on foot to capture the whole party." A runaway community near Marion, South Carolina, was attacked in June 1861.[59] There were no casualties, however, the slave hunters captured two Negro children, twelve guns, and one axe.

Confederate Brigadier-General R. F. Floyd asked Governor Milton of Florida on April 11, 1862, to declare martial law in Nassau, Duvar, Clay, Putnam, St. John's, and Volusia Counties "as a measure of absolute necessity, as they contain a nest of traitors and lawless Negroes."[60] In October 1862, a scouting party of three armed whites, investigating a maroon camp containing one hundred men, women, and children in Surry county, Virginia, were killed by these fugitives.[61] Governor Shorter of Alabama commissioned J. H. Clayton in January 1863, to destroy the nests in the southeastern part of the state of "deserters, traitors, and runaway Negroes."[62]

Colonel Hatch of the Union army reported in August 1864, that "500 Union men, deserters, and Negroes were . . . raiding towards Gainesville," Florida.[63] The same month a confederate officer, John K. Jackson, declared that

> Many deserters . . . are collected in the swamps and fastnesses of Taylor, La Fayette, Levy and other counties [in Florida], and have organized, with run-away Negroes, bands for the purpose of committing depredations upon the plantations and crops of loyal citizens and running off their slaves. These depredatory bands have even threatened the cities of Tallahassee, Madison and Marianna.[64]

A Confederate newspaper noticed similar activities in North Carolina in 1864.[65] It reported it

> difficult to find words of description . . . of the wild and terrible consequences of the Negro raids in this obscure . . . theatre of the war . . . In the two counties of Currituck and Camden, there are said to be from five to six hundred Negroes, who are not in the regularly military organization of the Yankees, but who, outlawed and disowned by their masters, lead the lives of banditti, roving the country with fire and committing all sorts of horrible crimes upon the inhabitants.
>
> This present theater of guerrilla warfare has, at this time, a most important interest for our authorities. It is described as a rich country, . . . and one of the most important sources of meat supplies that is now accessible to our armies. . . .

The account ends with a broad hint that white deserters from the Confederate army were fighting shoulder to shoulder with the self-emancipated Negroes.

The story of the American maroons is of interest not only because it forms a fairly important part of the history of the South and of the Negro, but also because of the evidence it affords to show that the conventional picture of slavery as a more or less delightful, patriarchal system is fallacious. The corollary of this fallacious picture—docile, contented slaves—is also, of course, seriously questioned. Indeed, taking this material on maroons in conjunction with that recently presented on servile revolts,[66] leads one to assert that American slavery was a horrid form of tyrannical rule which often found it necessary to suppress ruthlessly the desperate expressions of discontent on the part of its outraged victims.

Notes

This chapter originally appeared as an article of the same title in *The Journal of Negro History* 24: 2 (Apr. 1939), 167–84.

1. Charles W. Janson, *The Stranger in America,* London, 1807, pp. 328–30; William H. Russell, *My Diary North and South,* Boston, 1863, pp. 88–89; Frederick L. Olmsted, *Journey in Seaboard Slave States,* London, 1904, 2, pp. 177–78; Olmsted, *Journey in the Back Country,* London, 1860, pp. 30, 55; T. W. Higginson, *Army Life in a Black Regiment,* Boston, 1870, p. 248; James Parton, *Life of Andrew Jackson,* Boston, 1860, 2, pp. 397–98; W. H. Siebert, *The Underground Railroad,* N.Y., 1899, p. 25; S. M. Ellis, *The Solitary Horseman,* Kensington, 1927, p. 169; V. A. Moody in *Louisiana Historical Quarterly* (1924), 7, pp. 224–25; R. H. Taylor in *North Carolina Historical Review* (1928), 5, pp. 23–24; U. B. Phillips in *The South in the Building of the Nation,* Richmond, 1909, 4, p. 229.

2. See references in note 1, and an article by Edmund Jackson in *The Pennsylvania Freeman,* January 1, 1852; Harriet B. Stowe, *Dred,* 2 vols., Boston, 1856; Margaret Davis in *South Atlantic Quarterly* (1934), 33, pp. 171, 184.

3. W. Hening, *Statutes at Large of Virginia,* II, p. 299; P. A. Bruce, *Economic History of Virginia in 17th Century,* N.Y., 1896, 2, p. 115.

4. *Order Book,* Middlesex County, 1680–1694, pp. 526–27 (Virginia State Library); Bruce, *Economic History of Virginia in 17th Century,* N.Y., 1896, 2, p. 116.

5. E. C. Holland, *A Refutation of the Calumnies,* Charleston, 1823, p. 63; D. D. Wallace, *The History of South Carolina,* N.Y., 1934, 1, p. 372.

6. Virginia Manuscripts from British Record Office. Sainsbury, 9, p. 462, Virginia State Library.

7. *Council Journal* (MS.) 5, pp. 487, 494; 11, pp. 187, 383, South Carolina Historical Commission, Columbia, S.C.

8. D. D. Wallace, *The History of South Carolina,* N.Y., 1934, 1, p. 373.

9. *The Boston Chronicle,* October 3–10, 1768.

10. *The Colonial Records of Georgia,* ed. A. D. Candler, Atlanta, 1907, 12, pp. 146–47, 325–26.

11. M. D. Conway, *Omitted Chapters in History Disclosed in the Life and Papers of Edmund Randolph,* N.Y., 1888, pp. 50–51.

12. W. B. Stevens, *A History of Georgia,* Philadelphia, 1859, 2, pp. 376–78; C. G. Woodson, *The Negro in Our History,* Washington, 1928, p. 123; *Historical Manuscripts Commission, Report on American Manuscripts,* London, 1904, 2, p. 544.

13. C. C. Pinckney, *Life of General Thomas Pinckney,* Boston, 1895, p. 95; D. D. Wallace, *The History of South Carolina,* N.Y., 1934, 2, p. 415.

14. Letter dated Richmond, November 19, in *Boston Gazette,* December 17, 1792.

15. *Wilmington Chronicle* (Photostat, Library of Congress), July 3, 10, 17, 1795; *Charleston City Gazette,* July 18, 23, 1795; R. H. Taylor in *North Carolina Historical Review* (1928), 5, pp. 23–24.

16. *Raleigh Register* (State Library, Raleigh), June 1, 1802; *New York Herald,* June 2, 1802.

17. *Edenton Gazette,* March 22, 1811; G. G. Johnson, *Antebellum North Carolina,* Chapel Hill, 1937, p. 514.

18. J. W. Pratt, *Expansionists of 1812,* N.Y. 1925, pp. 92, 116, 192–95, 212.

19. T. F. Davis in *Florida Historical Quarterly* (1930), 9, pp. 106–07, 111, 138; *Niles' Weekly Register,* December 12, 1812, 3, pp. 235–37.

20. See, for example, *Richmond Enquirer,* July 10, 1816.

21. *Connecticut Courant,* September 10, 24, 1816; *State Papers,* 2d sess., 15 Cong., vol. 4; J. B. McMaster, *History,* 4, p. 431; McMaster's account is practically copied by H. B. Fuller, *The Purchase of Florida,* Cleveland, 1906, p. 228.

22. H. T. Cook, *Life and Legacy of David H. Williams,* N.Y., 1916, p. 130

23. Quoted in *New York Evening Post,* July 7, 1818.

24. *Raleigh Register,* November 13, 27, 1818.

25. G. G. Johnson, *Antebellum North Carolina,* Chapel Hill, 1937, p. 514.

26. U. B. Phillips, *Plantation and Frontier Democrats,* Cleveland, 1909, 2, p. 91.

27. *Edenton Gazette,* May 12, 1820, quoted by *New York Evening Post,* May 17, 1820.

28. *New York Evening Post,* June 11, 1821.

29. See petition of John H. Hill, Colonel Commandant of the Carteret Militia, dated December 1825, and accompanying memoranda in Legislative Papers, 1824–1825 (No. 366), North Carolina Historical Commission, Raleigh; R. H. Taylor, *North Carolina Historical Review* (1928), 5, p. 24; G. G. Johnson, *Antebellum North Carolina,* Chapel Hill, 1937, p. 514.

30. *New York Evening Post,* May 11, 1824.

31. *Washington National Intelligencer,* July 23, August 24, 1822.

32. Quoted in *New York Evening Post,* May 15, 1823.

33. *Ibid.,* May 29, June 5, June 30, 1823.

34. *Charleston City Gazette* quoted in *New York Evening Post,* October 24, 1823; *Niles' Weekly Register,* October 18, 1823, 25, p. 112; T. J. Kirkland and R. M. Kennedy, *Historic Camden,* Columbia, 1926, part 2, p. 190.

35. *Mobile Register,* June 20, 21, 1827, quoted in *New York Evening Post,* July 11, 12, 1827; U. B. Phillips in *The South in the Building of the Nation,* Richmond, 1909, 4, p. 229.

36. *New York Evening Post,* December 4, 1827.

37. *Ibid.,* August 10, 1829.

38. G. G. Johnson, *Antebellum North Carolina,* Chapel Hill, 1937, pp. 515, 517; R. H. Taylor, *North Carolina Historical Review* (1928), 5, p. 31.

39. See letter dated November 15, 1830, Newbern, from J. Turgwyn to Governor John Owen in Governor's *Letter Book,* Vol. 28, pp. 247–49, and letter from J. I. Pasteur to Governor Owen also dated Newbern, Nov. 15, 1830, in Governor's Papers No. 60, Historical Commission, Raleigh.

40. Quoted in *The (Boston) Liberator,* January 8, 1831.

41. *New York Sentinel,* quoted in *Liberator,* March 19, 1831.

42. *Richmond Enquirer,* August 30, 1831.

43. *Louisiana Advertiser,* June 8, 1836, quoted by *Liberator,* July 2, 1836.

44. *New Orleans Picayune,* July 19, 1837.

45. Grant Foreman, *Indian Removal,* Norman, 1932, pp. 366, 383; see also *Liberator,* March 18, 1837.

46. John T. Sprague, *The Origin, Progress and Conclusion of the Florida War,* N.Y., 1848, p. 309; J. R. Giddings, *The Exiles of Florida,* Columbus, 1858, pp. 121, 139.

47. *Wilmington Chronicle,* January 6, 1841, in *Liberator,* January 22, 1841.

48. *New Orleans Bee,* October 4, 1841.

49. *Lafourch (LA) Patriot* in *Liberator,* November 12, 1841.

50. *Hanesville Free Press,* March 1, 1844, cited by *Liberator,* April 5, 1844.

51. *New Orleans Picayune,* quoted in *Liberator,* December 4, 1846.

52. Giddings, *The Exiles of Florida,* Columbus, 1858, pp. 316, 334, 337.

53. Olmstead, *Journey in Seaboard Slave States,* London, 1904, 2,p. 177; *Journey in the Back Country,* London, 1860, pp. 30, 55.

54. Governor's *Letter Book,* No. 43, pp. 514–15, Historical Commission, Raleigh.

55. *Vicksburg Whig,* cited by *Liberator,* April 3, 1857.

56. *The Day Book,* Norfolk, October 13, 1859.

57. Laura White, in *Journal of Southern History,* 1 (1935), p. 47.

58. *New York Daily Tribune,* March 11, 1861.

59. H. M. Henry, *Police Control of the Slave in South Carolina,* Emory, 1914, p. 121.

60. *Official Records of the Rebellion,* Ser. 1, vol. 53, p. 233.

61. *Calendar of Virginia State Papers,* 11, pp. 233–36.

62. *Official Records of the Rebellion,* Ser. 1, vol. 15, p. 947; Georgia Lee Tatum, *Disloyalty in the Confederacy,* Chapel Hill, 1934, p. 63.

63. Tatum, *Disloyalty in the Confederacy,* Chapel Hill, 1934, p. 88.

64. *Official Records of the Rebellion,* Ser. 1, vol. 25, Part II, p. 607.

65. *Daily Richmond Examiner,* January 14, 1864.

66. Harvey Wish, *Journal of Negro History* (1937), 22, pp. 304–20; Aptheker, *Science and Society* (1937), 1, pp. 512–38; 2 (1938), pp. 386–91.

3

The Negro in the Abolitionist Movement

Cohesiveness, discipline, organization were vital if the abolitionist cause was to succeed, for its purpose was of a profoundly revolutionary nature.[1] Unless the effort is seen in this light its character is but dimly grasped, for the abolitionists set themselves the tasks of subverting and destroying a fundamental vested interest whose roots were deep and whose branches were far spread.

True it is that success finally came only after the maturing of a new face, a new class, the industrial bourgeoisie, whose interests were opposed to those of its predecessor, but this success was not automatic, did not come of itself. It was produced by men and women, Negro and white, who had for decades been sowing the seed, talking, writing, petitioning, voting, and who finally piloted an aroused America through the maelstrom of a four-year Civil War. How much work had to be done before the nation willingly set itself the task of excising the cancer of slavery from its vitals, before a long-legged Westerner named Lincoln would agree that the operation should continue even though it go on "until all the wealth piled by the bondsman's two hundred fifty years of unrequited toil shall be sunk, and until every drop of blood drawn by the lash shall be paid by another drawn with the sword!"

The job was not for the faint-hearted. The slave holders represented, for the first half of the nineteenth century, the most closely knit and most important single economic unit in the nation, their millions of bondsmen and millions of acres of land comprising an investment of billions of dollars. This economic might had its counterpart in political power, giving its possessors dominance within the nation and predominance within the South. Listen to the words of

James Hammond, a rich slave holder and leading South Carolina politician. He is commenting, in 1845, on the bitterness of the words passing between the slave holder and abolitionist groups, and to the latter he says:[2]

> But if your course was wholly different—if you distilled nectar from your lips and discoursed sweetest music, could you reasonably indulge the hope of accomplishing your object by such means? Nay, supposing that we were all convinced, and thought of Slavery precisely as you do, at what era of "moral suasion" do you imagine you could prevail on us to give up a thousand millions of dollars in the value of our slaves, and thousand millions of dollars more in the depreciation of our lands, in consequence of the want of laborers to cultivate them?

And the products driven out of the slaves and this land, the rice, sugar, cotton, tobacco, made up the blood and bones of the businesses of the merchant capitalists of the North; they, too, rested finally upon the broad black backs of the slaves, and so they allied themselves with their immediate exploiters. Thus it was that a partner in a large New York mercantile house called aside Samuel J. May, the abolitionist, one day in 1835, and said:[3]

> Mr. May, we are not such great fools as not to know that slavery is a great evil and a great wrong. But it was consented to by the founders of the Republic. It was provided for in the Constitution of our Union. A great portion of the property of the Southerners is invested under its sanction; and the business of the North as well as of the South, has become adjusted to it. There are millions upon millions of dollars due from the Southerners to the merchants and mechanics of this city alone, the payment of which would be jeopardized by a rupture between the North and the South. We cannot afford, sir, to let you and your associates succeed in your endeavor to overthrow slavery. It is not a matter of principle with us. It is a matter of business necessity. We cannot afford to let you succeed. And I have called you out to let you know, and to let your fellow laborers know, that we do not mean to allow you to succeed. We mean, sir, to put you Abolitionists down—by fair means, if we can, by foul means, if we must.

And if this were not enough, the slave holders did not fail to appreciate, and to point out to their northern class brothers, that the philosophy of Abolitionism—its equalitarianism, its progressivism, and above all, its attack upon the sanctity of private property—represented an ultimate threat to the interests of all exploiters. As a Virginian wrote in reply to the questioning of the institution of slavery that flowered following the Nat Turner cataclysm:[4]

> This is one thing we wish to be understood and remember—that the Constitution of this state, has made Tom, Dick, and Harry, *property*—it has made Polly, Nancy and Molly, *property;* and be that property is an evil, a curse, or what not, we intend to hold it. Property, which is considered the most valuable by the owners of it, is a nice thing; and for the right, thereto, to be called in question by an unphilosophical set of political mountebanks, under the influence of supernatural agency or deceit, is insufferable.

Somewhat later a wealthy Georgian warned that the "same torch" which, wielded by the abolitionists, threatened to consume the fabric of the slave South would, one day, "also cause the north-eastern horizon to coruscate with the flames of northern palaces."[5] The essence of the matter was more fully put, in an inimitable manner, by a religious and educational leader of South Carolina, Dr. James H. Thornwell, in 1850:[6]

> The parties in this conflict are not merely Abolitionists and slaveholders—they are atheists, socialists, communists, red republicans, Jacobins on the one side, and the friends of order and regulated freedom on the other. In one word, the world is the battleground—Christianity and atheism the combatants; and the progress of humanity the stake.

Yes, the abolitionists were attacking the lords of the lash who controlled the press and pulpit, represented stability and respectability, manipulated the political apparatus; and to conquer required wisdom, level-headedness, energy, organization, and above all, perfect courage, rooted in deep-seated, overwhelming conviction that human slavery was bad, evil, rotten—a courage and conviction that scorned compromise, detested opportunism, and gained strength from the enemy's resistance. Where would this conviction reside if not in the hearts and brains of Negro Americans? Who would better know slavery than those whose backs bore its stripes, into whose eyes had been blazoned its indignities and abominations? Who, while they spoke and wrote and agitated, were speaking and writing and agitating about that which, even while they labored, was oppressing their own people, often their own children, or their own parents?

From the era of the first American Revolution through the years of the second, Negroes were ever in the vanguard of the organized army attacking the slavocracy, seeking out and using to the uttermost whatever possibilities existed to advance the struggle.

Evidence of a concerted activity of an abolitionist nature on the part of the Negro people goes back at least the 1760s when, in Massachusetts, they attempted, by bringing an action of trespass against their masters, to challenge the entire legal concept of slavery.[7] The next decade was marked by a petition campaign, organized and carried on by Negroes themselves, in which provincial and state governing bodies were urged to destroy slavery, on the ground, as one of the documents put it: "That the God of Nature gave them life and freedom, upon the terms of most perfect equality with other men; That freedom is an inherent right of the human species, not to be surrendered, but by consent, for the sake of social life." There are extant records of eight such petitions, some signed by "a Grate Number of Blackes," in Massachusetts and New Hampshire from 1773 to 1779. One of these, that presented in 1775 by Negroes of Bristol and Worcester to the Committee of Correspondence of the latter county, led to the holding of a convention, on June 14, of many citizens, which went on record as abhorring Negro slavery and pledging to work for its abolition.[8]

This type of agitation was continued during the remaining years of the eighteenth century and, in addition, one may discern during the same period the beginnings of the Negro's contribution to the vast body of antislavery literature and the birth of Negro organizations of the same character. Particularly to be noted are the petitions of Prince Hall, a Massachusetts Negro, Masonic official, and veteran of the Revolutionary War, and of Absalom Jones, the Pennsylvania religious leader.

The former, signed by Prince Hall alone, was presented early in 1788 to the Massachusetts legislature and was aimed at getting that body to outlaw the slave trade. It attracted considerable attention, being the object of correspondence between such figures as Jeremy Belknap and Ebenezer Hazard, and being printed in full in the Boston *Spy* of April 24, 1788. Other petitions, from white people of a like nature followed, and this type of pressure and publicity was influential in bringing about the passage, that very year, of a state ban upon the trade.[9]

The latter was drawn up in 1799 and signed by "Absalom Jones and others, free men of color, of the city and county of Philadelphia," and presented on January 2, 1800, to the Congress of the United States by Representative Waln.[10] This asked for a federal anti-slave-trade law, the repeal of the Fugitive Slave Act of 1793, and "the adoption of such measures as shall in due course emancipate the whole of their brethren from their present situation." It provoked an exceedingly sharp and long debate, lasting two days, and was the means of focusing national attention upon the abomination. The petition was finally accepted and referred (and then, of course, buried), but only after the House had added the statement that the petitioners by their boldness and audacity, especially since they had asked Congress to abolish slavery, had earned the "disapprobation" of the members—and this by a vote of 85 to 1, Mr. Waln alone having the honor of casting a negative vote.

The pen was also wielded for the cause, even this early in the nation's history. One of the leading magazines in the country, the *American Museum*, published in Philadelphia by Mathew Carey, ran articles contributed by Negroes, one signed "Othello," the other "A Free Negro" in 1788 and 1789, denouncing slavery and demanding the realization in practice of the Declaration of Independence. The latter work was especially effective, stressing the fact that while white revolutionists were hailed as heroes and martyrs, Negroes who essayed the same task were greeted with derision and treated like depraved criminals. "Do rights of nature cease to be such when a Negro is to enjoy them?" this writer demanded. "Or does patriotism in the heart of an African rankle into treason?"[11]

Others, including Prince Hall, Benjamin Banneker, Absalom Jones, and Richard Allen published pamphlets in the 1790s in which every essential argument of the abolitionist movement was enunciated and developed. These works denied the inferiority of the Negro, gave the lie to the assertion that the slaves were happy and docile, and warned that the longer the evil was permitted to live, the more costly and catastrophic would be its destruction.[12]

The beginnings of Negro organization likewise go back to these years, and no matter what the ostensible purposes of these groups might be—religious, philanthropic, or literary—the very act on the part of these oppressed people of joining together was itself revolutionary, and they all, sooner or later, became part and parcel of the entire antislavery crusade. In the spring of 1787, Philadelphia Negroes, including Richard Allen, Absalom Jones, William White, Mark Stevenson, William Gray, and others, formed a Free African Society, whose original stated purpose was largely convivial, but which by 1790 devoted itself to antislavery agitation, the prevention of Negro kidnapping, and cooperation with emancipationist groups, such as state manumission societies and Quakers. Shortly after, Henry Stewart, a member of this society, moved to Newport, Rhode Island, and established in that community a similar association. Still another group was formed in New York City in 1795, and within three years still another African Society sprang up in Boston. The interests of the latter society are sufficiently indicated by the fact that it published, in 1808, a pamphlet entitled, *The Sons of Africa: An Essay on Freedom with Observations on the Origin of Slavery.*[13]

The first generation of the nineteenth century witnesses a significant expansion in the antislavery activity of the Negro people which did much to prepare the ground for the tilling and harvesting that was to come from the 1830s to the Civil War. Among the events and characters that stand out during this formative period is Peter Williams Jr., a minister in New York City, whose efforts to arouse his countrymen to the iniquities of slavery attracted attention as early as 1806. His work in this field continued for thirty years and led to his appointment in 1834 to the Board of Managers of the American Anti-Slavery Society.[14] Large-scale meetings of Negroes occurred in 1807 and 1808 in various northern cities, notably Philadelphia and New York, celebrating the passage, and the coming into force, of the federal anti-slave-trade law and contributing toward the publicizing of the cause of freedom.[15]

A few years later, another Negro whose career was to continue on into the thirties, James Forten of Philadelphia, made himself felt on behalf of his people's liberation. He gained notice in 1813 by his vigorous denunciation of projected Jim Crow regulations in Pennsylvania and in 1817, together with Russell Parrott, was important in bringing together 3,000 Philadelphia Negroes. These people went on record as decidedly opposed to the purposes of the recently launched American Colonization Society and as determined to win justice for themselves and their enslaved brethren here in their native land, not to seek a doubtful refuge elsewhere and so withdraw from the struggle for the slave's emancipation. In the words of the assembled thousands:[16]

> Let not a purpose be assisted which will stay the cause of the entire abolition of slavery in the United Sates, and which may defeat it altogether; which proffers to those who do not ask for them benefits, but which they consider injuries, and which must insure to the multitudes, whose prayers can only reach through us, misery, sufferings, and perpetual slavery.

This early meeting and expression of opinion are indicative of the consistently held viewpoint of the Negro people. Their well-nigh unanimous opposition was of the utmost importance in crippling the colonization movement (which received support and money from numerous wealthy individuals and even state legislatures, such as those of Maryland and Virginia) and in winning William Lloyd Garrison away from the snare and toward his unequivocal demand for immediate abolition of slavery.[17]

The next decade was marked by a worldwide development of progressivism, the most striking manifestation of which in the United States was the triumph of Jacksonianism and the lusty beginnings of a politically conscious labor movement. The growth of antislavery feeling was notable, particularly in Great Britain, and keen observers, such as Thomas Jefferson and John Quincy Adams, prophesied as early as 1820 the speedy crystallization of the struggle between the free and the slave systems.[18]

Negroes, ever in the forefront of those struggling against slavery, anticipated and did vital spade work for the flowering of the abolitionist movement, which came in the thirties. Of importance in the immediately preceding years were the Reverend Nathaniel Paul of the African Baptist Society in Albany, New York, whose radical speeches began to attract attention in 1827, the Reverend John Gloucester of Philadelphia, and William Whipper of the same city.[19] The latter was influential in beginning a Reading Room Society in Philadelphia in 1828, the purpose of which was the general education of its Negro members and, specifically, the development of antislavery sentiment. Similar groups (sometimes demonstrating by their names, as with the New York African Clarkson Society [1829], their emancipationist motive) sprang up elsewhere. Thus it was that by the time the national antislavery groups were formed early in the thirties, there already existed about fifty such Negro organizations spread throughout the country and eager to assist and join forces with the newcomers.[20]

The cause had sufficiently developed among the Negro people for them to be able to bring into existence and to support a weekly organ devoted to its enhancement. This appeared with the publication, beginning March 16, 1827, of the *Freedom's Journal* in New York City under the editorship of Samuel E. Cornish and John Russwurm. The journal had agents throughout New England, New York, Pennsylvania, Maryland, the District of Columbia, and even in Virginia and North Carolina, as well as Haiti, Canada, and England.[21]

One of the Boston agents of this paper was David Walker, a key figure in the history of the abolitionist movement. He had been born free in North Carolina on September 28, 1785, but the enslavement of his fellow men disgusted and enraged him and he decided he had to "leave this part of the country." He went to Boston where he earned his bread by dealing in old clothes. Here he became active in antislavery work, making at least one speech before the Colored Association of that city in December, 1828, and occasionally contributing to, as well as distributing, *Freedom's Journal*.[22]

In September 1829, he published his *Appeal*,[23] and from then, until his mysterious death sometime in 1830,[24] he supervised the distribution and reprinting of this work, which during the last year of his life went into its third edition. And David Walker, back in 1829, went as far as, and in some respects further than, abolitionist literature in general was to go for another twenty years. He used the Declaration of Independence with telling effect, flinging its immortal words into the teeth of those who upheld slavery. He denounced the colonizationists and affirmed the Negroes' right to the title of American. He excoriated the traitors among his own people, finding it difficult to find words damning enough with which to express his contempt for them. He waxed sarcastic and exuded bitterness as he contemplated the prevailing hypocrisy, with everyone talking about liberty and equality, while millions of human beings were treated worse than brutes. Rebel, he told the slaves, rebel and when "you commence make sure work—do not trifle, for they will not trifle with you—they want us for their slaves and think nothing of murdering us in order to subject us to that wretched condition—therefore, if there is an attempt made by us, kill or be killed."

At one point Walker left the immediate and the practical and this he did in order to utter this remarkable prophecy:[25]

> . . . for although the destruction of the oppressors God may not effect by the oppressed, yet the Lord our God will bring other destructions upon them—for not infrequently will he cause them to rise up one against another, to be split and divided, and to oppress each other, and sometimes to open hostilities with sword in hand.

Walker's *Appeal* was sent by him, through Negro and white sympathizers,[26] into the South and caused great excitement when discovered in Georgia, Louisiana, and North Carolina: it was a precipitant of slave conspiracy in the latter state, at least, in 1830.[27]

In 1829 appeared also the second Negro newspaper, the *Rights of All*, which Samuel E. Cornish brought out in New York shortly after Russwurm's renegacy had forced the *Freedom's Journal* to suspend publication. This was a radical paper of the highest integrity and quality, and while it lasted but a short time, it led the way for a host of other Negro newspapers that shortly followed and that, without exception, were devoted and valued adjuncts of the abolitionist movement.

Another major event that antedated the appearance of the *Liberator* and was a forerunner of similar events which were to play an important part during the years of the pre–Civil War generation was the assembling in September 1830, of the first national Negro Convention in Philadelphia. This convention denounced the American Colonization Society, called for slaves' liberation, advocated improved educational and industrial opportunities for Negroes, and set up the American Society for Free Persons of Colour to protect and assist such people and to secure a refuge for escaped slaves in Canada.[28] In December of the same year, a meeting of several hundred Negroes took place in Richard Allen's Philadelphia church, presided over by Ignatius Beek. Here was formed a Free Produce Society with a membership of about 230 people pledged to abstain from the use of slave-produced commodities,[29] a boycott movement which had played and was to continue to play a fairly large part in the general antislavery struggle, both in the United States and in Europe.

These independent efforts of the Negro people continued during the years when large numbers of white people entered into the battle. Thus there existed, in addition to the literary and social organizations to which reference has been made, all-Negro abolitionist societies in many parts of the country.[30] Some, like the Massachusetts General Colored Association, established in 1832 under the leadership of Thomas Dalton and William C. Nell, preceded the formation of the American Anti-Slavery Society. Many such organized bodies existed throughout the nation, more than one in cities like New York, Philadelphia, Boston, Newark, and Albany, and others in Rochester and Geneva, New York; Middletown, Connecticut; Nantucket, Massachusetts; Lexington, Ohio, and Lexington, Kentucky.[31]

There is, also, evidence of the existence of Negro societies having as their objective even more dangerous tasks than the sheltering of fugitives and the spreading of the literature and ideas of Abolitionism. These were dedicated to the aim of overthrowing slavery by every and any possible way, not escaping militant action, and to organizing the rescue of Negroes from slavery by entering the South and helping them escape. The dangerous character of the work of these groups and their illegality demanded secrecy, so that information concerning them is scarce. It does, however, seem clear that in 1844 the Reverend Moses Dickson of Cincinnati, together with eleven other Negroes, founded an "Order of Twelve of the Knights and Daughters of Tabor," which had the aims indicated above. In 1846, he started another secret association, the Knights of Liberty, with headquarters in St. Louis, which aided hundreds of slaves to escape.[32]

In addition to these permanent organizations, conventions of Negroes called to combat slavery, assist abolitionist societies and publications, fight Jim Crowism, and strive for the betterment of conditions for free Negroes, were regular features of America's antebellum years. National conventions were held annually from 1830 on, steadily growing in the number of delegates and the areas represented, the chief meeting places being New York and Philadelphia.[33] State conventions also frequently assembled in various parts of the country, while from time to time, as special issues such as colonization or battles against Jim Crowism, or aid to progressive forces, became acute, almost spontaneous, and always enthusiastic and well-attended meetings giving voice to the Negro's viewpoint were held.

Characteristic examples of each of these may be presented. The fifth annual convention of Negroes of New York state was held from September 18 to 20, 1844, in Schenectady. This was attended by over eighty delegates from eighteen cities and towns in the state, including Albany, Amsterdam, Ballston, Brooklyn, Constantia, Peterstown, Rochester, Syracuse, Troy, and Waterford. Men like the Reverend Henry Highland Garnet, Patrick H. Reason, Stephen Myers, and Dr. James McCune Smith were present, and resolutions demanding absolute equality, immediate emancipation, and total abstinence from slave-produced goods were adopted as the sentiments of the meeting.[34]

Reference has already been made to anti-colonization meetings on the part of Negroes soon after the launching of that obnoxious scheme. Similar affairs occurred whenever the movement showed signs of regaining vigor. This was particularly true in 1831 when, as a result of the marked increase of restlessness among the slaves, the master class turned to colonization with heightened ardor.

Typical was the meeting held in African Hall on Nassau Street in Brooklyn, New York, in May 1831, where the Negroes affirmed, "that we are *men,* we are *brethren,* that we are *countrymen* and *fellow citizens*" and found it strange indeed that the eminent gentlemen of the Colonization Society "can promise to honor and respect us in Africa, when they are using every effort to exclude us from all rights and privileges at home."[35]

Every Negro meeting and convention lambasted chauvinism, but some were wholly devoted to the subject or to some specific manifestation of the disease. Thus legal discrimination against New York Negroes with regard to the suffrage moved them to hold repeated meetings in the 1830s with men like Charles L. Reason and Thomas L. Jennings particularly prominent in protesting the disability. A petition campaign was organized, agents tramped through the country and succeeded in getting thousands of signatures, though success was not to crown their efforts for many years.[36] Similarly, in the forties, mass meetings and conventions were organized by Negroes in Ohio in order to secure the repeal of the Black Codes, with John M. Langston, George Carey, David Jenkins, and Dennis Hill leading the battle. This was successful, so that in 1849 the discriminatory legislation of the state of Ohio was repealed.[37]

Encouragement and assistance for progressive forces were often the main purposes of Negro meetings. Thus Philadelphia Negroes, led by Frederick Hinton, William Whipper, Robert Purvis, James Foren, and Junius C. Morell, met on March 1, 1831, only two months after the launching of the *Liberator,* pledged their support to it, and contributed to its maintenance. Such gatherings were common in various cities throughout that paper's life.[38]

A remaining and very important contribution made independently by the Negro people to the abolitionist movement came through their own publications, which included newspapers, magazines, pamphlets, and books. Record exists of well over a score of weekly newspapers owned, edited, and published by Negroes and very largely devoted to the antislavery movement. New York City was the favorite locale of these organizations, but they carried on in several other areas, such as Philadelphia, Pittsburgh, Albany, Troy, Rochester, Syracuse, Cincinnati, Cleveland, Baltimore, and San Francisco. There existed, too, beginning in 1841, magazines, both monthly and quarterly, produced by Negroes, in which more substantial contributions for the benefit of the same movement appeared.[39]

Of the antislavery books produced by Negroes (largely, though by no means wholly, autobiographical) one can here select for notice only a few of those which were most influential in creating and molding public opinion, for an attempt at compiling merely a list of all that flooded the bookstores would require many pages.[40] Restricting ourselves to single autobiographical works that were not equaled by any other single piece of writing so far as depicting the essence of the institution of slavery is concerned, we may note the narratives of Charles Ball,[41] Henry Bibb,[42] William Wells Brown[43] (this former slave also produced, prior to the Civil War, a travel book, a collection of antislavery songs, a novel, and a play), Lewis and Milton Clarke,[44] Josiah Henson[45] (his work so moved a lady named Harriet Beecher Stowe that in 1850 she visited and conversed with him in Boston—an important force behind the production, in 1852, of her epoch-making *Uncle Tom's Cabin*[46]), Jeremiah W. Loguen,[47] Solomon Northrup,[48] James W. C. Pennington[49] (the first edition of 6,000 copies of the life of this fugitive slave and militant abolitionist, who earned the degree of Doctor of Divinity from Heidelberg University, was sold within the year), Austin Steward,[50] Sojourner Truth,[51] Samuel R. Ward,[52] and in a class by itself in this literature or any literature, the perfectly forthright and magnificently moving autobiography of Frederick Douglass, first published in Boston in 1845. This classic was bought by 11,000 people within the United States by the end of 1847, went through in the same brief period nine editions in Great Britain, was translated into French and German,[53] and continued throughout the struggle as one of the most widely read works of all antebellum writings.

Important works of a historical and sociological nature aiding the cause of Abolitionism were also produced by Negroes. Especially noteworthy were two sharp and biting pamphlets published in New York in 1834 and 1838 by David Ruggles;[54] a pioneer historical work by James W. C. Pennington; an excellent brief work on Toussaint L'Ouverture by James McCune Smith; a full-length and still very useful study of the Negro's role in American history by William C. Nell; and a detailed socio-economic monograph by Martin D. Delany.[55] Near the end of the antebellum area, an "Afric-American Printing Company" was established in New Haven, this being "an association for the publication of Negro literature" which has to its credit the issuance of at least one good short historical work.[56]

Negroes did not, of course, restrict themselves to independent work, but struggled side by side with white people in the common effort. Thus, for example, the production and sustenance of the chief organ of the abolitionist movement, that ball of charged lightning, the *Liberator*, published in Boston from 1831 to 1865 by William Lloyd Garrison, were made possible by the encouragement and aid of Negroes. They wrote many letters to Garrison, beginning in 1830, giving not only moral stimulation, but that kind of stimulation without which any publication perishes, namely, money and subscriptions.[57] Indeed, in the earliest and most trying years the number of Negro subscribers far outweighed that of the whites, so that in 1831, out of 450 subscribers, fully 400 were Negroes, and in 1834 "of the whole number of subscribers [2,300] to the *Liberator*, only about one-fourth are white."[58]

Contributions to that paper and to all other joint abolitionist productions were exceedingly common. As an example may be noted the *Liberator* for February 12, 1831. About a third of the paper's space is taken up by articles by two Philadelphia Negroes, a call to an anti-colonization mass meeting of Negroes in Boston signed by James G. Barbadoes, Robert Roberts, Coffin Pitts, James T. Hilton, and Thomas Cole, and an account of a similar meeting recently held in New York, under the leadership of Samuel Ennals and Philip Bell. This is fairly typical of the entire thirty-five volumes of the paper. Again, in the first issue of a popular annual called *Autographs for Freedom* one finds a biographical sketch of a Scottish abolitionist, John Murray, by James McCune Smith and a sixty-seven-page history of the slave rebellion aboard the domestic slave trader Creole, by Frederick Douglass. And in the second issue of this work there are five articles on every phase of the movement by the Negro leaders Charles L. Reason, John M. Langston, William W. Brown, James M. Smith, and Frederick Douglass, and two poems by Charles Reason and George B. Vashon.[59]

Organizational work shows the same characteristics of joint participation. Three of the original signers of the declaration of the National Anti-Slavery

Convention, held in Philadelphia in December 1833, at which was formed the American Anti-Slavery Society, were Negroes: James G. Barbadoes, Robert Purvis, and James McCrummell;[60] the committee which drew up this immortal document included John G. Whittier, Samuel J. May, and William L. Garrison, who performed their task at the home of Frederick A. Hinton, a Philadelphia Negro.[61] It is, too, an arresting fact that the first presiding officer of the Philadelphia Female Anti-Slavery Society was a Negro and a man, the dentist James McCrummell. None of the ladies forming that organization felt competent to preside at a public meeting, and the only man they could find courageous enough to associate himself with two such slandered causes as abolitionism and the active participation of women in public affairs was this Dr. McCrummell.[62]

Four of the original members of the Board of Managers of the American Anti-Slavery Society were Negroes: Peter William, Samuel E. Cornish, Theodore S. Wright, and Christopher Rush; the last three were members of its Executive Committee.[63] In the later, more politically minded American and Foreign Anti-Slavery Society, five Negroes were members of the Executive Committee: Samuel E. Cornish, Christopher Rush, George Whipple, Charles B. Ray, and James W. C. Pennington.[64] In the organizational setup of the abolitionist movement, Vigilance Committees, local and state, were key bodies since they protected fugitive slaves, aided free Negroes, and organized mass demonstrations. The directors of these committees in the most important centers, New York and Philadelphia, were both Negroes—Theodore S. Wright and William Still—while the corresponding secretary of the New York State Vigilance Committee was Charles B. Ray.[65] Finally, it may be noted that in 1847 Frederick Douglass was appointed president of the New England Anti-Slavery Society.[66]

The record of the proceedings of any one of these abolitionist organizations is studded with accounts of contributions by Negroes. To take a few random examples: The 1849 meeting of the American and Foreign Anti-Slavery Society, held in New York City, was opened with an invocation by the Reverend Samuel R. Ward, a featured speaker was Henry Bibb, recently fled from Kentucky, and the entertainment was furnished by the four Luca boys, Negro youngsters who sang an antislavery song called "Car of Emancipation."[67]

Again, at the 1853 meeting of the American Anti-Slavery Society, held in Philadelphia, the audience heard a Negro gentleman of New Bedford, Massachusetts, the Reverend John J. Kelley, denounce slavery with great earnestness using "the plainest and most uncompromising language," and then was privileged to listen while Sojourner Truth sang "a plaintive song, touching the wrongs of the slave" and followed this with a speech, in her inimitably colorful manner, concerning "the wrong slavery had done to herself and others." And as an invigorating surprise, a Negro lady, introduced as a Mrs. Williams, said a few words. She lived in Wilmington, Delaware, and though free herself, had seen slavery at first hand. She had heard and read of the terrible abolitionists, inciters of violence, knaves, fools, fanatics, and decided to see these monsters for herself. Well, she had been sitting and listening, and she knew the Lord would bless them, for they were good and righteous folk. That is what she thought, and she did not care who knew it. Keep up the good fight, she said—and with this Mrs. Williams passes from history's pages.[68]

Another rank-and-filer, whose very name is unknown, provided the city of New York with an antislavery meeting all his own. In October, at Clinton Hall, the New York City Anti-Slavery Society was formed. The members of this meeting had managed to get out of the hall before a newspaper- and Tammany-incited proslavery mob arrived intent upon rooting out this subversive element. Frustrated by the emptiness of the hall, the mob pounced upon a passing Negro, constituted itself a mock abolitionist meeting, placed the man on the platform, and demanded a speech. They got one, or as much of one as they would permit.

> I am called upon to make a speech—said this unknown hero—You doubtless know that I am a poor ignorant man, not accustomed to make speeches. But I have heard of the Declaration of Independence, and have read the Bible. The Declaration says all men are created equal, and the Bible says God has made us all of one blood. I think, therefore, we are entitled to good treatment, that it is wrong to hold men in slavery, and that—

But here shouts and blows stopped him. Yet they had had their speech, had they not?[69]

But thus far we have merely touched upon the greatest part of the story. For the fate of the abolitionist movement rested essentially on the backs of those who followed the sublime profession of agitators of the people, those who personified the heart and the conscience of the masses, those who, in the words of one of them, Sojourner Truth, served as fleas, mosquitoes, biting and stinging away at the vast giant of America—and Canada and Europe—until it was aroused to its obligation and duty and interest, and acted accordingly.

Contemporaries were keenly aware of the significance of these itinerant Negro arousers and probers. Back in 1839 a paper had aptly remarked of them:[70]

> They have men enough in action now to maintain the antislavery enterprise and to win their liberty and that of their enslaved brethren—if every white Abolitionist were drawn from the field, McCune Smith, and Cornis, and Wright, and Ray, and a host of others—not to mention our eloquent brother, Remond of Maine, and Brother Lewis who is stay and staff of field antislavery in New Hampshire.

William Lloyd Garrison gave similar testimony:[71] "Who are among our ablest speakers? Who are the best qualified to address the public mind on the subject of slavery? Your fugitive slaves—your Douglasses, Browns and Bibbses—who are astonishing all with the cogency of their words and the power of their reasoning."

This cogency and power and eloquence were present because the speakers were talking about that which they knew, that which they had seen and felt, that which affected them more directly and more forcefully than it did anyone else. And the very facts of their appearance, their bearing, courage, and intelligence were devastating antislavery forces.[72]

They scoured the nation, visiting every state north of the Mason-Dixon line, searching out every nook and cranny, with the incessant cry—Let my people go! The list of these valiant fighters for freedom includes all those who have already been mentioned and many others—like William Jones, Frances E. W. Harper, Henry Foster, Lunsford Lane, Charles Gardens, Andrew Harris, Abraham D. Shadd, David Nickes, and James Bradley.

Had none of these people existed, however, with the exception of but one, his existence and participation in the abolitionist movement would justify the assertion that the Negro's role therein was decisive. That man is Frederick Douglass who, from his first public antislavery speech in 1841 to his organizing and recruiting activities during the war against the slavocracy, was the voice of America's millions of slaves. He, in the words of a white abolitionist, was what fighters in that movement had been praying for: one who had known slavery and was eloquent, impressive, truculent, energetic, and fearless.[73] There he stood, a magnificent figure of a man, impregnable, incorruptible, bearing slavery's scars upon his back, suffering, as he spoke, the anguish of knowing that a brother and four sisters were yet slaves. Those who once saw Douglass never forgot him. To Elizabeth Cady Stanton he appeared like an African prince, conscious of his dignity and power, grand in his physical proportions, majestic in his wrath, as with keen wit, satire, and indignation he portrayed the bitterness of slavery, the humiliation of subjection to those who in all human virtues and capacities were inferior to himself.[74] Wendell Phillips could only say, "He is one of our ablest men,"[75] while a tailor in Bristol, England, after hearing him, said he had never been so moved in his life and found it difficult to believe that such a man had been a slave just a few years before.[76]

When such a man met the despicable taunts concerning the inhumanity of the Negro uttered by the Tammany ward heeler, Police Captain Rynders, by facing him and demanding, "Am I a man?" the captain was left stumbling for a retort.[77]

He and his co-workers did not confine themselves to the United States. Negro fugitives in Canada formed the Windsor Anti-Slavery Society. The additional influx of Negroes after the Fugitive Slave Act of 1850 led to the formation in Toronto the next year of the Anti-Slavery Society of Canada under the leadership of Jeremiah W. Loguen and Samuel R. Ward. The importance of this work is graphically demonstrated by the fact that 40,000 Canadians enlisted in the Union Army during the Civil War.[78]

England, Scotland, and Ireland were often visited by Negro abolitionists like Nathaniel Paul, Ellen and William Craft, Samuel R. Ward, Sarah P. Remond, Alexander Crummell, William Wells Brown, James W. C. Pennington, Henry Highland Garnet, Frederick Douglass, and Charles L. Remond. The last named, after eighteen months' work, returned in 1841 with an antislavery petition signed by 60,000 men and women of Ireland headed by Daniel O'Connell.[79] The work was carried into France by William Wells Brown; in 1850, Henry H. Garnet and James W. C. Pennington helped set up an antislavery society in Frankfurt, Germany.[80]

The facts relating to the part played by the Negro people in the last acts of the drama of slavery's abolition, from John Brown's opening scene to the finale produced by Lincoln's army, have been developed elsewhere.[81] Of these it need merely be said here that both scenes were made possibly only through the Negro's participation. It was he who, in the words of Abraham Lincoln, when the final test came, "with silent tongue, and clenched teeth, and steady eye, and well-poised bayonet . . . helped mankind on to this great consummation."

From the first Negro rebels in what is now South Carolina back in 1526 to the earliest runaway slave and the first Negro antislavery petition, to the towering figures of men like Douglass and women like Tubman, to Green, Newby, Anderson, Leary, and Copeland who followed the Old Man into Harper's Ferry, to the 200,000 men who shouldered muskets in the Tall Man's Army of Liberation and the 36,000 among them who died in that army's battles, the story of the American Negro is one of unsurpassed heroism and titanic efforts to realize his aspiration, and the aspiration of all other men, for equality and freedom. Let our posterity know, said the Reverend Alexander Crummell,

> That we their ancestors, uncultured and unlearned, amid all trials and temptations, were men of integrity.—Recognized with gratefulness their truest friends dishonored and in peril. Were enabled to resist the seductions of ease and the intimidations of power. Were true to themselves, the age in which they lived, their abject race, and the cause of man. Shrank not from trial, nor from suffering:—but conscious of Responsibility and impelled by Duty, gave themselves up to the vindication of the high hopes and lofty aims of True Humanity![82]

Notes

1. In a preceding paper (*Science and Society*, vol. 5, No. 1) examination was made of certain facets of the crusade against human enslavement in the United States, with particular emphasis upon the role of the Negro therein. With the exception of some notice of the Underground Railroad, attention was focused upon the unorganized, spontaneous phases of that movement, and extraneous factors affecting its strength, rather than upon the movement itself.

2. Published in E. N. Elliott, ed., *Cotton is King* (August, 1860), pp. 140–41.

3. P. G. and E. Q. Wright, *Elizur Wright* (Chicago, 1937), p. 84. See also James Madison to Henry Clay, June 1833, *The Writings of James Madison*, Gaillard Hunt, ed., (New York, London, 1900–1910), 9, p. 517.

4. Letter signed "A. B. C. of Halifax City" in the *Richmond Whig*, April 13, 1832, emphases in original.

5. John W. H. Underwood to Senator Howell Cobb, Clarksville, Georgia, Feb. 2, 1844, "The Correspondence of Robert Toombs, Alexander H. Stephens, and Howell Cobb," *Annual Report of the American Historical Association 1911*, U. B. Phillips, ed., (Washington, 1913), 2, 54–54. This phase of the proslavery argument was enunciated at an early period. Thus, when the institution was threatened in Kentucky at the end of the eighteenth century, John Breckenridge wrote to Isaac Shelby (March 11, 1798): "If the envious, the discontented, or the needy . . . can by one experiment emancipate our slaves the same principle pursued will enable them at the second experiment to extinguish our land titles, for both are held by rights equally sacred." Bernard Mayo, *Henry Clay* (Boston, 1937), pp. 65–66.

6. Virginia Dabney, *Liberalism in the South* (Chapel Hill, 1932), p. 118. In 1851, Dr. Thornwell was appointed president of South Carolina College.

7. Charles F. Adams, ed., *The Works of John Adams* (Boston, 1856), 2, p. 200.

8. See *Collections of the Massachusetts Historical Society*, 5th series (Boston, 1877),

3, pp. 432–37; William Lincoln, *History of Worcester, Massachusetts* (Worcester, 1852), p. 99; Lorenzo Green, "Slave-holding New England and Its Awakening," in *Journal of Negro History* (1928), 13, pp. 492–533; Richard Upton, *Revolutionary New Hampshire* (Hanover, 1936), p. 214; Herbert Aptheker, *The Negro in American Revolution* (New York, 1940), pp. 9–10

9. "Belknap Papers" in *Collections of the Massachusetts Historical Society*, 5th series, 3, pp. 22, 24, 32, 55.

10. Annals of the Congress of the United States, 6th Cong., 1st sess., pp. 230–42.

11. *The American Museum*, 1788, 5, p. 72; 6, p. 80; see also 1, p. 463.

12. See Prince Hall, *A Charge Delivered to the Brethren of the American Lodge on the 25th of June, 1792* (Boston, 1792); *A Charge Delivered to the African Lodge, June 24, 1979, at Menotony* (n.p., 1797); [Absalom Jones and Richard Allen], *A Narrative of the Proceedings of the Black People* (Philadelphia, 1794); Carter G. Woodson, *The Mind of the Negro* (Washington, 1936), pp. xxiv-xxvii.

13. See Clarice A. Richardson, "The Antislavery Activities of Negroes In Pennsylvania," unpublished master's thesis, Howard University (Washington, 1937); Dorothy B. Porter, "Afro-American Writings before 1835," unpublished master's thesis, School of Library Service, Columbia University (New York, 1932); Sidney I. Pomerantz, *New York: An American City 1783–1803* (New York, 1938), p. 469. The Brown Fellowship Society, founded in Charleston, S.C., in 1790 was an exception in that, though a society for Negroes (mulattoes), it was proslavery. This, however, was an expression of class position, since membership was restricted to wealthy free men. The initiation fee was $50. See E. H. Fitchett, "The Traditions of the Free Negro in Charleston," *Journal of Negro History* (1940) 25, p. 144.

14. Charles H. Welsey, "The Negroes of New York in the Emancipation Movement," *Journal of Negro History* (1939) XXIV, pp. 68–69; G. H. Barnes and D. L. Dumond, eds., *Weld-Grimké Letters* (New York, 1934), 1, 275n. Mr. Williams was finally forced to resign from his committee position at the insistence of Bishop Onderdonk. Biographical data concerning him are scarce and conflicting. See above, and C. G. Woodson, *Negro Orators and Their Orations* (Washington, 1925), pp. 32–33.

15. See Peter Williams, *An Oration on the Abolition of the Slave Trade, Delivered in the African Church in the City of New York* (New York, 1808); N. S. Chase, "The Attitude of the Negro towards Slavery," unpublished master's thesis, Howard University (Washington, 1936).

16. C. G. Woodson, *Negro Orators*, pp. 52–53; Lewis Tappan, *The Life of Arthur Tappan* (New York, 1870), pp. 135–36, emphases in original.

17. *The American Anti-Slavery Almanac for 1836* (Boston, n.d.), no pagination, see entry for January; Bella Gross, "Freedom's Journal and the Rights of All," *Journal of Negro History* (1932) 17, pp. 244–45.

18. Josiah Quincy, *Memoir of the Life of John Quincy Adams* (Boston, 1858), pp. 103–4.

19. C. G. Woodson, *Negro Orators,* pp. 64–65; C. A. Richardson, "The Antislavery Activities of Negroes In Pennsylvania," unpublished master's thesis, Howard University (Washington, 1937), p. 12.

20. Dorothy B. Porter, "The Organized Educational Activities of Negro Literary Societies, 1828–1846," The *Journal of Negro Education* (1936), 5, pp. 557–58. There exists evidence of one or more such Negro societies in Albany, Baltimore, Boston, Buffalo, Cincinnati, Columbus, Detroit, Hartford, Newark, New Bedford, New York, Philadelphia, Pittsburgh, Poughkeepsie, Providence, Rochester, Schenectady, Troy, and Washington.

21. B. Gross, "Freedom's Journal and the Rights of All," *Journal of Negro History* (1932) 17, pp. 244–45; I. G. Penn, *The Afro-American Press* (Springfield, 1891), pp. 26–28.

22. *Freedom's Journal,* Dec. 18, 20, 1828; N. S. Chase, "The Attitude of the Negro towards Slavery," unpublished master's thesis, Howard University (Washington, 1936), pp. 14–16

23. (David) *Walker's Appeal, in Four Articles together with a Preamble to the Coloured Citizens of the World, but in particular, and very expressly to those of the United States of America, written in Boston, State of Massachusetts, September 28, 1829.* Third Edition, with additional notes, corrections, etc. (Boston, 1830). The three editions may be found in the Boston Public Library.

24. "A colored Bostonian" reported in the *Liberator,* Jan. 22, 1831, that it was believed Walker had been murdered. A rumor was current that some person or persons in the South offered $3,0000 reward to the individual who would kill him.

25. In contradistinction to the generally realistic and practical approach of Walker is to be noted the peculiar, mystical pamphlet issued in February 1829, by a New York Negro, Robert Alexander Young. An undertone of bitterness and militance appears here, but it is couched in Biblical language and conveyed by prophesying the coming of a Negro messiah, who is described in detail, endowed with invincibility, and will free his people [Robert A. Young]. *The Ethiopian Manifesto, Issued in Defense of the Black Man's Rights, in the Scale of Universal Freedom* (New York, 1829). The same year marked the appearance of George Moses Horton's *The Hope of Liberty Containing a Number of Poetical Pieces* (Raleigh, 1829). This was reprinted in Philadelphia in 1837.

26. One of the whites accused of circulating this bombshell was Elijah H. Burritt, a printer of Milledgeville, Ga., a brother of Elihu, the "learned blacksmith" of Massachusetts. He was forced to flee for his life. That he safely reached the North appears from a letter sent by S. S. Jocelyn to William L. Garrison, dated New Haven, July 12, 1832, asking that the *Liberator* be sent to Burritt at Berlin, Conn., "the gentleman who suffered so much on acc't of Walker's pamphlet" (MS. Letters to Garrison, Boston Public Library). See also U. B. Phillips, ed., "The Public Archives in Georgia," *Annual Report of the American Historical Association, 1903* (Washington, 1904), 1, p. 469; and Merle Curti, *The Learned Blacksmith* (New York, 1937), p. 118n. In May 1830, a Mr. James Smith of Boston (whether Negro or white is not stated) was convicted in New

Orleans of circulating the *Appeal,* fined $1,000 and sentenced to a year's imprisonment. *Niles' Weekly Register* (Baltimore), April 24, June 19, 1930, 38, pp. 157, 304.

27. *Journal of the House of Representatives of the State of Georgia, 1829* (Milledgeville, 1830), p. 353; James F. McRae, Magistrate of Police to Governor John Owen, Wilmington, Aug. 7, 1830, L. D. Henry to Governor Owen, Fayetteville, Sept. 3, 1830, in Governor's Letter Book and Governor's Papers, vol. 60, Historical Commission, Raleigh. See note 25, and Clement Eaton, "A Dangerous Pamphlet in Old South," *Journal of Southern History* (1936), 2, pp. 327–31. It has been said that Nat Turner was influenced by Walker's work but the evidence for this is unsatisfactory.

28. *Liberator,* Oct. 22, 1831; John W. Cromwell, *The Negro in American History* (Washington, 1914), p. 28ff.; C. H. Wesley, *Journal of Negro History* (1959), 24, pp. 72–73. Among the prominent delegates were Richard Allen, James Forten, Hezekiah Giles, Robert Douglass, John Gloucester, Austin Steward, James W. C. Pennington, and Junius C. Morrell.

29. Charles H. Wesley, *Richard Allen: Apostle of Freedom* (Washington, 1935), pp. 239–40.

30. As indicated, they too were actively antislavery and frequently contributed to the cause. For example, Garrison, while on a speaking tour in New England, made note of the fact that, in addition to receiving $30 from a Negro gathering in Providence, RI, three Negro societies, a "Female Tract Society," a "Female Literary Society," and a "Mutual Relief Society" donated $25 to assist the *Liberator.* Garrison to Isaac Knapp, dated New Haven, April 11, 1833, Garrison MSS.

31. Organizations, leadership, and dates of formation may be found in the third, fourth, and fifth *Annual Reports of the American Anti-Slavery Society* (New York, 1836–1838). See also Helen B. Whittaker, "The Negro in the Abolition Movement 1830–1850," unpublished master's thesis, Howard University (Washington, 1955); D. B. Porter, *Journal of Negro Education* (1956), 5. 555; letter to Garrison from Anne C. Smith and Susan Paul of the Negro Garrison Society of Boston, Nov. 23, 1833 (enclosing $15), Garrison MSS; George Howell and J. Tenney, *History of the County of Albany* (New York, 1886), p. 723.

32. This information is given in Booker T. Washington, *The Story of the Negro* (New York, 1909), 2, p. 158; and H. D. Whittaker, "The Negro in the Abolition Movement 1830–1850," unpublished master's thesis, Howard University (Washington, 1955) p. 63, but neither cites sources. Washington, who seems to have known Dickson, states that he served in the Union Army, and following the Civil War, was active in establishing the Lincoln Institute in Jefferson City, Mo. It is a fact that militant Abolitionism (a subject badly in need of intensive study) appears to have been adopted earlier and more readily by the Negroes than by the whites.

33. J. W. Cromwell, *The Negro in American History* (Washington, 1914), p. 28; C. H. Wesley, *Journal of Negro History* (1939), 24, pp. 72–75.

34. *Minutes of the Fifth Annual Convention of the Colored Citizens of the State of New York, held in the City of Schenectady, September 18–20, 1844* (Troy, 1844).

35. Ralph F. Weld, *Brooklyn Village 1816–1834* (New York, 1938), p. 297n. In 1825, the town of Brooklyn contained 870 Negroes. *Ibid.*, p. 274n. See, for a later example—this in Baltimore in 1840—*Tenth Annual Report of the Board of Managers of the Massachusetts Anti-Slavery Society, 1843* (Boston, 1842), pp. 20–21. Similar mass protest meetings of Negroes were reported in 1851 from Philadelphia, Columbia, Pittsburgh, Harrisburg, and Lewistown in Pennsylvania; New Haven, Lyme, and Middletown in Connecticut; Boston, Nantucket, and New Bedford in Massachusetts; and Baltimore, New York, Providence, Trenton, Washington, and Wilmington. See *First Annual Report of the New England Anti-Slavery Society, 1833* (Boston, 1833), pp. 36–40; *Liberator*, Feb. 12, March 26, June 25, Oct. 29, 1851. Note the remark of Elizur Wright: "If the honor of originating American Anti-Slavery as a plan of operations opposed to expatriation were now the matter in question, a strong claim might be urged in favor of some of our colored friends." *First Annual Report of the American Anti-Slavery Society, 1834* (New York, 1834), p. 45.

36. C. H. Wesley, *Journal of Negro History* (1939), 24, pp. 92–95.

37. John W. Cromwell, *The Negro in American History* (Washington, 1914), p. 37; similar events occurred somewhat later in Illinois. Arthur C. Cole, *The Era of the Civil War* (Springfield, 1919), p. 227. Suits, petitions, agitation, forcible resistance were everywhere employed against Jim Crowism by the Negro people. Here is another subject in need of serious study. Prominent in this were Frederick Douglass, Sarah Remond, Sojourner Truth, Robert Purvis, Theodore S. Wright, Charles L. Remond, David Ruggles, Archie P. Webb, and William C. Nell. See: *Tenth Annual Report of the Board of Managers of the Massachusetts Anti-Slavery Society* (Boston, 1842), pp. 72–75; Eliza Wigham, *The Anti-Slavery Cause in America* (London, 1863), p. 105; Parker Pillsbury, *Acts of the Anti-Slavery Apostles* (Boston, 1884), p. 238; C. G. Woodson, *The Mind of the Negro*, pp. 178–79; C. G. Woodson, *Negro Orators*, pp. 88, 96, 144; petition of Negro Seamen to House of Representatives, presented by J. Q. Adams, Feb. 7, 1842, in *Journal of the House of Representatives of the United States, 1841* (Washington, 1841–42), p. 325; letter from Augustus W. Hanson to Frances Jackson, Boston, Oct. 22, 1838, in MS. Letters to Garrison; W. S. Savage, "The Negro in the Westward Movement," *Journal of Negro History* (1940), 25, p. 535.

38. Helen Whittaker, "The Negro in the Abolition Movement 1830–1850," unpublished master's thesis, Howard University (Washington, 1955) pp. 6–7, 58. See also W. C. Nell's account of a convention in Boston of Negro adherents of the Free Soil Party, the Republican Party's immediate forebear. The *Liberator*, Dec. 10, 1842. The Reverend Samuel R. Ward was a delegate to the national nomination convention of that party in 1848. W. E. Smith, *The Francis P. Blair Family in Politics* (New York, 1933), 1, p. 236.

39. See I. G. Penn, *The Afro-American Press* (Springfield, 1891) passim; C. G. Woodson, *The Education of the Negro*, p. 281n; M. N. Work, "Charles B. Ray," *Journal of Negro History* (1919), 4, pp. 361–71; Charles S. Johnson, "The Rise of the Negro Magazine." *Ibid.* (1928), 12, pp. 7–21; F. A. Rollin, *Life and Public Services of Martin R. Delany*

(Boston, 1868), pp. 48–49. Among the outstanding newspapers may be mentioned Frederick Douglass' *North Star* of Rochester; Charles Ray's *Colored American* of New York; William G. Allen's and Henry H. Garnet's *National Watchman* of Troy; Samuel R. Ward's *Impartial Citizen* of Syracuse; and Martin Delany's *Mystery of Pittsburgh.* Magazines of note were the Philadelphia *Demosthenian,* edited by Benjamin Stanley; and three New York publications, the *Mirror of Liberty,* edited by David Ruggles, the *Review* by George Hogarth, and the particularly effective *Anglo-African,* by Thomas Hamilton.

40. For a partial list see M. A. Howe and R. E. Lewis, *A Classified Catalogue of the Negro Collection in the Huntington Library of Hampton Institute* (mimeographed, Hampton, 1940), especially pp. 66–69.

41. First published in Lewistown, Pa., in 1836, reprinted in New York in 1937 and 1859.

42. New York, 1849.

43. Boston, 1847, reprinted 1848.

44. Boston, 1845, reprinted 1846.

45. Boston, 1849, reprinted 1858.

46. Aileen Ward, "In Memory of 'Uncle Tom,'" in *Dalhousie Review* (1940), 20, pp. 335–38.

47. Syracuse, 1859.

48. New York, Auburn, London, 1853.

49. London, 1849.

50. Rochester, 1847.

51. Boston, 1850.

52. London, 1855.

53. *Rochester North Star,* Jan. 8, 1848; Ruth C. Brannum, "Frederick Douglass," unpublished master's thesis, Howard University (Washington, 1937), p. 44. It continued to be reprinted in the post–Civil War period, and a new edition is, while these words are written, soon to be issued by the Pathway Press of New York—thanks to the work of such worthy successors of Douglass as Angelo Herndon, Richard B. Moore, and Dr. L. D. Reddick.

54. These are well described by Charles Wesley in the *Journal of Negro History* (1939), 24, pp. 88–89.

55. These works are, respectively, J. W. C. Pennington, *A Textbook of the Origin and History of the Colored People* (Hartford, 1841); J. M. Smith, *A Lecture on the Haytien Revolution* (New York, 1841), W. C. Nell, *The Colored Patriots of the American Revolution with Sketches of Several Distinguished Colored Persons: to which is added a brief survey of the condition and prospects of colored Americans* (introduction by Harriet Beecher Stowe, Boston, 1833); M. R. Delany, *The Condition, Elevation, Emigration, and Destiny of the Colored People of the United States* (Philadelphia, 1852).

56. James T. Holly, *A Vindication of the Capacity of the Negro Race for Self-Government, and Civilized Progress* (New Haven, 1857). The quoted words are from the book's pref-

ace. Lectures based on this book were delivered by the author in 1855 and 1856 in Connecticut, Michigan, and Canada.

57. Particularly active in these respects were James Forten, Robert Purvis, Sarah Douglass, and Joseph Cassey of Philadelphia; George Cary of Cincinnati; John B. Vashon of Pittsburgh; Nathan Blount of Poughkeepsie; and Charles L. Remond of Salem. See letters to Garrison from James Forten, Dec. 31, 1830, Feb. 2, May 6, 1832; George Cary, June 6, 1831; Sarah Douglass, Dec. 6, 1852; Nathan Blount, Feb. 2, 1855; Joseph Cassey, Feb. 12, 1833; Charles Remond, April 10, 1854; and Garrison's letters to Samuel J. May, Feb. 14, 1851, to Henrey E. Benson, July 30, 1831, and to John B. Vashon, Aug. 15, Dec. 8, 1832, Nov. 5, 1833. Garrison MSS. Dorothy B. Porter published some of these letters in the *Journal of Negro History* (1927), 12, pp. 33–36; (1939) 24, pp. 199–205.

58. "Shall the *Liberator* Die," a printed appeal for funds, dated Boston, April 15, 1854, in Garrison MSS.; and *Liberator*, Jan. 5, 1855.

59. Julia Griffiths, ed., *Autographs for Freedom*, 1 (Boston, Cleveland, London, 1853); 2 (Auburn, Rochester, 1854).

60. *Liberator*, Dec. 14, 1833.

61. So said Mr. May, *Proceedings of the American Anti-Slavery Society at Its Second Decade, Held in the City of Philadelphia, December 3–5, 1853* (New York, 1854), p. 7.

62. Lloyd C. Hare, *Lucretia Mott* (New York, 1937), p. 92. Space does not permit a discussion of the Negro's role in the women's-rights movement. It was considerable, particularly on the part of Frederick Douglass and Sojourner Truth. See Benjamin Quarles, "Frederick Douglass and the Woman's Rights Movement." *Journal of Negro History* (1940), 25, pp. 35–44; Arthur H. Fauset, *Sojourner Truth* (Chapel Hill, 1938), pp. 127–34.

63. *First Annual Report of the American Anti-Slavery Society, 1834* (New York, 1834), pp. 35–36.

64. *Annual Report of the American and Foreign Anti-Slavery Society, Presented at New York, 1849* (New York, 1849), p. 1. Not only were Negro abolitionists generally militant (rejecting Garrisonian pacifism) but they were, as a rule, also keenly aware of the importance of political activity. See C. G. Woodson, *The Mind of the Negro*, pp. 172–74. Henry H. Garnet, Charles B. Ray, and Theodore S. Wright were pioneers in the formation of the Liberty Party. Samuel R. Ward's association with the Free Soil Party has been noted. James McCune Smith, George Whipple, and Frederick Douglass were leaders of the "Radical Political Abolitionists." See *Minutes of the Fifth Annual Convention of Colored Citizens in New York, 1844* (Troy, 1844); *Radical Abolitionist*, New York, August 1855, 1, p. 5; C. H. Wesley, *Journal of Negro History* (1939), 24, p. 101.

65. M. N. Work, *Journal of Negro History* (1919), 4, pp. 362–63; Henrietta Buckmaster, *Let My People Go* (New York, 1941), pp. 216–17.

66. Brannum, "Frederick Douglass," unpublished master's thesis, Howard University (Washington, 1937), p. 37.

67. *Annual Report of the American and Foreign Anti-Slavery Society, 1849* (New York, 1849).

68. *Proceedings of the American Anti-Slavery Society, Philadelphia, 1853* (New York, 1854), pp. 27, 73, 76.

69. Lewis Tappan, *The Life of Arthur Tappan* (New York, 1870), p. 171; Henrietta Buckmaster, *Let My People Go* (New York, 1941), p. 70. Such people as this unknown rank-and-file member of the abolitionist movement formed, of course, its backbone. But their anonymity makes the telling of their story exceedingly difficult in any way but as one sees its reflection in the leaders they raised up. One wishes, for example, to know more about the Negroes who offered their bodies as shields for Frederick Douglass when, as was common, he was mobbed (see his letter on this in the *National Anti-Slavery Standard*, New York, Aug. 19, 1847); or about the Negroes who, at night, stationed themselves about the home of the intrepid white Underground Railroad operator, Thomas Garrett, and, at the expense of their own sleep, saw to it that no harm came to him (Henrietta Buckmaster, *Let My People Go*, p. 150). And when all other meeting places were barred, a Negro church or hall was always available for abolitionists, though this often involved great danger. This was indicated, after such an episode, by Wendell Phillips in commenting on the fact that only the African Church in Boston was open to them: "The Monday evening meeting, I regretted to hold where we were compelled to, as it left the colored people exposed all night to the remains of the mob." Carlos Martyn, *Wendell Phillips* (New York, 1890), p. 303.

70. "The Herald of Freedom," in M. N. Work, *Journal of Negro History* (1919), 4, pp. 364–65.

71. W. P. and F. J. Garrison, *Life of Garrison* (Boston, 1885–1889), 3, p. 311.

72. Typical is a letter from Charles L. Remond to Wendell Phillips, dated Philadelphia, April 5, 1845 (in the *Liberator*, April 18, 1845): "Since arriving in this state, I have spent some time in Bucks and Montgomery counties, a portion of it in company with Stephen [S. Foster, a leading white abolitionist] and the remainder holding meetings and lecturing myself, and in most places mobs and rumors of mobs have been the order of the day; but receiving personal injury only in a single instance, I will pass them without comment." When a mob milled around Sojourner Truth and threatened to burn down any hall granted her, she shouted back at them, in her low, powerful voice, "Then I will speak upon its ashes!" A. H. Fauset, *Sojourner Truth* (Chapel Hill, 1938), p. 141.

73. Robert R. Raymond, "Outline of a Man," in Julia Griffith's *Autographs for Freedom*, 1 (Boston, Cleveland, London, 1853), pp. 148–60.

74. Alma Lutz, *Created Equal A Biography of Elizabeth Cady Stanton* (New York, 1940), p. 39. There is no biography of Douglass that begins to do the man justice. Read his autobiography, and see the summary of his career by Steve Kinston, recently issued by the National Negro Congress.

75. Wendell Phillips to Elizabeth Pease, Boston, Feb. 24, 1845, in Garrison MSS.

76. Quoted in a letter by Mary Carpenter to Garrison, dated Bristol, Sept. 3, 1846, in Garrison MSS.

77. Carlos Martyn, *Wendell Phillips* (New York, 1890), pp. 228–29; H. Buckmaster, *Let My People Go* (New York, 1941), p. 174.

78. Fred Landon, "The Anti-Slavery Society of Canada," *Journal of Negro History*, 4, pp. 33–40; "Negro Migration to Canada," *ibid.* (1920), 5, pp. 22–36.

79. *Tenth Annual Report of the Board of Managers of the Massachusetts Anti-Slavery Society, 1842* (Boston, 1842), p. 68.

80. *Annual Report of the American and Foreign Anti-Slavery Society, New York, 1851* (New York, 1851), pp. 96–97; *The Non-Slaveholder* (Philadelphia, October, 1850), 5, p. 221.

81. For brief treatments of these subjects and bibliographical references, see the present writer's "American Negro Slave Revolts," *Science and Society* (1937), 1, p. 533, and *The Negro in the Civil War* (New York, 1938).

82. Alexander Crummell, *A Eulogy on the Life and Character of Thomas Clarkson; Delivered in the City of New York, December, 1846* (New York, 1847), p. 21.

4

Militant Abolitionism

Three major schools of thought permeated various segments of the American abolitionist movement. These were: that dedicated to the use of moral suasion and nothing else; that which believed in moral suasion, or argument, plus political action; and that which believed in direct, militant action, in resistance. Members of the last school adopted at times, but not always, the methods of the first two as well.

Historical literature has neglected consideration of the last group. Its prevalence and importance demonstrate, however, that without careful examination of these militants the crusade against Negro slavery in the United States is but partially investigated. This paper assays the filling of this gap.

Among the earliest protests against American slavery may be found the kernel of this militancy in that the righteousness of the cause for which slaves conspired and fought was acknowledged. In the famous Germantown Protest of 1688 signed by four Quakers, including Francis Daniell Pastorius, the authors put this question: Suppose the slaves rebel here and now, as they have frequently done elsewhere, "will these masters and mastrisses take the sword at hand and warr against these poor slaves, licke, we are able to believe, some will not refuse to doe; or have these negers not as much right to fight for their freedom, as you have to keep them slaves?" Ten years later, again in Pennsylvania, this time Concord, another Quaker protest[1] against slavery, signed by Robert Pyle asked a similar question. Suppose our slaves do rebel, and blood is shed. The Friend wondered "whether your blood will cry innocent whether it will not be said you might have let them alone."

The Grand Jury of Charles Town, South Carolina, made the following interesting charge on March 17, 1741:

> We present as a Public Grievance a certain book or Journal sign'd by Hugh Brian, directed to ye Honble, the Speaker, and the rest of the members of the Commons house of Assembly in Charles Town, wch we have perused and find in general, contains sundry enthusiastic prophecys, of the destruction of Charles Town, and deliverance of the Negroes from their Servictude, and that by the Influence of ye said Hugh Brian, great bodys of Negroes have assembled together on pretence of religious worship, Contrary to ye laws, and destructive of ye Peace . . .

Other whites, Jonathan Brian, William Gilbert, and Robert Ogle, were also declared to possess opinion inimical to the security of a slave society. Mr. Brian's work was suppressed but what punishment, if any, was meted out to the individuals is not known.[2]

Some of the literature produced just before and during the Revolutionary War contained, as one might expect, passages justifying, if not actually urging, attempts on the part of the Negroes to liberate themselves by violence. The writings of James Otis, for example, particularly his famous pamphlet published in Boston in 1764, *The Rights of the British Colonies Asserted and Proved,* excoriated the institution of slavery, and affirmed the Negro's inalienable right to freedom.[3] The logical deduction was plain, and did not pass unnoticed, as John Adams testified:

> Young as I was, and ignorant as I was, I shuddered at the doctrine he taught; and I have all my life shuddered, and still shudder, at the consequences that may be drawn from such premises. Shall we say, that the rights of the masters and servants clash, and can be decided only by force? I adore the idea of gradual abolitions! But who shall decide how fast or how slowly these abolitions shall be made?[4]

Another popular pamphlet of this year, that by the Reverend Isaac Skillman entitled, *An Oration upon the Beauties of Liberty, or the Essential Rights of the Americans,* (published in Boston in 1772 and in its fourth printing by 1773) vehemently attacked the enslavement of the Negroes, demanded their immediate liberation, and affirmed, "Shall a man be deem'd a rebel that supports his own rights? It is the first law of nature, and he must be a rebel to God, to the laws of nature, and his own conscience, who will not do it."[5] Very much the same point was made by the Reverend Samuel Hopkins of Newport, Rhode Island, in a work first published in 1776.[6]

From then on, the action of the inhabitants of the American colonies in waging war for mere political and economic freedom was often referred to by militant abolitionists in order to support their own views justifying or urging Negro rebellion. One of the earliest writings of this type was produced by a "Free Negro," who denounced slavery, denied the oft-repeated idea concerning his people's "inferiority," and demanded, "Do the rights of nature cease to be such when a Negro is to enjoy them? Or does patriotism, in the heart of an African, rankle into treason?"[7]

A physician, Dr. George Buchanan, delivered a very militant speech on July 4, 1791, at Baltimore before a public meeting of the Maryland Society for Promoting the Abolition of Slavery. In the course of it occur these passages, spoken six weeks before the outbreak of the great Haitian Revolution:

> What then if the fire of Liberty shall be kindled amongst them? What, if some enthusiast in their cause shall beat to arms, and call them to the standard of freedom? Would they fly in clouds, until their numbers become tremendous, and threaten the country with devastation and ruin? . . .
>
> Led on by hopes of freedom, animated by the aspiring voice of their leader, they would soon find, that "a day, an hour of virtuous liberty, was worth a whole eternity of bondage."[8]

With the eruption of the Haitian Revolution many people felt called upon to declare their attitude towards it, and some, who gloried in the American and French Revolutions, found it but consistent and logical to welcome that which occurred in the West Indies. Typical of this group was the Bostonian, J. P. Martin, who wrote an article entitled, "Rights of Black Men."[9] Said this forthright individual: "We believe that freedom is the natural right of all rational beings, and we know that the blacks have never voluntarily resigned that freedom. Then is not their cause as just as ours? . . . Let us be consistent, Americans, if we justify our own conduct in the late glorious revolution; let us justify those who, in a cause like ours, fight with equal bravery."

A delegate to the Kentucky Constitution Convention of 1792, the Reverend David Rice, argued against the establishment of slavery, declaring it to be "a perpetual war, with an avowed purpose of never making peace," and an institution which would weaken the home front and strengthen an enemy. He pointed to the events then transpiring in the West Indies and declared, "There you may see the sable, let me say the brave sons of Africa, engaged in a noble conflict with their inveterate foes. There you may see thousands fired with a generous resentment of the greatest injuries, and bravely sacrificing their lives on the altar of liberty."[10]

A prominent resident of Connecticut went even further in a public speech delivered two years later, for he applied the case to the United States, itself. Warning of coming plots and rebellions, he went on:[11]

> And when hostilities are commenced, where shall they [the slave holders] look for auxiliaries, in such an iniquitous warfare? Surely, no friend to freedom and justice will dare to lend them his aid . . . Who then can charge the Negroes with injustice, or cruelty, when "they rise in all the vigor of insulted nature," and avenge their wrongs. What American will not admire their exertions, to accomplish their own deliverance?

Like sentiments were occasionally printed in the press, as the Hartford *Connecticut Courant* in 1796 and 1797.[12] In the latter year, too, a Massachusetts Negro, Prince Hall, a veteran of the Revolutionary War, a fighter against his people's enslavement, and a leader in the Masonic movement, expressed admiration for the militant activities of his brothers in Haiti.[13]

Early in the year 1804, a judge for the eastern district of Georgia, Jabez Bowen, Jr., created a sensation by his "inflammatory" charge to the grand jury of Chatham. The jury refused to have this charge published and bitterly condemned the judge. A resident of Savannah wrote shortly afterward that "Judge Bowen's charge related to the emancipation of the Negroes; and that he went to the length of declaring, that if the Legislature did not, their first session, pass a law liberating all slaves, he would put himself at the head of the Negroes and effect it, though at the expense of the lives of every white inhabitant of the State." In May the Judge was dismissed from office and imprisoned on a charge of inciting servile insurrection, but early in June he was released into the custody of his father, on the condition that he be sent out of the State. He was—to Rhode Island—but "he still swears vengeance against the white people of this place."[14]

A white Missourian, one Humphrey Smith, was indicted by the Howard County Grand Jury in 1819 for inciting servile insurrection,[15] but the outcome of this case is not clear. In October 1822, four white men were arrested and convicted of having encouraged the Negroes involved in the Vesey plot. These residents of Charleston represented four different nationalities: Andrew S. Rhodes, English; William Allen, Scotch; Jacob Danders, German; and John Igneshias, Spanish. Allen's motives alone were suspect since he was accused by a free Negro, named Scott, of expecting to reap a financial reward from the successful rebels. The others, however, hated slavery, and their crime consisted in letting the Negroes know this and in telling them, as the German put it, "they had as much right to fight for their liberty as the white people." All were sentenced to prison terms ranging from three to twelve months and to fines from one hundred to one thousand dollars, which had to be paid prior to release from jail.[16]

There appeared in the one year 1829 three works produced by Negroes which contained more or less open calls for, or justifications of, outright revolt.

The least open of these is the remarkable book of poems, called *The Hope of Liberty,* written by George Moses Horton, a slave in Chatham County, North Carolina, and published by Joseph Gales, editor of a leading newspaper, the *Raleigh Register.*[17] Occasional lines were fairly militant as, for example:

> Oh Liberty, thou golden prize,
> So Often sought by blood—
> We crave thy sacred sun to rise
> The gift of Nature's God!
> Bid Slavery hide her haggard face,
> And barbarism fly:
> I scorn to see the sad disgrace
> In which enslaved I lie.

A truculent note of foreboding and militance was struck by the peculiar, mystical pamphlet issued in February 1829, by a New York Negro, Robert Alexander Young.[18] This appears especially in the work's prophecy of the coming of a Negro savior who, by his invincibility, will lead his people to freedom.

David Walker's work, written in clear, unmistakable prose and containing no far-fetched allusions, appeared in the closing months of the year. Not much is known of this very interesting person, but these facts appear well-established:[19] He was born of a free mother in Wilmington, North Carolina, on September 28, 1785. The enslavement of his fellow men disgusted and enraged him. In 1828 he wrote:

> If I remain in this bloody land, I will not live long, as true as God reigns, I will be avenged. This is not the place for me, no, I must leave this part of the country. It will be a great trial for me to live on the same soil where so many men are in slavery, certainly I cannot remain where I must hear their chains continually, and, where I must encounter the results of their hypocritical enslavers. Go I must.

He went to Boston where he earned his bread by dealing in old clothes. Here he became active in anti-slavery work, making at least one speech before the Colored Association in the city in December 1828, serving as Boston agent for the fighting New York anti-slavery newspaper edited and published by Negroes, *Freedom's Journal,* and occasionally contributing to it.

In September 1829, he published his *Appeal,*[20] and from then until his mysterious death sometime in 1830,[21] supervised the distribution and reprinting of this work, which during the last year of his life went into its third edition.

It is certain that copies of this work were sent into the South with the object of getting them into the hands of slaves. And it reached them at a moment when they were displaying great unrest. Note of this is made by Governor John Forsyth, of Georgia, in a communication to the state legislature on December 21, 1829, when he referred to a recent conspiracy in Georgetown, South Carolina, and "the late fires in August and Savannah" set by the slaves.[22] These occurrences, said the Governor, added to the importance of a letter he had just received from W. T. Williams, the Mayor of Savannah, "informing me that sixty pamphlets of a highly seditious and insurrectionary character, had been seized by the police of the city." The description that follows identifies this as the work of Walker, and then appears the information that they had been "carried to Savannah by the Steward of some vessel (a white man), and delivered by him to a negro preacher for distribution."

A printer in Milledgeville, Georgia, Elijah H. Burritt, brother of Elihu, the famous "learned blacksmith," was accused in February 1830, of introducing this work within the State[23] and "was finally forced to flee for his life in the middle of the night when a hostile mob attacked his dwelling."[24] Some copies were also discovered early in 1830 in New Orleans. In May, a Mr. James Smith of Boston (whether Negro or white is not stated) was convicted of circulating the *Appeal,* fined one thousand dollars, and sentenced to a year's imprisonment.[25]

The pamphlet's appearance in Walker's native state, where disaffection was rife at the time, created much excitement. First mention of it came from Wilmington in August 1830, when a free Negro brought a copy to the police. A slave, unnamed, who had acted as distributor of the disconcerting booklet was arrested, but refused—although it is a good guess that very persuasive tactics were used—to implicate others or tell how many he had dispersed.[26] Spies were used in Fayetteville in order to discover whether the pamphlet had appeared there, but, said a report to the governor of September 3, "altho this plan has been sometime in operation, it has yet developed nothing that ought to excite our alarm."[27]

The stirring contents of Walker's *Appeal* justified the fears of the slavocracy. He used the Declaration of Independence with telling effect, flinging its immortal words into the teeth of those whose upheld slavery. He denounced the colonizationists and affirmed the Negro's right to the title of American. He excoriated the traitors among his own people, finding it difficult to find words damning enough with which to express his contempt for them. He waxed sarcastic and exuded bitterness as he contemplated the prevalent hypocrisy, with everyone *talking* about liberty and equality:[28]

> But we (coloured people) and our children are *brutes!!* And of course are, and *ought to be* Slaves to the American people and their children forever!! To dig their mines and work their farms; and thus go on enriching them, from one generation to another with our *blood* and our *tears!!!!* [Rebel, he said, rebel and] if you commence, make sure work—do not trifle, for they will not trifle with you—they want us for their slaves, and think nothing of murdering us in order to subject us to that wretched condition—therefore, if there is an *attempt* made by us, kill or be killed.

At one point did David Walker leave the immediate and the practical, and this he did in order to utter this prophecy:

> for although the destruction of the oppressors God may not effect by the oppressed, yet the Lord our God will bring other destructions upon them—for not infrequently will he cause them to rise up one against another, to be split and divided, and to oppress each other, and sometimes to open hostilities with sword in hand.

The ensuing years witness a sharply accelerating growth in militant abolitionism as the struggle between pro- and anti-slavery forces became more acute. In 1831, William Lloyd Garrison expressed his opinion on this subject and maintained it throughout his long devotion to the cause. He wrote Le Roy Sunderland on September 8 of that year that he did not advocate servile rebellion, since he believed in non-resistance to evil, but, "Of all men living, however, our slaves have the best reason to assert their rights by violent measures, inasmuch as they are more oppressed than others."[29]

His newspaper did, in line with its editor's belief in freedom of expression, occasionally print material that bore no signs of non-resistance, as, for example, a poem "supposed to be sung by slaves in insurrection," contributed by "V" and published one month before the Turner uprising.[30] Portions of this work went as follows:

> See, tyrants see; your empire shakes;
> Your flaming roofs the wild wind fans;

Stung to the soul, the Negro wakes:
He slept, a brute—he wakes, a man!
His shackles fall,
Erect and tall
He glories in his new found might,
And wins with bloody hand his right.

Up, Afric, up; the land is free
It sees no slave to despot bow.
Our cry is Liberty—
On; strike for God and vengeance now
Fly, tyrants fly,
Or stay and die.
No chains to bear, no scourge we fear;
We conquer, or we perish here.

Once a revolt started Garrison could not help wishing it success and the bitterness of his language condemning the hypocrisy of the slave holders who habitually expressed sympathy with rebels in Greece or France or Belgium or Poland, but contempt for those on their very plantations, could not be exceeded. Thus, following the Turner uprising Garrison, in his inimitable style, wrote:

> Ye patriotic hypocrites! Ye panegyrists of Frenchman, Greeks, and Poles! Ye fustian declaimrs for liberty! Ye valiant sticklers for equal rights among yourselves! Ye haters of aristocracy! Ye assailants of monarch! Ye republican nullifiers! Ye treasonable disunionists! Be dumb! Cast no reproach upon the conduct of the slaves, but let your lips and cheeks wear the blisters of condemnation![31]

A visitor to the city of Petersburg, Virginia, a Mr. Robinson, was indiscreet enough to remark in the course of a private talk, at the height of the terror evoked by Nat Turner in September 1831, that, while he deprecated the rebellion yet, he felt compelled to acknowledge that "black men have, in the abstract, a right to their freedom." His opinion became known, a mob of over one hundred persons ("some of them . . . men of fortune") dragged him from his residence, lashed and stripped him, and, in this condition, drove him from the town. A Mr. Carter, who was the victim's host, was also compelled to leave. "Not the least disgraceful feature in the case was, that the civil authorities, though applied to, declined interfering."[32]

At about this time James Forten, the well-to-do and courageous Philadelphia Negro reformer, congratulated Garrison for having withstood unflinchingly the campaign of intimidation let loose against him, particularly after Turner's attempt. He asserted that the cause of servile rebellion was in the South, not in *The Liberator,* and that the latest revolt would strengthen the anti-slavery movement by "bringing the evils of slavery prominently before the public. . . . Indeed we live in stiring [sic] times, and every day brings news of some fresh effort for liberty, either at home or abroad—onward, onward, it is indeed the watchword."[33]

Others were moved to write, print, and send into the South letters such as following, dated Albany [N.Y. ?] Sept. 15, 1831:

> Sir—As our Constitution says that all men are created equal; [sic] and as God has made of one flesh all the nations of this earth; and as the Negroes are no worse when born than the Whites; and as there is no good prospect that a voluntary release of the slaves will be effected to any (great) degree—I hereby make known that for these and other reasons, I will, as an individual, use all honorable means to sever the iron band that unites the slaves to their masters. And as long as this national ulcer (slavery) remains upon a part of the republic, a disunion is highly desirable. It is a disgrace to the United States. It is looked upon as such by most of Europe. What? A republic, boasting its equal rights, when a worse system of slavery is hardly (if at all) to be found. It is a shame. Yours Respectfully, Sherlock P. Gregory.[34]

In April 1835, at a Boston anti-slavery meeting the question, "Would the slaves be justified in resorting to physical violence to obtain their freedom?" was submitted for discussion. The position generally adopted was very much like that held by Garrison.[35] The Reverend Samuel J. May and George Thompson, the British abolitionist, declared that if any human being could justly employ violence it would be the slave in an endeavor to gain freedom, but both agreed that pacifism was, in all cases, even in that of slaves, right, and thus replied to the question in the negative. A Mr. Parker, of the Newton Theological Institution, came around to an agreement with this predominant feeling, although early in the discussion he had felt differently. He had permitted himself to say: "If the masses of the slaves would occasionally rise, like men and patriots, and assert their rights, would not these attempts hasten the day of total and complete emancipation?" He had, moreover, declared that to the vast majority of the slaves the message of true Christianity had not been brought, and the Bible remained a closed book. "As heathens, then would they not be justified in revolting against their oppressors, especially as their object would be to obtain an immense good—liberty and the Bible?"

Only one man, apparently, a Mr. Weeks, expressed and maintained disagreement with the accepted philosophy, and even he opposed violence. He did this, however, merely on the ground of expediency, and argued that the Bible could be used as easily to sanction the rising of the slaves as not.[36]

Following the slave plots of the summer of 1835 and the accusations leveled against the abolitionists, there appeared, as already noted, denials on their part of advocacy of rebellion. It is, nevertheless, interesting to note that the disavowals were not considered complete or satisfactory by some connected with the movement. This appears, for example, in a letter from William Oakes to Samuel Sewell:

> I have looked with great anxiety to see under the signatures of the most respectable & best known abolitionists in Boston, a statement of their principles, and especially a *full* & not to be misunderstood denial in general & particular, of insurrectionary doctrines, or practices of any kind—Let it be fully understood that 3/4 of the Abolitionists do not believe even in defensive war, much less in the "sacred right of insurrection."[37]

There was much thinking, talking, and writing among abolitionists in 1837 concerning this perplexing question of non-resistance. It arose in the annual meeting of the Massachusetts Anti-Slavery Society held in Boston in January. A Negro, identified merely as a Mr. Johnson who had once been a slave, spoke at this meeting and informed the audience that he had read Walker's pamphlet. He went on to express similar convictions, remarking that the white people in the United States had fought for liberty and were revered as heroes for so doing. Moreover, said Mr. Johnson, in his sparkling style, even a bug will try to bite when stepped upon.

William Lloyd Garrison followed and conceded that when Mr. Johnson pointed to the inconsistency of the white Americans in denouncing slave rebellion and glorying in their own Revolution, his argument was unanswerable. Garrison also noted the fact that several of the state constitutions, as those of Maryland and Tennessee, contained the words, "The doctrine of non-resistance to oppression is absurd, slavish, and destructive of the good and happiness of mankind." Yet, he said, this was not his opinion and he could but reiterate his belief in the evil of violence and the duty of non-resistance.

This appeared to be the dominant sentiment of the meeting. Indeed, a Negro abolitionist of Boston, the Reverend Hosea Easton, offered the following resolution, meant in a complimentary sense, and it was adopted—though its statement of fact is open to grave doubt: "Resolved, That the spirit of insurrection and insubordination of the slave population of this country, is restrained more by the influence of the free colored people thereof, than by all the oppressive legislative enactments of the slave-holding states."[38]

The determined resistance to mob attacks offered by the anti-slavery editor, Elijah Lovejoy, and his friends (Lovejoy himself being killed November 7, 1837) and the fact that the abolitionist societies did not deprecate the resistance then offered aroused considerable comment. The famous radical ladies from South Carolina, Sarah and Angelina Grimké, wrote a joint letter to Theodore Weld referring to the use of violence in this episode and to the absence of an expression of regret over this on the part of the American Anti-Slavery Society.[39] "Surely to be consistent," said these earnest young women, "abolitionists sh'd go South and help the slaves to obtain their freedom at the point of the bayonet."

Charles Marriott, a Hicksite Quaker whose anti-slavery agitation was to lead to his disownment, wrote an illuminating letter, headed "private," to Garrison in December.[40] Marriott declared:

> I & some other of my friends called soon after [the Lovejoy tragedy] at the A.S. office to urge the necessity of disavowing this resort to arms—all the satisfaction we could obtain was that abolitionists were divided on the subject of defensive war, and that they could not say what they did not believe in. A division on this point, seems almost inevitable. *Fighting & pacific* Abolitionists! Your Mass. Society has done nobly, as also has Benja. Lundy, Wm. Goddell, H. C. Wright, and some other individuals, but from the spirit manifested by not a few abolitionists, Slavery is not like to be terminated by a *moral* conflict *only.*

A communication from Putnam, Ohio, of a little later date revealed growing uncertainty as to the wisdom of pacifism and appealed to Garrison for philosophic ammunition to hurl at the doubters.[41] The subject of force was discussed at the town's lyceum, and it was discovered that while about half the inhabitants of the community opposed slavery, only some three or four individuals were non-resistants.

The same question was discussed in 1837 in a Negro newspaper, the *Colored American,* published in New York City, in a series of articles by William Whipper. Mr. Whipper's essay took a pacifistic stand, but it is interesting to observe that the editor, Samuel E. Cornish, in introducing the series wrote: "But we honestly confess that we have yet to learn what virtue there would be in using moral weapons, in defense against kidnappers or a midnight incendiary with a torch in his hand."[42]

The first militant abolitionist to actually discuss details of a plan for putting his ideas into practice, so far as this writer has seen, was Jabez D. Hammond of Cherry Valley, New York. In the Spring of 1839 he told Gerrit Smith (who did not then agree) of his belief in the justice of the use of force in this case, and suggested the establishment of military schools for young Negroes in Canada and Mexico. "I believe that young men thus educated . . . would be the most successful Southern missionaries."[43]

By 1841, however, Gerrit Smith had moved to the point of urging slaves to flee and take whatever they needed and to blast away all obstacles in order to succeed in their effort at self-liberation. The organization which heard his words, the American Anti-Slavery Society, while not committing itself to an approval of them, did feel impelled to go on record as declaring that its members would not aid in suppressing Negro insurrection.[44]

David Ruggles, a leading New York Negro abolitionist, headed an open letter announcing an anti-slavery convention with the motto, "Know ye not who would be free, Themselves must strike the first blow!" In the text of the letter itself were these words:[45] "Our condition is everywhere identical. Rise, brethren, rise! Strike for freedom, or die slaves!"

An exceedingly severe note of bitterness enters the writings of the great Theodore Weld at about this time. Thus, in a letter to his wife in the midst of a severe economic depression in the South, and threats of war against Great Britain (which, should they materialize might culminate, he thought, in freedom for the Negroes) Weld wrote:[46]

> The slaveholders of the present generation, if cloven down by God's judgments, cannot plead that they were *unwarned.* Warnings, reproofs, and the foreshadows of coming retribution have for years freighted the very air, and should sudden destruction come upon them at last, well may the God of the oppressed cry out against them, "because I have called and ye have refused . . . Therefore will I laugh at your calamity and mock when your fear cometh."

The rebellion in October 1841, of the slaves aboard the domestic trader, *Creole,* whilst en route from Hampton Roads, Virginia, to New Orleans, the sterling character displayed by the Negroes, their success in getting the ship to Bermuda and the resulting international complications, brought the question of pacifism amongst abolitionists once more to the fore.

One of the country's most eminent fighters against slavery, the Ohio congressman, Joshua R. Giddings, made his position clear in a resolution introduced in the House of Representatives in 1842 opposing the treatment of the rebellious slaves as common criminals. The resolution maintained that slavery existed only by positive, local law, not by a Federal Statute. Once the ship, therefore, had reached the high seas and left the jurisdiction of any slave state, the Negroes were no longer slaves, and they had reasserted a natural right in rebelling against those who pretended to own them. In attempting to secure their freedom, said Representative Giddings, the Negroes did what was commendable and proper. For daring to introduce such a resolution Mr. Giddings was censured by his colleagues, by a vote of 126 to 69, and immediately resigned. But, and this marked an important milestone in the abolitionist movement, the determined gentleman was promptly reelected by his constituents as their Representative.[47]

The year 1843 is marked by the flaming speech made by one of the best-known Negroes of that day, the Reverend Henry Highland Garnet, before a Negro convention meeting in Buffalo, New York. This remarkable person had been born a slave in Kent County, Maryland, in 1815, and had, with his parents, escaped to New Hope, Pennsylvania, in 1824. That same year, however, his sister was retaken by slave catchers, and the Garnets moved to New York City in 1825. Here Garnet studied at elementary and high school, and met and was greatly influenced by the Negro radical, the Reverend Theodore S. Wright. He then, together with Alexander Crummell, attended a school at Canaan, New Hampshire. Both, however, were driven out by a mob, at which time Garnet seems to have lost any faith he may have had in the efficacy of non-resistance, for he used a shotgun in his own defense.

From thence, Garnet went to Oneida Institute at Whitesboro, New York, and studied under Beriah Green. Completing his work there, he taught in Troy from 1840 to 1842, and later became pastor of the Negro Presbyterian Church in that city. He was holding that position when he delivered "An address to the slaves of the United States of America" before a convention of colored citizens in Buffalo.

Henry Highland Garnet's speech delivered in his characteristically effective manner advanced ideas beyond which the abolitionist movement was never to go. He said to his brethren, "If you must bleed, let it all come at once." He reminded them of their martyrs, men like Denmark Vesey and Nat Turner, and affirmed, "it is your solemn and imperative duty to use every means, both moral, intellectual, and physical, that promises success." He was specific:

> Brethren, arise, arise! Strike for your lives and liberties. Now is the day and the hour. Let every slave throughout the land do this, and the days of slavery are numbered. You can not be more oppressed than you have been: you can not suffer greater cruelties than you have already. *Rather die freemen than live to be slaves.*

Should these sentiments be broadcast throughout the land as coinciding with those of the convention itself? This question was debated, with a comparative newcomer to the ranks of the Negro abolitionists, one Frederick Douglass, taking, at this stage of his career, the negative, and carrying the convention with him. But this was done by a vote of 19 to 18, the closeness of which is indicative of the fact that militance developed earlier and was more widespread among the Negro abolitionists—so many of whom had themselves felt the lash—than among their white fellow workers.[48]

Desperation rather than philosophic conviction sometimes led to the expression of militant views. The difficulties of the struggle and the weakness and splits that plagued the abolitionists led some among them at moments to doubt that verbal or even political action would bring essential improvement. This mood was expressed by William Birney in a letter to his father, James, dated Cincinnati, June 14, 1843: "When I witness these ill-considered movements on the part of the friends of the Slave, I do feel that our hope is not in a man or in a political action but in the flames of insurrection, or of foreign war."[49]

It has been asserted that in 1844, a Negro, the Reverend Moses Dickson of Cincinnati, together with eleven other Negroes, founded an "international Order of Twelve of the Knights and Daughters of Tabor" for the purpose of accomplishing the overthrow of slavery in any and every way possible. In 1846 the same individual is supposed to have started another secret organization, called the Knights of Liberty, which used St. Louis as its headquarters and aided hundreds of slaves to flee, but whether it was active in aiding or provoking conspiracies and rebellions is not clear.[50]

A comment made early in 1844 by the Presidential candidate of the political abolitionists, in defending his position, is indicative of a developing school of thought. James G. Birney asked, rhetorically, whether it was not a fact that all just men rejoice "when they hear that the oppressed of any land have achieved their liberty, at whatever cost to their tyrants?"[51] And while this former slave holder did not actually express the deduction that logically followed from his words, the conclusion could hardly have been more plain even if specifically drawn.

From the wing of the non-political abolitionists during the same year came the blast against the Constitution delivered by the Bostonian, Francis Jackson, on the Fourth of July. Mr. Jackson publicly renounced his allegiance to this expression of the fundamental law, and he did so particularly because of its fourth article guaranteeing Federal aid for the suppression of domestic violence,[52]

> Which [as he saw it] pledges to the South the military force of the country, to protect the masters against their insurgent slaves, and binds us, and our children, to shoot down our fellow-countrymen, who may rise, in emulation of our revolutionary fathers, to vindicate their inalienable "right to life, liberty, and the pursuit of happiness,"—this clause of the Constitution, I say distinctly, I will never support.

Mr. Jackson's position was adopted at a convention of the New England Workingmen's Association held in January 1846, at Lynn, Massachusetts. These laborers resolved, "That while we are willing to pledge ourselves to use all means in our power, consistent with our principles, to put down wars, insurrections and mobs, and to protect all men from the evils of the same, we will not take up arms to sustain the Southern slave-holders in robbing the one-fifth of our countrymen of their labor."[53] They urged, moreover, that "our brethren speak out in thunder tones, both as associations and individuals, and let it no longer be said that Northern laborers, while they are contending for their rights, are a standing army to keep three millions of their brethren and sisters in bondage at the point of the bayonet."

An individual who was soon to put his philosophic convictions into practice and thereby attract the attention of the world and help precipitate the Second American Revolution, John Brown, had by this period arrived at those convictions. In the year 1847, Frederick Douglass visited Brown in his humble Springfield, Massachusetts, home. The two men spoke of means wherewith to eradicate slavery. Brown, with perfect confidence in the discreetness and integrity of Douglass, did not hesitate to tell him that, in his opinion, nothing but force could overthrow the institution of human bondage. And he told him, too, of his plan for the most effectual use of force, the employment of small units of men, Negro and white, to penetrate the slave area, establish themselves in the Appalachian Mountains and there serve as bases from which marauding expeditions against nearby slave plantations might set out, and to which slaves might flee.[54]

Douglas thought the plan had "much to commend it,"[55] but was not yet convinced that moral suasion might not convert the nation as a whole, even the slave holders, to the anti-slavery viewpoint. Nevertheless, Brown's arguments, that slavery was a state of war, and that the owners of human property would never voluntarily relinquish it, impressed Douglass so that, as he said, "My utterances became more and more tinged by the color of this man's strong impressions."

The Federal House of Representatives heard strange words in 1848—words such as even he who now uttered them, Joshua R. Giddings, had not hitherto used. That Ohio Congressman praised Captain Drayton of the Pearl who, for attempting to carry to freedom a group of Washington slaves, had been caught and jailed. Indeed, Mr. Giddings thought it right for an American Representative to visit such a man in his cell and to congratulate him personally on his courage. This, as might be expected, raised a whirlwind of protest. Mr. Haskell of Tennessee asked his interesting colleague whether he actually felt it to be proper for a slave to flee from his master. Mr. Giddings said yes, and more than yes, for he declared "that it was not only the right of the oppressed to obtain their liberty if they could do so, even by slaying their oppressors, but it was the unquestioned duty, even to the taking of the life of every man who opposed them."[56]

As the weeks and months wore on these thoughts were becoming less and less strange and unique, more and more frequently expressed. Frederick Douglass, by 1849, was moving towards Garnet's position that he had, six years before, opposed. In Fanueil Hall, Boston, this striking individual, who bore the marks of enslavement upon his back, and whose four sisters and one brother were still in chains, denounced the oppression of his people, cited the revolutionary heritage of America,[57] and found himself saying that "in view of these things, I should welcome the intelligence tomorrow, should it come, that the slaves had risen in the South, and that the sable arms which had been engaged in beautifying and adoring the South were engaged in spreading death and destruction here." Meanwhile, that same year the Liberty Party resolved that it was preferable to send the slaves compasses and pistols than Bibles.[58]

During the next decade such militant ideas were so frequently expressed that one is justified in declaring that, among anti-slavery folk, they became commonplace. It is, indeed, a moot question whether the hitherto dominant pacifist or non-resistance wing in the movement (so far, at least, as its articulate members were concerned) was not overshadowed and outweighed, in the decade of crisis, by activists and believers in resistance.

A convention of Negro adherents of the Free Soil Party which met in Boston in 1852 heard the Reverend J. B. Smith of Rhode Island, whose own father had been killed while attempting to flee, declare,[59] "He believed that resistance to tyrants was obedience to God, and hence, to his mind, the only drawback to the matchless Uncle Tom of Mrs. Stowe was his virtue of submission to tyranny—an exhibition of grace which he (the speaker) did not covet."

That year, another Negro, Martin R. Delany, ended a letter to Garrison with these lines:

> Were I a slave, I would be free,
> I would not live to live a slave;
> But boldly *strike* for LIBERTY—
> For FREEDOM or a Martyr's grave.[60]

The New York abolitionist and correspondent of Gerrit Smith whose militance was observed as early as 1839, retained the same views and let Mr. Smith hear them again in 1852. He affirmed the righteousness of the forcible overthrow of slavery and maintained, with great optimism, that, "An organized army of 10,000 men with an able commander, and arms munitions of war and provisions for 50,000 men would march through the Southern States and liberate every slave there in six months."[61]

At about this time the Reverend George W. Perkins wrote an article entitled, "Can Slaves Rightfully Resist and Fight?" in which he warned that quick emancipation alone would spare future bloodshed. And, while himself inclining towards the non-resistant school, he confessed, as did Garrison, that, "*If* it was right in 1776 to resist, fight, and kill to secure liberty,—it is right to do the same in 1852. *If* three millions of whites might rightfully resist the powers ordained by God, then three millions of blacks may rightfully do the same."[62]

The Reverend J. W. Loguen, the Syracuse Negro who gained fame for his public defiance of the Fugitive Slave Act of 1850 and his prominence in the Jerry Rescue in 1851, wrote Garrison an informative letter early in 1854 concerning his own attitude, and that which seemed to be most prevalent among Negroes, generally:

> I want you to set me down as a *Liberator* man. Whether you will call me so or not, I am with you in heart. I may not be in hands and head—for my hands will fight a slaveholder—which I suppose THE LIBERATOR and some of its good friends would not do . . . I am a fugitive slave, and you know that we have strange notions about many things.[63]

Charles Francis Adams, also, at this time, made an interesting generalization when he asserted that while personally he opposed rebellion on the part of the slaves, he believed that, "Probably few of them [abolitionists] entertain any doubt of the abstract *right* of the slave to free himself from the condition in which he is kept against his own consent, in any manner practicable."[64]

One of the series of conventions of free Negroes called for the purpose of battling Jim Crowism and aiding the abolitionist movement, held in Philadelphia in the spring of 1854, adopted a most radical resolution. This declared as the sense of the gathering that "those who, without crime, are outlawed by any Government can owe no allegiance to its enactments;—that we advise all oppressed to adopt the motto, 'Liberty or Death.'"[65]

A widely-read work copyrighted in 1855 and issued simultaneously in 1856 by four publishers in London, Boston, New York, and Cleveland, opened with sentences modeled after those of the manifesto of 1776, but specifically applied to the American Negro:

> When in any State, the oppression of the laboring portion of the community amounts to an entire deprivation of their civil and personal rights, when it assumes to control their will, and to punish with bodily tortures the least infraction of its mandates, it is obvious that the class so overwhelmed with injustice, are necessarily, unless prevented by ignorance from knowing their rights and their wrongs, the enemies of the government. To them, insurrection and rebellion are primary, original duties.[66]

The Kansas War stimulated the spread and acceptance of these ideas, so that while in 1849 only a rather restricted group like the Liberty Party would resolve that pistols were more important to the Southern slaves than Bibles, by the years of the Kansas excitement a minister who earnestly strove to say what he felt people wanted to hear, Henry Ward Beecher, was sending pistols into the troubled territory and calling them his Bibles. Gerrit Smith, too, exemplifies the drift. "Hitherto," he declared, "I have opposed the bloody abolition of slavery. But now, when it begins to march its conquering bands into the Free States, I and ten thousand other peace men are not only ready to have it repulsed with violence, but pursued even unto death, with violence."[67]

The influential Frederick Douglass also definitely committed himself to the same side at this time. While affirming that it was still one's duty to use "persuasion and argument" and any other instrumentality that offered promise of ending slavery without violence,[68]

> we yet feel that its peaceful annihilation is almost hopeless . . . and contend that the slave's right to revolt is perfect, and only wants the occurrence of favorable circumstances to become a duty . . . We cannot but shudder as call to mind the horrors that have marked servile insurrection—we would avert them if we could; but shall the millions for ever submit to robbery, to mur-

der, to ignorance, and every unnamed evil which an irresponsible tyrant can devise, because the overthrow of that tyrant could be productive of horrors? We say not. The recoil, when it comes, will be in exact proportion to the wrongs inflicted; terrible as it will be, we accept and hope for it.

John Henry Hill, a slave who escaped from Richmond in 1853, expressed to the Negro director of the Philadelphia station of the underground railroad, the typical opinion of one who had himself worn the chains. "Our Pappers," he wrote, "contain long details of insurrectionary movements among the slaves of the South . . . I beleve that Prayers affects great good, but I beleve that the fire and sword would affect more good in this case."[69]

At a time when old John Brown had fully matured his plans for an invasion of the slave area, another abolitionist, Lysander Spooner of Boston, developed, quite independently, put into writing, and finally into print, a proposal strikingly similar to the ideas of Brown. Spooner printed a long circular,[70] one side of which contained an appeal "To The non-Slaveholders of the South" calling upon them to overthrow the domination of the Bourbons and thus assure their own well-being and advancement, as well as the liberation of the slaves. The other side contained "A Plan for The Abolition Of Slavery" which envisaged the sending of money and arms to the slaves, the inciting of rebellion, the use of arson, flogging, and kidnapping to destroy the property and morale of the slave holders, the formation throughout the nation of Leagues of Freedom, the members of which, finally, were to descend upon the slave-holding area, declare freedom for all, and, if necessary, wage a war of liberation. Moreover, said Spooner, should such a war be necessary, the property of the slave owners was to be confiscated and given to the slaves as some compensation for their years of unrequited toil, and in order to make certain that their rights as free men would be retained after the war.

Some copies of the amazing document were distributed,[71] but John Brown learned of it, and upon his informing Spooner that continued publicity and distribution would injure the possibilities of the successful carrying out of his own plan (of which Spooner heard for the first time) its dispersion was stopped.[72]

Happily, for those anxious to learn of the development of militant abolitionism, Spooner sent copies of his circular (in manuscript form) to several anti-slavery leaders and received and preserved answers from nine of them. Only one, J. R. French, writing from Painesville, Ohio, utterly and completely repudiated the idea. He felt it to be "*Quixotic* in the extreme" and found it hard to believe that a "sober man of reason," as he knew lawyer Spooner to be," would have "any faith in such a scheme," fit for "the crased [sic] brain of *S. S. Foster.*"[73]

Three others, Lewis Tappan, Hinton Rowan Helper, and Francis Jackson, felt that they could not go along with Mr. Spooner in his choice of means to accomplish their common end. Lewis Tappan acknowledged that the Negroes had every right to their freedom, and would be as justified in obtaining it by violence as any people, including those engineering the American Revolution, but, as for himself, he was "a Christian, and a peace-maker, and abjure all resort to deadly weapons to secure our rights."[74]

Francis Jackson, a seventy-year-old veteran of the crusade, told Spooner he could not "accept your 'Plan' or join your 'League.'"[75] He had, he wrote, been laboring with the Garrisonians for twenty-five years and was "loaded down to the gunwales with their apparatus" and believed their "doctrine of Non-Resistance is true." Yet, he declared, "I shall neither encourage, [n]or discourage you, because I know your motives are true to your own light, and conviction of duty" and ended, "I have but little strength left, but if I had ever so much, I could not ask, or encourage others to go, where I was not ready and willing to go myself."

Hinton Rowan Helper preceded the salutation of his letter with the words, "Immature—Impractical—Impolitic" which, he went on, succinctly expressed his "candid criticism of the circular in regard to which you did me the honor to request my opinion."[76] He urged that it not be distributed, "or, to say the least, that you will withhold it from the public until after the next Presidential campaign." His closing paragraphs are interesting enough to warrant a full quotation:

> For several months past I have had in contemplation to issue a circular especially designed to reach the South in the right way; and if I am not failed or prejudiced in my aims and efforts, I think I shall, in connection with other Southerners, who are willing and anxious to cooperate with me, be successful in accomplishing more in that direction within the next two or three years than has been accomplished within the last fifty.
>
> My friend, Prof. Hedrick,[77] has seen your circular and fully concurs in the opinion which I have expressed in reference to the same. Neither the Professor nor myself, however, desire to be taken as criterions to go by. Probably it would be well for you to consult others.

Wendell Phillips, Theodore Parker, Thomas Wentworth Higginson, Stephen S. Foster, and Dr. Daniel Mann expressed agreement in principle, and the last two very largely in detail, with Spooner.

The earliest reply in the whole series came from Wendell Phillips, whose letter was dated July 16, 1858. His idea is summarized in the sentence, "Your scheme would be a good one if it were only *practicable.*" He doubted, however, that enough men would enlist "to save the attempt from being ridiculous" and added that if the opposite were true and a fairly

> Considerable number did rally round you it would be treason & the Govt. would at one move & array all its power to crush the enterprise—before it made head enough to be able to compete with an organized despotism like ours. In such circumstances, I cannot see any present availability & use in the proposal.

Yet Phillips did not completely shut the door for he ended by remarking that he always heard Spooner's elaboration of his own plans "with interest & respect & sometime we will steal an hour & talk it over." This must indeed have been an interesting conversation, if it occurred, but no record of it has been seen.

Theodore Parker's letter, written some months later, while considerably more brief than that of Phillips, said much the same thing. "Your paper," he declared, "is very well thought & expressed as indeed are all your writings. If it were widely circulated at the South, it would strike a panic terror into those men, whose $2 billion is invested neither in land nor things. But I think you can't get a Corporal's Guard to carry you plan into execution. When I am well enough I will come & talk with you about it"[78]—another undoubtedly fascinating conversation which apparently was never recorded.

On the same day, Thomas Wentworth Higginson, who had demonstrated his resistance philosophy in fugitive slave rescues, wrote Spooner from Worcester a very long and highly informative letter of approval. The circular had his "general approbation." He felt that "the increase of interest in the subject of Slave Insurrection is one of the most important signs of the time," and was convinced "that, within a few years, that phase of the subject will urge itself on general attention, and the root of the matter be thus reached. I think that this will be done by the action of the slaves themselves, in certain localities, with the aid of secret co-operation from the whites." This, he believed, was "greatly to be desired" as it would terrorize the slave holders, force them to the defensive in the national struggle and stimulate thinking in the North "on the fundamental question of Liberty."

He reaffirmed, then, his sympathy with Spooner's aim. "My only criticism on your plan, is, that I think in Revolutions the practical end always comes first & the theory afterwards; just as our fathers, long after the Battle of Bunker Hill, still disavowed the thought of separation—and honestly." There followed a sentence whose truth John Brown's exploit was soon to confirm: "For one man who would consent to the proposition of a slave insurrection, there are ten who would applaud it, when it actually came to the point. People's hearts go faster than their heads. . . . In place therefore of forming a Society or otherwise propounding insurrections as *plan*, my wish would be to assure it as a *fact*."

Higginson vaguely hinted at the coming Brown attempt in which he was already deeply concerned by remarking, "Were I free to do it, I could give you assurances that what I say means something, & that other influences than these of which you speak are even now working to the same end. I am not now at liberty to be more explicit." He closed by affirming that Spooner's work had considerable value in preparing the public mind for servile rebellion, something that he always did in his speeches and had urged other agitators to do.

Another Worcester man, Stephen S. Foster, whose contempt for compromise and expediency had led even sympathetic folk to think him, at best, eccentric, though opening his letter with remarks concerning a severe rheumatic attack, proceeded to give his opinion in an essay of some one thousand words.[79] He had long seen, he declared, the need for new methods among the friends of freedom.

> The grand defect in our present policy is that it sets our practice in direct conflict with our principles and preachings. We proclaim the great truth of the equality of the races, & maintain with words the equal right of the slaves with ourselves to liberty & personal protection: but in practice, with few exceptions we essentially ignore these theories, & either unite politically with their masters in active measures for the destruction of their liberty, or fold our arms & refuse them the protection we demand for ourselves.

In typical unyielding fashion Foster said that if we claim the products of our own labor, we must assert the slaves' right to the property of their owners, and help them get possession of it. And if we believe in taking life,

> Under any circumstances, we must teach him to cleave down his tyrant master, & aid him in the work. If we refuse allegiance to a government which tramples upon our own liberty, we must put our help upon the government which yokes him with the brute. That abolitionism which comes short of this is essentially defective; & if persisted in when property enlightened, is shown to be tainted & spurious.

While, according to Foster, the ultimate solution resided in the formation of a national party gaining mass support and power in order to put these principles into action, yet concerning Spooner's proposal he wrote:

> Entertaining these views I cannot but regard your plan of action, in the main, as a step in the right direction.... To aim at such a result is to quicken the nation's sense of justice; & thus to pave the way to the final overthrow of the whole system.... Every supporter of the government must be held responsible for the entire slave system, & made identical in moral turpitude with the master, & both must be outlawed.

A physician friend of Spooner's, Daniel Mann, who had recently moved to Painesville, Ohio, wrote the most enthusiastic letter of all those preserved.[80] He thanked Lysander Spooner for himself and "in behalf of the cause, for which you have done a great job, in making a *great beginning.*" He referred to America's revolutionary history, and the audacity of the slave holders. Then came these observations:

> Truth should not disarm her champions, yet such seems to be the effect of her humanizing & evaluating influences. We learn to hate fighting & therefore are not "valiant for the truth." War has been employed so long only in behalf of wrong, that the idea of its use in behalf of right has become obsolete. Yet war is wicked only when its purpose is not worthy. A war, in whatever form, & to whatever extent, however desperate & bloody against slavery would be a holy war.... My trust in God is stronger when I put some trust in myself & keep my powder dry. Garrisonism (which is only a new name for what Christianity once meant) would, & yet will plant the wilderness of this world with the rose of Sharon, but there needs a rough breaking up team to prepare the way. The ugly dragons heads must be cut off & their necks seared & their dens destroyed. No people are worthy of freedom who will not fight in its behalf. There may be higher truths than this, but this is as high as I can climb at present.

Language like that makes more understandable the glorification of old John Brown, and the steadfastness and high courage shown by hundreds of thousands, Negro and white, in fighting that the nation might "have a new birth of freedom."

In 1859, a commercial publisher, A. B. Burdick of New York, who had become famous two years earlier as the publisher of Helper's *Impending Crisis,* saw fit to issue a book openly advocating the inciting of a servile rebellion. This was the work of a former *Tribune* editorial writer, James Redpath, and it was dedicated to John Brown, prior to the raid on Harper's Ferry.[81] The author was one of those who took seriously the resolution of the Liberty Party in 1849 that pistols and compasses, not Bibles, were what the slaves most needed, and during several months in 1854 and 1855 he traveled through Virginia, the Carolinas, and Georgia in order to put that resolution into effect.[82]

In his introductory pages Redpath boldly announces:

> I do not hesitate to urge the friends of the slave to incite insurrections, and encourage, in the North, a spirit which shall ultimate in civil and servile wars. . . . What France was to us in our hour of trial, let the North be to the slave today. . . . If the fathers were justified in *their* rebellion, how much more will the slaves be justified in *their* insurrection? You, Old Hero! [John Brown] believe that the slave should be aided and urged to insurrection; and hence do I lay this tribute at your feet. . . . I am a Peace-man and something more. I would fight and kill for the sake of peace. Now, slavery is a state of perpetual war. I am a Non-Resistant—and something more. I would slay every man who attempted to resist the liberation of the slave. I am a Democrat—and nothing more. I believe in humanity and human rights. I recognize nothing as so sacred on earth.

Similar appeals are scattered through the work it ends on the same note. "There are men who are tired of praising French patriots—who are ready to *be* Lafayettes and Kosciuskos to the slaves."[83] Guerrilla warfare, using the mountains and swamps as bases, is the method, and the young men who gained experience in the Kansas fighting should be the leaders. "*Will you aid them—will you sustain them? Are you in favor of a servile insurrection?* Tell God in acts."

A consistent pacifist, Adin Ballou was troubled by this swing towards militance just before John Brown crashed onto the scene. But that event, as he confessed, and as Higginson had prophesied to Spooner, by turning the abstract into the concrete, dealt, for that period, a death blow to non-resistance.[84]

Directly implicated in Brown's pleas were, of course, many prominent individuals, like Frank Sanborn, Theodore Parker, Thomas Wentworth Higginson, Gerrit Smith, Frederick Douglass, Harriet Tubman, Henry Highland Garnet, and others.[85] Perhaps the aspect of the affair most indicative of the turn in sentiments is the fact that two of the men who were with Brown at Harper's Ferry, the brothers Edwin and Barclay Coppoc, were of Quaker families and while one of them, Edwin (hanged for his part in the raid) had earlier been disowned by the Friends for nonattendance at meetings, the other one, Barclay, was still a member in good standing of the Society while shouldering a gun for the liberation of a people. This unique Quaker escaped from Virginia and returned to Iowa where he was disowned January 11, 1860, for bearing arms.[86]

Glorious Henry David Thoreau was moved to utter a "Plea for John Brown" in which he hailed the man as the possessor of a high aim and the performer of a noble act,[87] while Wendell Phillips, speaking in Brooklyn, New York, on November 1, 1859, publicly affirmed his belief that the slaves had both the right and the duty of rebelling.[88]

Striking, indeed, was the shift in attitude on the part of the Reverend Henry C. Wright. In the forties this man had written the "Non-Resistance" column in *The Liberator.* By 1851, however, he felt it to be the duty of abolitionists to go into the South and aid the slaves to flee.[89] In 1859, as he wrote to the imprisoned John Brown from Nattick, Massachusetts, on November 21, he presided at[90]

> a very large and enthusiastic meeting of the citizens of this town, without regard to political and religious creeds, [which] was held last evening, for the purpose of considering and acting upon the following resolution:—
>
> Whereas, resistance to tyrants is obedience to God, therefore, *Resolved,* That it is the right and duty of the slaves to resist their masters, and the right and duty of the North to incite them to resistance, and to aid them.

This resolution, said Mr. Wright, was adopted "without a dissenting voice," and was mailed to the Governor of Virginia.

Lamentations by more moderate anti-slavery men also indicate the trend. This appears, for example, in a letter from David D. Barnard to Hamilton Fish complaining of the growth of militance in the abolitionist movement, and the spreading of the idea that for both white and Negroes it was a duty to destroy all slave holders.[91]

In May, 1850, James Redpath wrote to a convention of the Massachusetts Anti-Slavery Society that he would not attend as he "had no faith in conventions, but only in the sword and insurrection," and that he was "pledged to the work of inciting an armed insurrection among the slaves of the South, and therefore could have nothing to do with peaceful agitation."[92]

He did, however, organize his own meeting, but this was to be held on the anniversary of Brown's martyrdom and its dominant note was to be rededication to the aims and purposes of the Old Man. Interestingly enough, William Lloyd Garrison, one of the founders of the Non-Resistance Society back in 1838, was asked to speak, but declined on the grounds of indisposition. He did, however, send Redpath a long letter in lieu of his personal appearance, and while reiterating his own belief in the inviolability of human life which disarmed "alike the oppressor and the oppressed," made strong and repeated appeals to those who were not, in principle, pacifists, to aid in servile rebellions. A few examples, among many of such passionate sentences are:[93]

> Brand the man as a hypocrite and dastard, who, in one breath, exults in the deeds of Washington and Warren, and in the next, denounces Nat Turner as monster for refusing longer to wear the yoke and be driven under the lash and for taking up arms to defense his God-given rights. . . . Let Hancock and Adams be covered with infamy, or the black liberators who aided John Brown be honored in history. . . . were I a convert to the doctrine of '76, that a resort to the sword is justifiable to recover lost liberty, then would I plot insurrection by day and by night, deal more in blows and less in words, and seek through blood the emancipation of all who are groaning in captivity at the South.

As this philosophy of resistance gathered disciples, as the danger of civil war increased, and as reports of slave uprisings and plots became more and more frequent, serious consideration was given in the North to the question of its obligation to aid, if called upon, in the suppression of Negro insurrections. In September 1860, Senator James R. Doolittle, of Wisconsin, asserted that if the slaves rose in rebellion the Constitution "binds us to put them down with ball and bayonet. The truth is, and we may as well open our eyes to the fact, that the strong arm of the federal government may be invoked to hold them for their masters to work them."[94]

He who believed this and possessed firm anti-slavery convictions was forced into the position—as were the Garrisonians—of denouncing the Constitution and advocating disunion. There were some, however, like William Jay and Lysander Spooner,[95] who professed to see no pro-slavery bias or bent of any kind in the Constitution, and denied that the obligation to suppress slave insurrections was there contained. In addition, others, like John Quincy Adams, contended that the method by which the federal government ended rebellion—or, specifically, a servile rebellion—was nowhere specified.[96] And, if this might best be done by granting the demands of the insurgents—in the case of slaves by granting them their freedom—the federal government, in the exercise of its war powers, might do that.

This, in essence, was the reply of Joshua R. Giddings to Senator Doolittle.[97] He said, in part: "If necessary to protect the people the army may be used to shoot down the slaves; but if the insurgent slaves can be pacified by having their freedom, the Executive may protect the people by giving the slaves their liberty, or be sending them out of the State or country, as was practiced in the Florida war by Generals Scott, Jessup, and Taylor." Mr. Diggins called this a "remedy" for slave revolts but it certainly was not one calculated to increase the slave holders' devotion for the Union, nor to allay the disaffection of their victims—assuming it reached their ears.

The years of the ultimate triumph of the philosophy of resistance saw its frequent application to the slave population. In the earliest days of the Civil War suggestions for the provoking of Negro insurrection appeared. Thus *The Liberator* of April 25, 1861, printed a letter by "Insurrectionist" advocating servile rebellion as the quickest and surest way of conquering the slavocracy, although Garrison did not fail to record his dissent from the views of this writer. Yet a much stiffer tone of protest came from that pioneer when he learned of General Benjamin F. Butler's offer to Governor Andrew of Maryland to aid in suppressing a threatened uprising.[98]

In May 1861, certain unnamed free Negroes of Pennsylvania offered to go down into the South for the purpose of provoking slave rebellions,[99] but Governor Curtin refused to sanction this. "A Voice from the Under Current" rising from Texas at the same time told of considerable discontent and mass flight among the slaves and advised their arming as the quickest way to end the war.[100] In subsequent months similar demands were made.[101]

The next year the idea of arming of the Negroes was put forth with increasing urgency[102] and, finally, in August 1862, the enlistment of free Negroes as soldiers was initiated. The Preliminary Emancipation Proclamation, issued September 22, 1862, promised that, on the first day of the new year, the Government of the United States "will recognize and maintain the freedom" of people held in bondage by rebels and "will do no act or acts to repress such persons, or any of them, in any efforts they may make for their actual freedom."

On the designated day the president declared such persons free "and that the Executive Government, including the military and naval authorities thereof, will recognize and maintain the freedom of such persons." The great pronouncement went on to urge these individuals, "to abstain from all violence, unless in necessary self-defense."

And an abolitionist, General Rufus Saxton, commanding Negro troops in South Carolina, had the pleasure of calling his men together and fulfilling the vision of Walker and Garnet and Brown, for he told them, after reading the Proclamation:

> It is your duty to carry this good news to your brethren who are still in slavery. Let all your voices, like merry bells join loud and clear in the grand chorus of

> liberty, "We are free," "We are free"—until listening, you shall hear its echoes coming back from every cabin in the land—"We are free," "We are free."[103]

In addition to those who wrote and spoke militantly there were some who acted by actually entering the South and bringing the message of freedom to the slaves. How much influence was thus brought to bear on the production of slave plots and uprisings is not certain but it does appear probable that some was exerted.[104] The activity of these people was, of course, illegal and carried possibilities of great personal danger. Secrecy was, therefore, characteristic, thus making its recording very difficult, and, no doubt, fragmentary.

The names, at least, of some of these people are, however, known. Mention has already been made of John Brown and James Redpath. Other white people who carried on this type of work are Alexander M. Ross, William L. Chaplin, Charles Torrey, Calvin Fairbank, Richard Dillingham, Delia Webster, and John Fairfield.[105]

The latter, a native Virginian, whose years of activity as a liberator extended from approximately 1844 to 1856, believed that every slave was justly entitled to freedom, and that if any person came between him and liberty, the slave had a perfect right to shoot him down.[106] He always went heavily armed himself, and did not scruple to use his weapons whenever he thought the occasion required their use.

This man, who is supposed to have led hundreds of slaves to freedom from every southern state, and to have taken part in several pitched battles, was captured only once and jailed in Bracken, Kentucky, but managed to escape within a short time. It was the belief of his friend, Levi Coffin, that Fairfield was one of the whites hanged in Tennessee in 1856 because of complicity in slave plots. This is not certain, though it is a fact that this remarkable person drops out of the picture in that year.

Free Negroes and escaped slaves were especially active in this type of endeavor. For example, Harriet Tubman, one of the most amazing women that ever lived,[107] carried on her personal emancipation crusade in a fashion very similar to that of John Fairfield, but she, happily, lived to see total emancipation a fact and did not pass away, indeed, until the year 1910. Others who went into the dragon's mouth were Josiah Henson, William Still, Elijah Anderson, and John Mason. Indeed, the leading authority on the subject has estimated that, from Canada alone, in 1860, five hundred Negroes went into the South to rescue their brothers and carry the word of liberty among them.[108]

Some idea of the effect upon the Negro population of the mere presence of a sincere anti-slavery person, who did little more than make clear her sentiments, appears in a letter from a former resident of Massachusetts, Mrs. Louisa Leland, to her Boston friend, Mary Ann Halliburton.[109] Mrs. Leland begins by assuring her friend that her residence in the South has, far from altering her abolitionist views, rather strengthened them, and that she has therefore refrained from using slave labor. As a servant she hired a Negro woman, Rose,

> A very intelligent black woman, who had just purchased her freedom by her own exertion—She was glad to remain in the neighborhood of her children whom she is endeavoring to free also and as we assured her of protection and high wages she gladly came to live with us—It would gladden your heart to hear her speak of the abolitionists of the North—I was reading to my husband a letter from Mrs. Childs not observing that Rose was in the room until on looking up I perceived her whole countenance glowing with delight and her eyes sparkling—As soon as my husband had gone she said to me—Do you know Mrs. Childs[110]—Do tell me about her—I wish her benevolent heart may often receive as much pleasure as I did in witnessing the gratitude and interest in which this woman heard the story of her goodness. She sat in perfect silence—but when I ceased only exclaimed fervently—God will bless her—the names of Garrison, Phillips and others whom we have so often heard together are often spoken by the slaves with deepest feeling . . .
>
> The first of August is generally observed among the slaves whenever they can do it without incurring [sic] punishment[111]—Knowing this, I told Rose to celebrate the day at our plantation[112] where they could be secure from interruption—I have heard eloquence and seen deep feeling manifested at the North on this day—but I never was so deeply moved as on witnessing this scene—They had raised a little arbor—which was decorated with flowers, where a few of the speakers stood—Never shall I forget the sight—An old man nearly eighty years old, blind and very infirm had been brought by his children to the meeting—They had succeeded in purchasing his freedom, which they preferred to their own—and now by the kind help of some Northern abolitionists, they had purchased their own and had within a few days received their free papers and were on the point of starting for the Land of Freedom. The old man took the most earnest farewell of his friends around, and then knelt in prayer—The Whole assembly fell on their knees on the green turn—and a prayer ascended to Heaven, which it seemed to me must call down angels to help them. Tears streamed from his sightless eyes, as he thanked God for this day of freedom and prayed that its blessing might be

extended over the whole race—Then he prayed for their masters, and with the voice and manner of a saint, he lifted his hands to heaven and exclaimed, "Father forgive them, for they know not what they do"—and alas, I thought have they even that excuse to plead?

Conclusion

The data here presented point to the conclusion that the existence of militant Abolitionism was widespread and deep-rooted. It appears to have been particularly common among the Negro people themselves, especially those who had escaped from the delights of the patriarchal paradise. In the decade of crisis, 1850–1860, the acceptance of this philosophy was fairly general among all abolitionists.

The narrative of its development is an important part of the entire story of the anti-slavery crusade, and makes more understandable the growth of a temperament in the North necessary to a people who successfully waged a terribly bloody Civil War, and whose chosen leader, in the midst of the carnage, declared that "if God wills that it continue until all the wealth piled by the bondsman's two hundred and fifty years of unrequited toil shall be sunk, and until every drop of blood drawn with the lash shall be paid by another drawn with the sword, as was said three thousand years ago, so it still must be said 'the judgments of the Lord are true and righteous altogether'."

Notes

1. Aptheker, "The Quakers and Negro Slavery," in *The Journal of Negro History*, 1940, 25, pp. 336, 338. Observe Jefferson's note to Governor James Monroe of Virginia after the Gabriel plot, urging mercy in the punishment of the rebels: "The other states & the world at large will forever condemn us if we indulge a principle of revenge, or go one step beyond absolute necessity. They cannot lose sight of the rights of the two parties, & the object of the unsuccessful one." Letter dated Monticello, September 20, 1800, in *The Writings of Thomas Jefferson*, P. L. Ford, ed., (New York, 1903), 7, pp. 457–58.

2. MS Council Journal, 8, p. 13, South Carolina Historical Commission, Columbia, S.C.

3. See Louis Hartz, "Otis and anti-slavery doctrine," in *The New England Quarterly*, 12, 1939, pp. 745–47.

4. John Adams to William Tudor, dated Quincy, June 1, 1818, in *The Works of John Adams*, C. F. Adams, ed., 1850–56, 10, p. 315; incorrectly quoted by Hartz in "Otis and anti-slavery doctrine," in *The New England Quarterly*, 1939. Observe the remark of

Mrs. John Adams in a letter to her husband, dated Boston, September 22, 1774, telling of the discovery of a slave plot: "I wish most sincerely there was not a slave in the province; it always appeared a most iniquitous scheme to me to fight ourselves for what we are daily robbing and plundering from those who have as good a right to freedom as we have." *Letters of Mrs. Adams, the Wife of John Adams,* C. F. Adams, ed., 3d edit., Boston, 1841, 1, p. 24.

5. Quoted by Alice M. Baldwin, *The New England Clergy and the American Revolution,* Durham, 1928, p. 119.

6. Reprinted often, as Samuel Hopkins' *Timely Articles on Slavery,* Boston, 1854.

7. *The American Museum,* Philadelphia, 1789, 6, p. 80. Note the statement of James Madison, made in 1783, in connection with the capture of a runaway slave belonging to him: "[I] cannot think of punishing him by transportation merely for coveting that liberty for which we have paid of price of so much blood, and have proclaimed so often to be the right, & worthy the pursuit of every human being." Quoted by Abbot E. Smith, *James Madison,* N.Y., 1937, p. 221.

8. William F. Poole, *Anti-Slavery Opinions Before the Year 1800,* Cincinnati, 1873, p. 17.

9. *The American Museum,* 1791, 12, pp. 299–300.

10. David Rice, *Slavery Inconsistent with Justice and Good Policy,* London, 1793, p. 9 (originally published in Philadelphia, 1792).

11. Theodore Dwight, *An Oration Spoken Before the Connecticut Society for The Promotion of Freedom and the Relief of Persons Unlawfully Holden in Bondage Convened in Hartford on the 8th Day of May, A.D. 1794,* pp. 20, 23. See Mary S. Locke, *Anti-Slavery in America from the Introduction of African Slaves to the Prohibition of the Slave Trade (1619–1808),* Boston, 1901, pp. 169–71.

12. Locke, op. cit., points out items of this nature in issues of December 12, 1796, and August 28, 1799; see also, issues of August 21, and September 4, 1799.

13. "A Charge, Delivered to the African Lodge," June 24, 1799, at Menotomy, by the Right Worshipful Master, Prince Hall, n.p., 1799, pp. 11–12; Benjamin Brawley, *The Negro Genius,* N.Y., 1937, pp. 30–31. An earlier charge, however, is in large part devoted to advising against plots or rebellions—see, *A Charge Delivered to the Brethren of the African Lodge on the 25th of June, 1792, at the Hall of Brother William Smith in Charlestown, by the Right Worshipful Master, Prince Hall, Boston, 1792,* passim.

14. Letters from Savannah dated April 28, June 12, and two not dated, but same approximate days of 1804 in the *New York Evening Post,* May 8, 9, June 2, July 3, 1804. U. B. Phillips mentions fears of rebellion in Georgia 1804—*American Negro Slavery,* N.Y., London, 1918, p. 476. A work published in Washington in 1804, by W. T. Washington, contains this sentence: "It is a melancholy reflection that while the energies of white men directed to shake off impositions, merely on trade, in every part of the world, meet with applause, the struggles of the blacks for liberty should meet with death if unsuccessful." *Political Economy Founded in Justice and Humanity,* in a letter to a friend, pp. 3–4.

15. *St. Louis Enquirer,* October 20, 1819, in Harrison A. Trexler, *Slavery in Missouri,* Baltimore, 1914, p. 114.

16. Lionel H. Kennedy and Thomas Parker, *An Official Report of the Trials of Sundry Negroes Charged with an Attempt to Raise an Insurrection in the State of South-Carolina . . .,* Charleston, 1822, appendix. The editor of the *Portland (Maine) Christian Mirror,* John L. Parkhurst, demanded, in the issue of September 2, 1825, the immediate abolition of slavery. He raised the question of insurrection and, in regard thereto, said: "Calamitous as such a struggle must be to our citizens, dreadful as must be the horrors of servile war, we should regard even these as less to be deplored than the perpetual existence of slavery in our land."—Calvin M. Clark, *American Slavery and Maine Congregationalists,* Bangor, 1940, p. 28.

17. As originally issued this was called *The Hope of Liberty, containing a number of political pieces,* by George Horton (Raleigh). Printed by Gales & Son, 1829. This is mentioned by G. B. Johnson, *Antebellum North Carolina,* Chapel Hill, 1937, p. 826, but this writer has not seen the original. He has seen a copy published in Philadelphia in 1837, called *Poems by a Slave,* George M. Horton, Second Edition, which owed its existence to the fact that an abolitionist, Joshua Coffin, came across the original and reprinted it. The work was published in the hope of raising money to purchase Horton's freedom, but this failed. Gales said he was an "honest and industrious slave," but Collier Cobb (*An American Man of Letters*—reprint from *University of North Carolina Magazine,* October, 1909) has Horton merely loafing away his time, and feels that his anti-slavery poems were "playing to the grand-stand." This was based on the recollections of whites in 1909! How a slave "played to the grand-stand" by denouncing slavery in a slave state is not clear.

18. [Robert Alexander Young] *The Ethiopian Manifesto, issued in defense of the black man's rights, in the scale of universal freedom,* New York, 1829.

19. *Freedom's Journal,* December 18, 20, 1828; Bella Gross, "Freedom's Journal," in *The Journal of Negro History,* 1932, 17, p. 259n; N. B. Chase, "The attitude of the Negro toward slavery: a study in opinion 1828–1850," unpublished master's thesis, Howard University, 1936, pp. 14–16.

20. Walker's (David) *Appeal, in four articles together with a preamble to the colored citizens of the world, but in particular, and very expressly to those of the United States of America,* written in Boston, State of Massachusetts, September 28, 1829. Third edition, with additional notes, corrections, etc., Boston, 1830. The three editions may be found in the Boston Public Library.

21. "A colored Bostonian" reported in *The Liberator,* January 22, 1831, that it was believed Walker had been murdered. A rumor was current that some person or persons in the South offered a large reward to the individual who would kill him. A recent writer has asserted that Walker's death was due to "natural causes," he does not document this. Robert A. Warner, *New Haven Negroes,* (New Haven, 1940), p. 100.

22. *Journal of the House of Representatives of the State of Georgia,* at an annual session of the General Assembly begun and held in this Town of Milledgeville, on

Monday the second day of November, 1829, Milledgeville, 1830, p. 353. See Clement Eaton, "A dangerous pamphlet in the old south," in *The Journal of Southern History,* 2, 1936, pp. 327–28.

23. U. B. Phillips, "The public archives of Georgia," in *The Annual Report of the American Historical Association for the Year 1903,* Washington, 1904, 1, p. 469.

24. The quoted words are those of Merle Curti, *The Learned Blacksmith, the Life and Journals of Elihu Burritt,* N.Y. 1937, p. 118n. Professor Curti does not, however, mention the Walker pamphlet. That Elijah safely reached the north appears in a letter from S. S. Jocelyn to W. L. Garrison, dated New Haven, July 12, 1832, asking that *The Liberator* be sent to Burritt at Berlin, Connecticut, "the gentleman who suffers so much on acct of Walkers pamphlet. I had an interview with him yesterday—he is a noble soul—lived 20 years in Geo.,—has facts on the subject of slavery most horrible."—MS Letters to Garrison, 2, Boston Public Library.

25. *Niles' Weekly Register* (Baltimore), 38, April 24, 1830, p. 157; June 19, 1830, 38, p. 304.

26. James F. McRae, Magistrate of Police to Governor John Owen, dated Wilmington, August 7, 1830, in Governor's Letter Book, Historical Commission, Raleigh.

27. L. D. Henry to Gov. Owen, in Governor's Papers, vol. 60, N.C. Hist. Comm. See Clement Eaton, "A dangerous pamphlet in the old south," in *The Journal of Southern History,* 1936, 2, pp. 330–31. A prominent North Carolinian, Calvin Jones of Wake Forest, drawn from his "secluded retreat" by "the great excitement and alarm that exists in several portions of the state as to an apprehended insurrection of the slaves," urged the Governor in a letter of Dec. 28, 1830, among other things, to be sure to get hold of Walker (in case, he added, he still was alive). *Ibid.*

28. Walker's *Appeal, in four articles together with a preamble to the colored citizens of the world, but in particular, and very expressly to those of the United States of America,* written in Boston, State of Massachusetts, September 28, 1829. pp. 5–6, 29. William Lloyd Garrison who, of course, did not agree with Walker's call for violence, affirmed that he personally knew that Walker himself wrote the *Appeal*—*The Liberator,* January 29, 1831. See Carter G. Woodson, *The Mind of the Negro as Reflected in Letters written during the crises, 1800–1860,* Washington, 1926, p. 224.

29. Original letter as well as a printed clipping are in MS Letters by Garrison, 1, Boston Public Library.

30. *The Liberator,* July 23, 1831.

31. *The Liberator,* September 3, 1831. For a striking instance of what Garrison was lambasting see "The Call of Poland" by Thomas Campbell on the editorial page of the *Richmond Enquirer,* August 23, 1831, containing lines asking whether "the hell-mark of slave must still blacken their name" and asserting "the call of each sword upon Liberty's aid Shall be written in gore on the steel of its blade!"

32. Robert Dale Owen in the *Free Enquirer,* N.Y., September 23, 1831; the account in *The Liberator* of the same day is also very full. A. B. Hart, *Slavery and Abolition, 1831–41,* N.Y., 1906, p. 236, gives the date of this incident as 1832.

33. James Forten to Garrison, Philadelphia, October 21, 1831, MS Letters to Garrison, 1.

34. This, all of which was printed except the month, day, signature, and the word "great" which was written, was enclosed in a letter to Governor Montfort Stokes of North Carolina by James Somervell, dated Warrenton, October 2, 1831. Mr. Somervell was postmaster of Warrenton, and stated that he believed the same circular had been sent to every postmaster in the State. Governor's Papers, vol. 52, Historical Comission, Raleigh.

35. Garrison's pacifism greatly influenced Tolstoy, to whom, in turn, Gandhi is indebted. See Leo Tolstoy, "Garrison and non-resistance" in *The Independent*, 59, 1905, pp. 881–883; Henry R. Mussey, "Gandhi the non-resistant," in *The Nation*, 1930, 130, p. 608.

36. *The Liberator*, April 11, 18, 1835. See also *George Thompson, Letters and Addresses . . . 1834–35*, Boston, 1837, pp. 58–60, 95. Certain remarks by Mr. Thompson make him out to be, at this time, rather a conservative than a radical anti-slavery man. Thus at the 1835 New York Anti-Slavery Society meeting he declared he opposed the immediate liberation of the slaves without outside control—"All we ask is, that the control of masters over their slaves may be subjected to supervision, and to legal responsibility." Op. cit., p. 72. According to Claude G. Bowers, George Thompson "proposed that the slaves should arise and cut their masters' throats"—*The Party Battles of the Jackson Period*, Boston, N.Y., 1928, p. 434. Arthur Y. Lloyd says the same thing,—*The Slavery Controversy*, Chapel Hill, 1940, p. 115, and cites James Schouler. That historian, however, merely says that Thompson used "imprudent language"—*History of the United States under the Constitution*, N.Y., 1894, rev. edit., 4, pp. 217–18. The fact is that George Thompson did not advocate servile rebellion, and never said what these writers claim he did.

37. Dated Ispwich, August 20, 1835, in Letters to Garrison, 5.

38. *Fifth Annual Report of the Board of Managers of the Massachusetts Anti-Slavery Society, with some account of the annual meeting, January 25, 1837, Boston, 1937, pp. xxvii, xxv, xxix.* Yet Vernon Loggins, op. cit., p. 90, citing Easton's work, *A Treatise on the Intellectual Character . . . Condition . . . of the Coloured People of the United States*, Boston, 1837, says it is, as compared with Walker's *Appeal*, "equally radical." A comparison of the works does not substantiate this characterization.

39. Dated Brookline, November 30, 1937, in Gilbert H. Barnes and Dwight L. Dumond, *Letters of Theodore Dwight Weld, Angelina Weld, and Sarah Grimké 1822–1844*, N.Y., London, 1934, 1, p. 486.

40. Dated Hudson, N.Y., 12 mo 21st 1837, emphasis in original, Letters to Garrison, 6. The same complaint came from Samuel J. May to Garrison in a letter dated South Seituate, December 26, 1837, and from the Buckingham Female Anti-Slavery Society in a letter to Garrison from J. P. Magill, dated Bucks County, Pennsylvania, January 18, 1838, Letters to Garrison, 6, 7.

41. George Helmick to Garrison, dated Putnam, February 3, 1838, Letters to Garrison, 7.

42. Quoted by Vernon Loggins, op. cit., p. 70.

43. Hammond to Smith, Cherry Valley, May 18, 1839, in Ralph V. Harlow, *Gerrit Smith Philanthropist and Reformer,* N.Y., 1939, p. 260.

44. *New York Daily Tribune,* January 29, 1841; W. Sherman Savage, *The Controversy Over the Distribution of Abolition Literature 1830–1860,* Washington, 1938, p. 109.

45. *The Liberator,* August 13, 1841; Loggins, op. cit., p. 79; Woodson, *The Mind of the Negro as Reflected in Letters written during the crises, 1800–1860,* Washington, 1926, p. 252. In a letter from the Pennsylvania abolitionist, Edward M. Davis, written while on a visit to England and dated London, Sept. 19, 1840, and addressed to Elizabeth Pease, a leading British abolitionist, there is enclosed a printed tribute, including a portrait, to Joseph Cinque, leader of the slaves who rebelled aboard the *Amistad* in 1839, as one deserving honor, since he "prefers death to slavery." Letters to Garrison, 9.

46. *Letters of Theodore Dwight Weld, Angelina Weld, and Sarah Grimké 1822–1844,* Barnes and Dumond, eds., N.Y., London, 1934, 2, pp. 911–12. See also Dwight L. Dumond, *Antislavery Origins of the Civil War in the United States,* Ann Arbor, 1939, p. 111.

47. George W. Julian, *The Life of Joshua R. Giddings,* Chicago, 1892, pp. 118–19; J. R. Giddings, *Speeches in Congress,* Boston, 1853, pp. 19, 22, 24; Dumond, *Antislavery Origins of the Civil War in the United States,* Ann Arbor, 1939, p. 99. An interesting eulogy of Madison Washington, leader of the *Creole* slaves, written by Frederick Douglass and entitled "The Heroic Slave" appeared in *Autographs for Freedom,* Julia Griffiths, ed., Boston, London, 1853, 1, pp. 174–239.

48. W. M. Brewer, "Henry Highland Garnet," in *The Journal of Negro History,* 1928, 13, pp. 36–52; Carter G. Woodson, *Negro Orators and Their Orations,* Washington, 1925, pp. 149–56; V. Loggins, op. cit., p. 192; Brawley, *The Negro Genius,* N.Y. 1937, p. 49. Walker's *Appeal* and Garnet's *Address* were issued in one volume in 1848. Brewer, Loggins, and Woodson state that John Brown paid attention to its publication.

49. Dwight L. Dumond, ed., *Letters of James Gillespie Birney 1831–1857,* N.Y., London, 1938, 2, p. 742.

50. This information is given in Booker T. Washington, *The Story of the Negro,* N.Y. 1909, 2, p. 158; and Helen Whittaker, "The Negro in the Abolitionist Movement 1830–1850," unpublished master's thesis, Howard University, 1935, p. 63, but neither cites sources. Washington, who seems to have known Dickson, states he served in the Union Army and, following the Civil War, was active in establishing Lincoln Institute in Jefferson City, Missouri.

51. James G. Birney to William E. Austen, et al., dated Lower Saginaw, Michigan, February 23, 1844, in Dumond, ed., *Letters of James Gillespie Birney 1831–1857,* N.Y., London, 1938, 2, p. 790.

52. Francis Jackson to Governor George N. Briggs, Boston, July 4, 1844, in *The*

Anti-Slavery Examiner, N.Y., 1845, 11, p. 123. Mr. Jackson is reiterating the resolution adopted in 1841 by the American Anti-Slavery Society. He is not, and it did not, however, advocate servile rebellion. It did denounce the obligation to suppress such rebellion. According to Thomas Wentworth Higginson, his friend, Dr. Samuel Gridley Howe, who had been active in Greek and Polish revolutions, had asserted, in 1844, "That in his opinion some movement of actual force would yet have to be made against slavery, and that but for the new duties he had assumed by his marriage (1843) he should very likely undertake some such enterprise himself."—*Contemporaries,* Boston, N.Y., 1899, pp. 294–95.

53. Herman Schlüter, *Lincoln, Labor, and Slavery,* N.Y., 1913, pp. 58–59; Charles H. Wesley, *Negro Labor in the United States 1850–1835,* N.Y., 1927, p. 73. A Boston workingmen's paper, *The New Era of Industry,* July 27, 1848, declared, "Slavery must be extinguished. . . . We go for direct and internecine war with the monster." Quoted by Norman Ware, *The Industrial Worker 1840–1860,* Boston, N.Y., 1924, p. 226.

54. Such activity on the part of Indians and fugitive slaves had recently required the United States Army seven years (1836–43) to overcome. Guerrilla warfare waged by outlying runaway Negroes was also everywhere a regular part of the slave institution. It is likely that Brown knew something of this. See this writer's, "Maroons within the present limits of the United States," in *The Journal of Negro History,* 1939, 24, pp. 167–84.

55. *Life and Times of Frederick Douglass,* Hartford, 1882, p. 217.

56. Julian, *The Life of Joshua R. Giddings,* Chicago, 1892, p. 243.

57. Woodson, *Negro Orators and Their Orations,* Washington, 1925, p. 191.

58. Octavius B. Frothingham, *Gerrit Smith,* N.Y., 1879, p. 190.

59. Reported by William C. Nell in *The Liberator,* December 10, 1852. Earlier "A Colored American" (Henry Bibb?) published a pamphlet the title of which referred to the Vesey martyrs as "patriots"—*The Late Contemplated Insurrection in Charleston, S.C., with the Execution of Thirty-Six of the Patriots,* N.Y., 1850.

60. Dated Philadelphia, May 14, 1852, in *The Liberator,* May 21, 1852, and in Woodson, *The Mind of the Negro as Reflected in Letters written during the crises, 1800–1860,* Washington, 1926, p. 293. Martin Robison Delany studied medicine at Harvard University, served as newspaper editor for several years in Pittsburg, and was a Major in the Union Army during the Civil War. See Frank A. Rollin (Frances E. R. Whipper), *Life and Public Service of Martin R. Delany,* Boston, 1868.

61. Jabez D. Hammond, to Smith, February 28, 1852, in Harlow, *Gerrit Smith Philanthropist and Reformer,* N.Y., 1939, p. 304.

62. *Autographs for Freedom,* Julia Griffiths, ed., Boston, London, 1853, 1, p. 34. Emphases in original.

63. Loguen to Garrison, April 28, 1854, in Woodson, *The Mind of the Negro as Reflected in Letters written during the crises, 1800–1860,* Washington, 1926, p. 267.

64. *Autographs for Freedom,* Julia Griffiths, ed., Auburn, Rochester, 1854, 2, p. 132.

The same volume contains a long eulogistic poem on the Haitian rebel, Vincent Ogé, by a Negro, George B. Vashon.

65. *New York Tribune,* June 16, 1854, quoted by Charles Wesley, *Negro Labor in the United States 1850–1835,* N.Y., 1927, p. 58.

66. Benjamin Drew, *A North-Side View of Slavery,* p. 1.

67. Letter to Syracuse *Journal,* May 31, 1856, in Harlow, *Gerrit Smith Philanthropist and Reformer,* N.Y., 1939, p. 350.

68. Frederick Douglass' Rochester newspaper of November 28, 1856, quoted in William Chambers, *American Slavery and Colour,* London, N.Y., 1857, p. 174. Chambers in introducing Douglass' remarks asserts very few abolitionists held this viewpoint, but the evidence herewith presented refutes that idea.

69. Dated Hamilton, Canada, January 5, 1857, in William Still, *Underground Railroad Records,* revised edition, Philadelphia, 1886, pp. 191, 200.

70. A printed copy of this circular will be found on page 73 of the collection of Lysander Spooner manuscripts in the Boston Public Library. Several handwritten drafts are also there. There is a brief sketch of Spooner in the *Dictionary of American Biography,* but the MSS in the Boston Library are not mentioned, nor is this episode of his life, with which the MSS very largely deal.

71. The *Boston Courier,* January 28, 1859, reporting the contents of the circular, stated it had received copies from a friend in Georgia, and from an unnamed Congressman. It was also noted in the *New York Tribune,* January 28, 1859, and the *Boston Post,* January 29, 1859. The latter paper and the *Boston Courier* of January 31, 1859, thought the circular to be a joke, or in the language of the day, a "quiz." The *Boston Atlas and Bee* of January 31, 1859, decided it was "too absurd to be treated seriously and too silly to be laughed at."—clippings in the Spooner MSS; that of the *Tribune* enclosed in a letter to Spooner from Hinton R. Helper, dated New York, January 31, 1859.

72. So declared Spooner in a letter to Governor Henry A. Wise of Virginia, signed "The Author of the Circular," dated November 2, 1859. He wrote in order to clear Brown of any suspicion of being the author for, "I apprehend that the Circular may be considered more disrespectful, offensive, and insulting to the slaveholders personally, than Brown's enterprise itself. . . ." Spooner MSS.

73. Dated December 25, 1858. This was probably the printed circular, for Francis Jackson in a letter of December 3 already referred to it as printed. French had formerly been associated with the New Hampshire leader, Nathaniel P. Rogers, in the publication of the *Herald of Freedom.*

74. Dated New York City, October 7, 1858.

75. Dated Boston, December 3, 1858.

76. Dated New York, December 18, 1858.

77. This reference to Professor Benjamin S. Hedrick of the University of North Carolina, who was forced to leave the South in 1856 because of his free soil views

and his expressed preference for John C. Frémont in the Presidential election of that year. A good brief account is in Clement Eaton, *Freedom of Thought in the Old South,* Durham, 1940, pp. 202–204. As appears in a letter from Helper to Spooner of January 31, 1859, requesting another copy of the circular, Professor Hedrick kept the one Spooner originally sent him. On October 28, 1859, Helper asked Spooner to send a copy of his letter of December 18, 1858, opposing the circular, in order to help convince those who suspected him of complicity with John Brown of his non-involvement.

78. Dated November 30, 1858.

79. Dated January 8, 1859.

80. Dated January 16, 1859; the information concerning Mann is in J. R. French's letter to Spooner dated Painesville, December 25, 1858. Mann wrote in pencil at the end of his letter, "Use, as you choose."

81. *The Roving Editor: or Talks with Slaves in the Southern States,* N.Y., 1859.

82. *Ibid.,* pp. 10, 129. In view of later historical writing it is interesting to note these words in this work: "The second American Revolution has begun. Kansas was its Lexington. . ."—p. 300. Redpath wrote the first biography of John Brown, and later published other volumes including a collection of the speeches of Wendell Phillips. For his relations with Lincoln, see Carl Sandburg, *Abraham Lincoln, The War Years,* N.Y., 1939, 1, p. 578.

83. Redpath, op. cit., p. 306; see also pp. 84, 269.

84. William S. Heywood, ed., *Autobiography of Adin Ballou,* Lowell, 1896, pp. 417–22. Ballou was particularly shocked at the fact that the Massachusetts Anti-Slavery Society adopted a resolution praising Brown, and that William Lloyd Garrison specifically associated himself with that set.

85. Carlos Martyn, *Wendell Phillips: The Agitator,* N.Y., London, 1890, p. 299; R. V. Harlow, *Gerrit Smith Philanthropist and Reformer,* N.Y., 1939, p. 410ff.; Oswald G. Villard, *John Brown, a biography fifty years after,* N.Y., 1909, p. 323.

86. Louis T. Jones, *The Quakers of Iowa,* Iowa City, 1914, p. 197.

87. Henry S. Canby, *Thoreau,* Boston, 1939, Chapter 24. Mr. Canby aptly states (p. 391): "Subtly, slowly as is happening with so many idealists in the twentieth century, the belief in justified violence has been capturing Thoreau's mind. Passive resistance was not enough in a state that had ceased to recognize human rights and was overriding personal integrity."

88. Martyn, *Wendell Phillips: The Agitator,* N.Y., London, 1890, pp. 295–96.

89. *The Liberator,* January 10, 1851.

90. Henry C. Wright, *The Natick Resolution; or, Resistance to Slaveholders the Right and Duty of Southern Slaves and Northern Freeman,* Boston, 1859, passim. On the day of Brown's execution, Wright, in a letter, pointed out to Governor Wise that the state seal of Virginia itself attested Brown's righteousness. Senator Henry Wilson was present at the Natick meeting but denied, on the floor of the Senate, December 6, 1859, that he favored rebellion.

91. Letter dated January 22, 1860, in Allen Nevins, *Hamilton Fish, The Inner History of the Grant Administration,* N.Y., 1936, p. 77.

92. William E. Smith, ed. *The American Civil War, An Interpretation,* by Carl Russell Fish, London, N.Y., 1937, pp. 53–54.

93. Garrison to Redpath, December 1, 1860, in MS Letters by Garrison, 5.

94. Report in the N.Y. *Evening Post,* September 27, 1860.

95. See Bayard Tuckerman, *William Jay and the Constitutional Movement for the Abolition of Slavery,* N.Y., 1894; T. W. Higginson, *Contemporaries,* Boston, N.Y., 1899, p. 264.

96. *Speech of John Quincy Adams on the Joint Resolution for Distributions to the Distressed Fugitives from Indian Hostilities in the States of Alabama and Georgia.* Delivered in the House of Representatives, May 25, 1836, Washington, 1836, pp. 5, 7.

97. Letter dated October 15, 1860, in *Principia,* N.Y., November 3, 1860. Note an editorial in the *New York Weekly Tribune,* Dec. 13, 1856, in which are these words, "They ask for more territory to be subject to the taskmaster and his cruelties, to the slave and his insurrections . . . What claim will the South have on the North when insurrections do come?"

98. *The Liberator,* May 24, 1861. In January 1861, Gerrit Smith went to Canada to protest the attempt by Missouri to extradite a fugitive slave, John Anderson, on a charge of murder, the Negro having killed his master who had tracked him to Ohio. Smith based the defense on, as he saw it, man's right to be free. In killing the person who attempted to enslave him, the Negro had done, said Smith, "a manly, heroic deed, entitling the man to praise and not to punishment." The extradition request was denied. Harlow, *Gerrit Smith Philanthropist and Reformer,* N.Y., 1939, p. 425; Frothingham, *Gerrit Smith,* N.Y., 1879, p. 116.

99. *New York Daily Tribune,* May 11, 1861.

100. *Ibid.* June 16, 1861.

101. Letter from T. Bourne, *ibid.,* July 27; from M. T. V., *ibid.,* August 3; editorial, *ibid.,* Sept. 19, 1861.

102. *Ibid.,* January 15, 20, 1862; Elizur Wright to Salmon P. Chase, Boston, November 13, 1862, in Philip G. and Elizabeth Q. Wright, *Elizur Wright,* Chicago, 1937, p. 217.

103. *New York Daily Tribune,* January 1, 1863.

104. Many who entered the South did so in order to help slaves flee. The existence of the possibility of gaining liberty via flight probably acted as a safety valve and cut down the number of mass uprisings.

105. For information on this see A. M. Ross, *Memoirs of a Reformer,* Toronto, 1893, *passim;* Annie Abel and Frank Klingberg, *A Side-Light on Anglo-American Relations,* N.Y., 1927, p. 258; D. L. Dumond, ed., *Letters of James Gillespie Birney 1831–1857,* N.Y., London, 1938, 1, pp. 388n, 527; Harlow, *Gerrit Smith Philanthropist and Reformer,* N.Y., 1939, p. 275; J. W. Coleman, Jr., *Slavery Times in Kentucky,* Chapel Hill, 1940, pp. 142ff.; Eliza Wigham, *The Anti-Slavery Cause in America and its Martyrs,* London, 1863, pp. 63, 64, 81. Torrey's work led to his being sentenced to six years' imprisonment in

Baltimore in 1844, but he died in that jail in 1846. See his letter to J. M. McKim, dated Baltimore Jail, November 29, 1844, asking that he thank several Philadelphia Negroes who had sent money for his defense—MS Letters to Garrison, 14. Calvin Fairbanks aided Lewis Hayden to escape and for this was jailed in Lexington, Kentucky, in 1848. Hayden learned that his owner would, for $650, sign a petition to pardon Fairbanks, and so within sixty days Hayden raised the money, by public and private appeals, and in August 1849, Fairbanks was freed. In 1851 he was sentenced to fifteen years' imprisonment, again for aiding slaves to secure freedom. For thirteen years he rotted in a Kentucky prison, until pardoned in 1864. See an undated manuscript signed by Francis Jackson and Ellis G. Loring in MS Letters to Garrison, 18.

106. *Reminiscences of Levi Coffin,* London, Cincinnati, 1876, pp. 428–446.

107. Earl Conrad of New York City has compiled much material on the life of Harriet Tubman. Some of this has been published in *The Negro World Digest,* 1940, 1, pp. 46–50, (August), pp. 15–16 (December).

108. W. H. Siebert, *The Underground Railroad,* N.Y., 1899, pp. 28, 152. Not a few residents of the South, Negro and white, aided in this work. See also, John H. Russell, *The Free Negro in Virginia,* Baltimore, 1913, p. 165n; Helen T. Catterall, *Judicial Cases Concerning the Negro and American Slavery,* Washington, 1926–35, 1, pp. 188, 216–221, 247, 441; 2, pp. 67, 511; 3, pp. 187, 200; 4, pp. 222, 232.

109. Dated Charleston, S.C., February 1, 1844, in MS Letters to Garrison, 14.

110. This refers to the abolitionists and author, Lydia Maria Child, whose *Appeal for that Class of Americans Called Africans,* published in Boston in 1833, was particularly popular and influential. A good brief sketch of this lady is in Higginson, *Contemporaries,* Boston, N.Y., 1899, pp. 108–141.

111. August 1, 1834, was the day upon which the British act emancipating the slaves of the West Indies took effect.

112. Above the word "plantation" in another hand is written "country seat."

5

Class Conflicts in the South—1850–60

The great attention given to the spectacular struggles between the North and the South in the decade before the Civil War has tended to befog the equally important contests which went on during the same period within the South itself.

Writers have dealt at considerable length with the national scene, have demonstrated a growing conflict between an agrarian, slave-labor society and an increasingly industrial, free-labor society as to which should direct public opinion, enact and administer the laws, appropriate the West—in short, which should control the state. In 1860, the grip of the slave civilization upon the national government was very considerably loosened and clearly seemed destined to complete annihilation. The slavocracy therefore turned to bullets.

But there was more to it than that. The facts are that not only did the slavocrats see their external, or national, power seriously menaced by the Republican triumph of 1860, but they also observed their internal, local power greatly threatened by increasing restlessness among the exploited classes—the non-slaveholding whites and the slaves.

There were three general manifestations of this unrest: (1) slave disaffection, shown in individual acts of "insolence" or terrorism, and in concerted, planned efforts for liberation; (2) numerous instances of poor white implication in the slave conspiracies and revolts, showing a declining efficiency in the divide-and-rule policy of the Bourbons; (3) independent political action of the non-slaveholding whites aimed at the destruction of the slavocracy's control of the state governments. In the opinion of the writer, this growing internal disaffection is a prime explanation for the desperation of the slaveholding class which drove it to the expedient of civil war.

Factors tending to explain the slave unrest of the decade are soil exhaustion, leading to greater work demands, improved marketing facilities, having the same result, and economic depression from 1854–56 throughout the South, approaching, especially in 1855, the famine state. These years witnessed, too, a considerable increase in industrialization and urbanization within the South. These phenomena were distinctly not conducive to the creation of happy slaves.[1] As a slave holder remarked, "The cities is no place for niggers. They get strange notions into their heads, and grow discontented. They ought, every one of them, to be sent back to the plantations."[2] As a matter of fact, there was for this reason, during this decade, an attempt to foster a "back-to-the-plantation" movement.

It is also true, as Olmsted observed, that: "Any great event having the slightest bearing upon the question of emancipation is known to produce an unwholesome excitement" among the slaves.[3] The decade is characterized by such events as the 1850 Compromise, the sensation caused by *Uncle Tom's Cabin,* the Kansas War, the 1856 elections, the Dred Scott decision, Helper's *Impending Crisis,* Brown's raid, the election of 1860. If to this is added the political and social struggles within the South itself (to be described later), it becomes apparent that there were many occasions for "unwholesome excitement."

Combined with all this is a significant change in the abolitionist movement. Originally this aimed at gradual emancipation induced by moral suasion. Then came the demand for immediate liberation, but still only via moral suasion. Then followed a split into those favoring political action and those opposed. Finally, and most noticeably in this decade, there arose a body of direct actionists whose idea was to "carry the war into Africa."

The shift is exemplified in the person of Henry C. Wright. In the forties, he wrote the "Non-Resistant" column for Garrison's *Liberator;* by 1851 he felt it was the duty of the abolitionists to go South and aid the slaves to flee; and by 1859 he was convinced that it was "the right and duty of the slaves to resist their masters, and the right and duty of the North to incite them to resistance, and to aid them."[4] By November 1856, Frederick Douglass was certain that the "peaceful annihilation" of slavery was "almost hopeless" and therefore contended "that the slave's right to revolt is perfect, and only wants the occurrence of favorable circumstances to come a duty. . . . We cannot but shudder as we call to mind the horrors that have marked servile insurrections—we would avert them if we could; but shall the millions for ever submit to robbery, to murder, to ignorance, and every unnamed evil which an irresponsible tyranny can devise, because the overthrow of that tyranny would be productive of horrors? We say not. . . . terrible as it will be, we accept and hope for it."[5]

And while John Brown's work was the most spectacular, he was by no means the only Northern man to agitate among the slaves themselves; there were others, the vast majority unnamed, but some are known, like Alexander Ross, James Redpath, and W. L. Chaplin.[6] But the exceedingly dangerous work was mainly done by Northern or Canadian Negroes who had themselves escaped from slavery. A few of these courageous people are known—Harriet Tubman, Josiah Henson, William Still, Elijah Anderson, John Mason. It has been estimated that, from Canada alone, in 1860, 500 Negroes went into the South to rescue their brothers.[7] What people can offer a more splendid chapter to the record of human fortitude?

The obvious is at times elusive and it is therefore necessary to bear in mind when trying to discover the causes of slave disaffection that one is indeed dealing with *slaves.* We will give but one piece of evidence to indicate something of what is meant. In January 1854, the British consul at Charleston, in a private letter wrote, "The frightful atrocities of slave holding must be seen to be described. . . . My next-door neighbor, a lawyer of the first distinction, and member of the Southern Aristocracy, told me himself that he flogged all his own Negroes, men and women, when they misbehaved. . . . It is literally no more to kill a slave than to shoot a dog."[8]

There is considerable evidence pointing to a quite general state of insubordination and disaffection, apart from conspiracies and revolts, among the slave population.

A lady of Burke County, North Carolina, complained in April 1850, of such a condition among her slaves and declared, "I have not a single servant (slave) at my command." Three years later a traveler in the South observed "in the newspapers, complaints of growing insolence and insubordination among the negroes."[9] References to the "common practice of slaves" of harboring runaways recur, as do items of the arrest of slaves caught in the act of learning to read. A paper of 1858 reported the arrest of ninety Negroes for that "crime." It urged severe punishment and remarked, "Scarcely a week passes, that instrument of writing, prepared by Negroes, are not taken from servants (slaves) in the streets, by the police."[10]

A Louisiana paper in 1858 reported "more cases of insubordination among the Negro population . . . than ever known before," and a Missouri paper of 1859 commented upon the "alarmingly frequent" cases of slaves killing their owners. It is added that "retribution seems to be dealt out to the perpetrators with dispatch and in the form to which only a people wrought up to the highest degree of indignation and excitement would resort."[11]

Examples of such retribution with their justification are enlightening. Olmsted tells of the burning of a slave near Knoxville, Tennessee, for the offense of killing his master and quotes the editor of a "liberal" newspaper as justifying the lynching as a "means of absolute, necessary self-defense." The same community shortly found six legal executions needed for the stability of its society.[12] Similarly, a slave killed his master in Mt. Meigs, Alabama, in August 1854, and, according to the Vigilance Committee, boasted of his deed. This slave, too, was burned alive. "The gentlemen constituting the meeting were men of prudence, deliberation and intelligence, and acted from an imperative sense of the necessity of an example to check the growing and dangerous insubordination of the slave population." Precisely the same things happened in the same region in June 1856, and January 1857.[13] Again, in August 1855, a patrolman in Louisiana killed a slave who did not stop when hailed and this was considered proper since "recent disorders among the slaves in New Iberia had made it a matter of importance that the laws relative to the police of slaves, should be strictly enforced."[14]

A common method by which American slaves showed their "docility" was arson. This occurred with striking frequency during the ten years under scrutiny. For example, from November 26, 1850, to January 15, 1851, one New Orleans paper reported slave burnings of at least seven sugar houses. For a similar period, January 31, 1850, to May 30, 1851, there were seven *convictions* of slaves in Virginia for arson.[15]

Burnings were at times concerted. Thus the *Norfolk Beacon* of September 21, 1852, declared that the slaves of Princess Ann County, Virginia, had excited alarm and that an extra patrol had been ordered out. And,

> On Sunday night last, this patrol made a descent upon a church where a large number of Negroes had congregated for the purpose of holding a meeting, and dispersed them. In a short time, the fodder stacks of one of the party who lived near were discovered on fire. The patrol immediately started for the fire, but before reaching the scene it was discovered that the stacks of other neighbors had shared a like fate, all having no doubt been fired by the Negroes for revenge. A strict watch law is now kept over them, and most rigid means adopted to make every one know and keep his place.

The *Federal Union* of Milledgeville, Georgia, on March 20, 1855, told of incendiary fires set by slaves that month in South Carolina and three counties of Georgia. Property damage was considerable and "many persons were seriously injured."[16]

The fleeing of slaves reached very great proportions from 1850 to 1860 and was a constant and considerable source of annoyance to the slavocracy. According to the census estimates 1,011 slaves *succeeded* in escaping in 1850 and 803 *succeeded* in 1860. At current prices that represented a loss of about $1,000,000 each year. But that is a very small part of the story. First, the census reports were poor. The census takers were paid a certain sum for each entrant and so tended to make only those calls that were least expensive to themselves. City figures were therefore more reliable than those for rural communities. Moreover, Olmsted found census taking in the South "more than ordinarily unreliable" and told of a census taker there who announced that he would be at a certain tavern at a certain day "for the purpose of receiving from the people of the vicinity—who were requested to call upon him—for the information it was his duty to obtain!"[17]

According to Professor W. B. Hesseltine, "Between 1830 and 1860 as many as 2,000 slaves a year passed into the land of the free along the routes of the Underground Railroad," and Professor Siebert has declared that this railroad saw its greatest activity from 1850 to 1860.[18] And this is but a fraction of those who fled but did not succeed in reaching a free land, were captured, or forced to turn back. When people pay as high as $300 for one bloodhound the fleeing of slaves is a serious problem indeed.[19]

It is also to be noted that the decade witnessed a qualitative as well as quantitative change in the fugitive slave problem, for now not only did more slaves flee, but more often than before they fled in groups; they, as South papers, stampeded.[20]

Another piece of evidence of the growing unrest of the slave population is afforded by the figures for money appropriated by the state of Virginia for slaves owned by her citizens who were *legally* executed or banished from the state.[21] For the fiscal year 1851–52, the sum equaled $12,000; for 1852–53, the sum was $15,000; 1853–54, $19,000 was appropriated and the same for 1854–55. For the year 1855–56, $22,000 was necessary and this was duplicated the next year. For 1857–58, the sum was $35,000 and stayed at that same high level for 1858–59. For each of the next two years prior to the Civil War, 1859–60, 1860–61, $30,000 was appropriated. Thus "bad" slaves, legally disposed of, cost the one state of Virginia in ten years the sum of $239,000.

There was still another manifestation of slave disaffection: conspiracy or revolt. Some of the episodes already described, as that in Virginia in 1852 or in Georgia in 1855, may perhaps be thought of as conspiracies. The decade witnessed many more, the most important of which follow.

A free Negro, George Wright, of New Orleans, was asked by a slave, Albert, in June 1835, to join in a revolt.[22] He declared his interest and was brought to a white man, a teacher by the name of Dyson, who had come to Louisiana in 1840 from Jamaica. Dyson trusted Wright, declared that one hundred whites had agreed to aid the Negroes in their bid for freedom, and urged Wright to join. Wright did—verbally. He almost immediately betrayed the plot and led the police to the slave Albert. The slave at the time of arrest, June 13, carried a knife, a sword, a revolver, one bag of bullets, one pound of powder, two boxes of percussion caps, and $86. The patrol was ordered out, the city guard strengthened, and twenty slaves and Dyson were instantly arrested.

Albert stated that 2,500 slaves were involved. He named none. In prison he declared that "all his friends had gone down the coast and were fighting like soldiers. If he had shed blood in the cause he would not have minded the arrest." It was indeed reported that "a large number of Negroes have fled from their masters and are now missing," but no actual fighting was mentioned. Excitement was great along the coast, however, and the arrest of one white man, a cattle driver, occurred at Bonnet Clare. A fisherman, Michael McGill, testified that he had taken Dyson and two slaves carrying what he thought were arms to a swamp from which several Negroes emerged. The Negroes were given the arms and disappeared.

The New Orleans papers tended to minimize the trouble, but did declare that the city contained "malicious and fanatical" whites, "cutthroats in the mane of liberty—murderers in the guise of philanthropy" and commended the swift action of the police, while calling for further precautions and restrictions. The last piece of information concerning this is an item telling of an attack by Albert upon the jailer in which he caused "the blood to flow." The disposition of the rebels is not reported.

The year 1856 was one of extraordinary slave unrest. The first serious difficulty of the year was caused by maroons in North Carolina. A letter[23] of August 25, 1856, to Governor Thomas Bragg signed by Richard A. Lewis and twenty-one others informed him of a "very secure retreat for runaway Negroes" in a large swamp between Bladen and Roberson Counties. There "for many years past, and at this time, there are several runaways of bad and daring character—destructive to all kinds of Stock and dangerous to all persons living by or near said swamp." Slave holders attacked these maroons August 1, but accomplished nothing and saw one of their own number killed. "The Negroes ran off cursing and swearing and telling them to come on, they were ready for them again." The *Wilmington Journal* of August 14 mentioned that these Negroes "had cleared a place for a garden, had cows, etc., in the swamp." Mr. Lewis and his friends were "unable to offer sufficient inducement for Negro hunters to come with their dogs unless aided by other sources." The Governor suggested that magistrates call for the militia, but whether this was done or not is unknown.

A plot involving over two hundred slaves and supposed to mature on September 6, 1856, was discovered in Colorado County, Texas, shortly before that date.[24] Many of the Mexican inhabitants of the region were declared to be implicated. And it was felt "that the lower class of the Mexican population are incendiaries in any country where slaves are held." They were arrested and ordered to leave the county within five days and never to return "under penalty of death." A white person by the name of William Mehrmann was similarly dealt with. Arms were discovered in the possession of a few slaves. Every one of the two hundred arrested was severely whipped, two dying under the lash. Three were hanged. One slave leader, Frank, was not captured.

Trouble involving some three hundred slaves and a few white men, one of whom was named James Hancock, was reported in October from two counties, Ouchita and Union, in Arkansas, and two parishes, Union and Claiborne, across the border in Louisiana. The outcome here is not known. On November 7, "an extensive scheme of Negro insurrection" was discovered in Lavaca, DeWitt, and Victoria Counties in the southeastern part of Texas and very near Colorado County, seat of the October conspiracy. A letter from Victoria of November 7 declared that: "The negroes had killed off all the dogs in the neighborhood, and were preparing for a general attack" when the betrayal came. Whites were implicated, one being "severely horsewhipped," and then others driven out of the county. What became of the slaves is not stated.[25]

One week later a conspiracy was disclosed in St. Mary parish, Louisiana. It was believed that "favorite family servants" were the leaders.[26] Slaves throughout the parish were arrested. Three white men and one free Negro were also held. The slaves were lashed and returned to their masters, but the four others were imprisoned. The local paper of November 22 declared that free Negro "and at least one of the white men, will suffer death for the part taken in the matter."

And in the very beginning of November trouble was reported from Tennessee.[27] A letter of November 2 told of the arrest of thirty slaves and a white man named Williams, in Fayette County at the southwestern tip of the state. It was believed that the plot extended to "the surrounding counties and states." Confirmation of this soon came. Within two weeks unrest was reported from

Montgomery County in the north central part of the state, and across the border in the iron foundries of Louisa, Kentucky. Again, many slaves and one white man were arrested. Shortly thereafter, plots were discovered in Obion, at Tennessee's western tip, and in Fulton, Kentucky, as well as in New Madrid and Scott Counties, Missouri.

In December, plots were reported, occasionally outbreaks occurred, slaves and whites were arrested, tortured, banished, and executed in virtually every slave state. The discontent forced its way through, notwithstanding clear evidence of censorship. Thus a Georgia paper confessed that slave disaffection was a "delicate subject to touch" and that it had "refrained from giving our readers any of the accounts of contemplated insurrections."[28]

The Washington correspondent of the *New York Weekly Tribune* declared on December 20, that "The insurrectionary movement in Tennessee obtained more headway than is known to the public—important facts being suppressed in order to check the spread of the contagion and prevent the true condition of affairs from being understood elsewhere." Next week the same correspondent stated that he had "reliable information" of serious trouble in New Orleans leading to the hanging of twenty slaves, "but the newspapers carefully refrain from any mention of the facts."

Indeed, the *New Orleans Daily Picayune* of December 9 had itself admitted that it had "refrained from publishing a great deal which we receive by the mails, going to show that there is a spirit of turbulence abroad in various quarters." December 23 it said the same thing about "this very delicate subject" but did state that there were plots for rebellion during the Christmas holidays "in Kentucky, Arkansas, and Tennessee, as well as in Mississippi, Louisiana, and Texas" and that recent events "along the Cumberland River in Kentucky and Tennessee and the more recent affairs in Mississippi, approach very nearly to positive insurrection."

To this may be added Maryland, Alabama, Virginia, North Carolina, South Carolina, Georgia, and Florida.[29] Features of the conspiracies are worth particular notice. Arms were discovered among the slaves in, at least, Tennessee, Kentucky, and Texas. Preparations for blowing up bridges were uncovered. Attacks upon iron mills in Kentucky were started but defeated. At least three whites were killed by slaves in that same state. The date for the execution of four slaves in Dover, Tennessee, was pushed ahead for fear of an attempt at rescue, and a body of 150 men was required to break up a group of about the same number of slaves marching to Dover for that very purpose.

Free Negroes were directly implicated as well as slaves in Kentucky, and they were driven out of several cities such as Murfreesboro, Tennessee, Paducah,

Kentucky, and Montgomery, Alabama. Whites, too, were often implicated. Two were forced to flee from Charles County, Maryland. One, named Taylor, was hanged in Dover, Tennessee, and two others driven out. One was hanged and another whipped in Cadiz, Kentucky. One was arrested in Obion, Tennessee. The *Galveston News* of December 27 reported the frustration of a plot in Houston County and stated, "Arms and ammunition were discovered in several portions of the country, given to them, no doubt, by white men, who are now living among us, and who are constantly inciting our slaves to deeds of violence and bloodshed."

A letter, passed along by whites as well as slaves, found December 24, 1856, on a slave employed on the Richmond and York Railroad in Virginia, is interesting from the standpoint of white cooperation and indicates, too, a desire for something more than bare bodily freedom. The letter reads:

> My dear friend: You must certainly remember what I have told you—you must come up to the contract—as we have carried things thus far. Meet at the place where we said, and don't make any disturbance until we meet and don't let any white man know anything about it, unless he is truth-worthy. The articles are all right and the country is ours certain. Bring all your friends; tell them, that if they want freedom, to come. Don't let it leak out; if you should get in any difficulty send me word immediately to afford protection. Meet at the crossing and prepare for Sunday night for the neighborhood—
> P.S. Don't let anybody see this—
>
> Freedom—Freeland
> Your old friend
> W. B.[30]

Another interesting feature of the plots of November and December 1856, is the evidence of the effect of the bitter presidential contest of that year between the Republican, Frémont, and the Democrat, Buchanan. The slaves were certain that the Republican Party stood for their liberation and some felt that Colonel Frémont would aid them, forcibly, in their efforts for freedom. "Certain slaves are so greatly imbued with this fable that I have seen them smile when they were being whipped, and have heard them say that, 'Frémont and his men can hear the blows they receive'." One unnamed martyr, a slave iron worker in Tennessee, "said that he know all about the plot, but would die before he would tell. He therefore received 750 lashes, from which he died."[31]

Of the John Brown raid nothing may be said that has not already been told, except that to draw the lesson from the attempt's failure that the slaves were docile, as has so often been done, is absurd. And it would be absurd even if we did not have a record of the bitter struggle of the Negro people against slavery. This is so for two main reasons: first, Brown's raid was made in the northwestern part of Virginia, where slavery was of a domestic, household nature and where slaves were relatively few; secondly, Brown gave the slaves absolutely no foreknowledge of his attempt. The slaves had no way of judging Brown's changes or even his sincerity, and, in that connection, let it be remembered that slave stealing was a common crime in the Old South.

The event aroused tremendous excitement. The immediate result is well described in this paragraph.

> A most terrible panic, in the meantime, seizes not only the village, the vicinity, and all parts of the state, but every slave state in the Union. . . . Rumours of insurrection, apprehensions of invasions, whether well-founded or ill-founded, alters not the proof of the inherent and incurable weakness and insecurity of society, organized upon a slave-holding basis.[32]

Many of these rumors were undoubtedly false or exaggerated both by terror and by anti–"Black Republican" politicians. Bearing this in mind, however, there yet remains good evidence of real and widespread disaffection among the slaves.

Late in November 1859, there were several incendiary fires in the neighborhood of Berryville, Virginia. Two slaves, Jerry and Joe, of Col. Francis McCormick, were arrested on the charge of conspiracy and convicted. An effort was made to save these slaves from hanging as it was felt that the evidence against them was not conclusive and that since "We of the South, have boasted that our slaves took no part in the raid upon Virginia, and did not sympathize with Brown,"[33] it would look bad to hang two slaves now for the same crime. Others, however, urged their executions as justified on the evidence and necessary as an example, for "there are other Negroes who disserve just as much punishment." The slaves' sentences were commuted to imprisonment, at hard labor, for life.

In December, Negroes in Bolivar, Missouri, revolted and attacked their enslavers with sticks and stones. A few whites were injured and at least one slave was killed. Later,

> A mounted company was ranging the woods in search of negroes. The owner of some rebellious slaves was badly wounded, and only saved himself by flight. Several blacks have been severely punished. The greatest excitement prevailed, and every man was armed and prepared for a more serious attack.[34]

Still later advices declared that "the excitement had somewhat subsided."

Early in July 1860, fires swept over and devastated many cities in Northern Texas. Slaves were suspected and arrested.[35] White men were invariably reported as being implicated, and frequent notices of their beatings and executions together with slaves occur. Listing of the counties in which plots were reported, cities burned, and rebels executed will give one an idea of the extensiveness of the trouble and help explain the abject terror it aroused: Anderson, Austin, Dallas, Denton, Ellis, Grimes, Hempstead, Lamar, Milam, Montgomery, Rusk, Tarrant, Walker, and Wood. The reign of terror lasted for about eight weeks.

And before it was over reports of disaffection came from other areas. In August, a conspiracy among the slaves, again with white accomplices, said to have been inspired by a nearby maroon band, was uncovered and crushed in Talladega County, Alabama.[36] About one hundred miles south of this, in Pine Level, Montgomery County, of the same state, in that same month, the arrest of a white man, a harness maker, was reported for "holding improper conversations with slaves."[37] Within five months serious difficulty is reported from that region.

Meanwhile, still in August, plots were uncovered in Whitfield, Cobb, and Floyd Counties in Northwest Georgia. Said the *Columbus* [GA] *Sun,* of August 29: "By a private letter from Upper Georgia, we learnt that an insurrectionary plot has been discovered among the Negroes in the vicinity of Dalton and Marietta and great excitement was occasioned by it, and still prevails." The slaves had intended to burn Dalton, capture a train, and crash on into Marietta some seventy miles away. Thirty-six of the slave leaders were imprisoned and the entire area took on a warlike aspect. Again it was thought that "white men instigated the plot," but, since Negro testimony was not acceptable against a white man, the evidence against them was felt to be insufficient for conviction. Another Georgia paper of the same month, the *Augusta Dispatch,* admitting, "we dislike to allude to the evidences of the insurrectionary tendency of things. . . ," nevertheless did deign barely to mention the recent history of a plot among the slaves of Floyd County, about forty miles northwest of Marietta.

In September, a slave girl betrayed a conspiracy in Winston County, Mississippi. Approximately thirty-five slaves were arrested and yet again it was discovered that whites were involved.[38] At least one slave was hanged as well as one white man described as a photographer named G. Harrington.

Late in October, a plot first formed in July was disclosed among the slaves of Norfolk and Princess Anne Counties, Virginia, and Currituck County, North Carolina.[39] Jack and Denson, slaves of a Mrs. David Corprew of Princess Anne, were among the leaders. Others were named Leicester, Daniel, Andrew, Jonas, and William. These men planned to start the fight for freedom with their spades and axes and grubbing hoes. And it was understood, according to a slave witness, that "white folks were to come in there to help us," but in no way could the slaves be influenced to name their white allies. Banishment, that is, sale and transportation out of the state, was the leaders' punishment.

In November, plots were disclosed in Crawford and Habersham Counties, Georgia.[40] In both places whites were involved. In Crawford a white man, described as Northern tinsmith, was executed, while a white implicated in Habersham was given five hours to leave. How many slaves were involved is not clear. No executions among them were reported. According to the Southern papers the rebels were merely "severely whipped."

December finds the trouble back again in the heart of Alabama, in Pine Level, Autaugaville, Prattville, and Hayneville. A resident of the region declared it involved "many hundred Negroes" and that "the instigators of the insurrection were found to be the lowdown, or poor, whites of the country."[41] It was discovered that the plot called for the redistribution of the "land, mules, and money." Said another source, the *MontgomeryAdvertiser* of December 13:

> We have found out a deep laid plan among the Negroes of our neighborhood, and from what we can find out from our Negroes, it is general all over the country . . . We hear some startling facts. They have gone far enough in the plot to divide our estates, mules, lands, and household furniture.

The crop of martyrs in this particular plot numbered at least twenty-five Negroes and four whites. The names of but two of the whites are known, Rollo and Williamson.

There is evidence of the existence in December 1860, of a wide-spread secret organization of slaves in South Carolina, dedicated to the objective of freedom.[42] Said J. R. Gilmore, a visitor in the region:

> . . . there exists among the blacks a secret and wide-spread organization of a Masonic character, having its grip, password, and oath. It has various grades of leaders, who are competent and *earnest* men and its ultimate object is FREEDOM.

Gilmore warned a slave leader, Scipio, that such an organization meant mischief. "NO," said Scipio, "it means only RIGHT and JUSTICE."

Scipio's parting words were a plea that Gilmore let the North know that the slaves were panting for freedom and that poor whites, too, were victims of the same vicious system.

Notes

This chapter was originally published in *The Communist,* February and March, 1939.

1. G. Johnson, *Antebellum North Carolina,* Chapel Hill, 1937, p. 478; J. Redpath, *The Roving Editor,* N.Y., 1859, p. 127.
2. J. S. C. Abbott, *South and North,* N.Y., 1860, p. 124
3. F. L. Olmsted, *A Journey in the Back Country,* London, 1860, pp. 474–75.
4. *The Liberator,* (Boston) Jan. 10, 1851; H. Wright, *The Natick Resolution,* Boston, 1859, passim.
5. Quoted in W. Chambers, *American History and Colour,* London, 1857, pp. 154–55.
6. A. Ross, *Memoirs of a Reformer,* Toronto, 1893; Redpath, *The Roving Editor,* N.Y., 1859; A. Abel & F. Klingberg, *A Sidelight on Anglo-American Relations,* New York, 1927, p. 258.
7. W. H. Siebert, *The Underground Railroad,* N.Y., 1899, pp. 28, 152.
8. *Journal of Southern History* (1935), 1, p. 33; see also R. Ogden, *Life and Letters of E. L. Godkin,* N.Y., 1907, 1, pp. 122, 143; Olmsted, *A Journey in the Back Country,* London, 1860, pp. 62, 82, 446.
9. Johnson, *Antebellum North Carolina,* Chapel Hill, 1937, p. 496; Olmsted, *Journey to the Seaboard Slave States,* N.Y., 1904, 1, p. 32.
10. *Richmond Daily Dispatch,* September 5, 1856, Aug. 24, 1858; J. Stirling, *Letters from Slave States,* London, 1857, p. 295.
11. *Liberator,* Jan. 29, 1858, citing *Franklin Sun,* and July 8, 1859, citing *St. Louis Democrat.* See also *Freeman's Journal* (Phila.), Aug. 7, 1852, citing *Fredericksburg Herald;* Chambers, *American History and Colour,* London, 1857, appendix; H. Trexler, *Slavery in Missouri,* p. 72.
12. Olmsted, *Back Country,* pp. 445–46.
13. *New York Weekly Tribune,* Sept. 16, 1854, Apr. 19, 1856, Feb. 7, 1857, citing *Montgomery Journal.*
14. H. T. Catterall, *Judicial Cases Concerning Slavery,* Washington, 1932, 3, p. 648.
15. *Louisiana Historical Quarterly* (1924), 7, p. 230, citing *Daily True Delta;* Document No. 46, *House of Delegates,* 1852, Virginia State Library, Richmond.
16. For other examples see *Executive Papers* for Dec. 1859, and Jan., Nov., Dec., 1860, in archives division, State Library, Richmond; New Orleans *Daily Picayune,* Nov. 25, 30, Dec. 2, 1856.
17. Siebert, *The Underground Railroad,* N.Y., 1899, p. 26; S. Mitchell, *Horatio Seymour,* Cambridge, 1938, p. 482; Olmsted, *Seaboard,* 2, p. 150.

18. Hesseltine, *A History of the South,* N.Y., 1936, p. 258; Siebert, *The Underground Railroad,* N.Y., 1899, p. 44.

19. Olmstead, *Seaboard,* I, p. 182.

20. Richmond *Daily Dispatch,* Sept. 17, 1856; *Annual Report of American Anti-Slavery Society . . . for year ending May 1, 1859,* N.Y., 1860, p. 84.

21. Citation in detail for these figures would require too much space. They are taken from the *Acts of the General Assembly of Virginia* for each of the years mentioned.

22. The sources used for this are the *New Orleans Daily Picayune,* June 14, 15, 16, 23, 1853; *The Liberator,* June 24, July 1, 8, 1853, citing other Southern newspapers.

23. *Governor's Letter Book* (MS), No. 43, pp. 514–15, Historical Commission, Raleigh, N.C.

24. Austin *State Gazette,* Sept. 27, 1856; F. Olmsted, *A Journey Through Texas,* N.Y., 1860, pp. 503–4, quoting other Texan papers.

25. *New York Weekly Tribune,* Nov. 15, 1856, citing Outchita, La., *Register; Austin State Gazette,* Nov. 15, 1856; *New Orleans Daily Picayune,* Nov. 16, 1856.

26. *New Orleans Daily Picayune,* Nov. 27, Dec. 2, 1856.

27. *Liberator,* Nov. 28, Dec. 12, 1856, citing local papers.

28. *Milledgeville Federal Union* quoted in U. Phillips, *Plantation and Frontier,* 2, p. 116.

29. Support for this and the following paragraph will be found in *Letter Books* of the Governors of North Carolina (MS), T. Bragg, No. 43, pp. 635, 636, 639, 653, 654, located in Raleigh; *New Orleans Daily Picayune,* Dec. 12, 13, 23, 24, 25, 26, 1856; *Richmond Daily Dispatch,* Dec. 9, 10, 11, 12, 15, 1856; *New York Weekly Tribune,* Dec. 13, 20, 1856, Jan. 3, 1857; *Liberator,* Dec. 12, 1856; *Ann. Rept. Amer. Anti-Slavery Society 1857–1858,* pp. 76–77; J. Stirling, *Letters from Slave States,* London, 1857, pp. 51, 59, 91, 294, 297–98; Olmstead, *Back Country,* pp. 474–75; *Journal of Southern History,* 1, pp. 43–44. An escaped German revolutionist, Adolph Douai, published an abolitionist paper in San Antonio, Texas, from 1852 until 1855, when he was driven out. See M. Hillquit, *History of Socialism in U.S.,* N.Y., 1910, p. 171.

30. Copied by Richard H. Coleman in a letter, asking for arms, dated Caroline country, Dec. 25, 1856, to Governor Henry Wise, in *Executive Papers,* archives division, State Library, Richmond. Other letters in this source show that the Governor in Dec. 1856, received requests from and sent arms to fifteen counties.

31. Letter from Montgomery County, Tenn. Originally in *The New York Times,* reprinted in *Liberator,* Dec. 19, 1856; see also *New York Weekly Tribune,* Dec. 20, 27, 1856, quoting local papers, and *Atlantic Monthly* (1858), 2, pp. 732–33.

32. *Principia,* N.Y., Dec. 17, 1859.

33. Letters quoted are to Governor Letcher from P. Williams, Jan. 5, 1860, and C. C. Larue, Jan. 17, 1860, in *Executive Papers,* State Library, Richmond.

34. *Principia,* N.Y., Jan. 7, 1860, quoting *Missouri Democrat.* Karl Marx read reports of this revolt. See his comment and Engels' reply in *The Civil War in the United States,* N.Y., 1937, p. 221.

35. *Austin State Gazette,* July 14, 28, Aug. 4, 11, 18, 25, 1860; John Townsend, *The Doom of Slavery,* Charleston, 1860, pp. 34–38.

36. *Journal of Southern History,* 1, p. 47.

37. *Liberator,* Aug. 24, 1860.

38. *St. Louis Evening News* quoted in *Liberator,* Oct. 26, 1860.

39. Material on this is in *Executive Papers,* Nov. 1860, State Library, Richmond.

40. R. B. Flanders, *Plantation Slavery in Georgia,* Chapel Hill, 1933, p. 275.

41. *New York Daily Tribune,* Jan. 3, May 28, Aug. 5, 1861.

42. Edmund Kirke (J. R. Gilmore), *Among the Pines,* N.Y., 1862, pp. 20, 25, 59, 89, 90–91, 301.

6

Notes from Negro History: The Struggle within the Ranks

White chauvinism is a problem only for the exploited; for the exploiters it is a weapon—carefully forged and regularly refurbished.

The ideology of white supremacy is not new; on the contrary it was born of slavery and has been American reaction's trump card for three centuries. The struggle against it also is not new, and progressives today who understand this to be a life and death matter would do well to study something of that history.

As a beginning toward this aim I shall examine some of the evidence of the presence of white supremacist thinking within two of the major progressive efforts of the past—the abolitionist and the early labor movement—and shall focus attention upon the struggles against this evil conducted by Negro participants.

The entire movement against chattel slavery was permeated with the fight against white supremacist thinking. For essential to that system was its rationalization—"if it could be proved," said a slave holder to the visiting English author, Harriet Martineau, "that Negroes are more than a link between man and brute, the rest follows course, and I must liberate all of mine."

From before the Revolution to the enactment of the Thirteenth Amendment, Negroes devoted themselves to refuting this slander. "You complain of British tyranny," wrote "An African" to the American colonists in 1774, but "are not your hearts also hard, when you hold men in slavery who are entitled to liberty by the law of nature, equal as yourselves? . . . pray, pull the beam out of thine own eye, that you may see clearly to pull the mote out of thy brother's eye." "There could be nothing more natural," wrote the Negro abolitionist, Hosea Easton, in 1837, "than for a slave-holding nation to indulge in a train of thoughts and conclusions that favored their idol, slavery. . . . 'The love of money is the root of all evil'; it will induce its votaries to teach lessons to their little babes, which only fits them for the destroyers of their species in this world, and for the torments of hell in the world to come." And, in 1860, a committee of New York Negroes, in appealing for universal male suffrage, asked questions terribly relevant today: "What stone has been left unturned to degrade us? What hand has refused to fan the flame of popular prejudice against us? What American artist has not caricatured us? What wit has not laughed at us in our wretchedness? What songster has not made merry over our depressed spirits? What press has not ridiculed and condemned us? Few, few, very few. . . ."

Such an atmosphere was not without its effect upon white abolitionists: many of them thought of the Negro as not quite human, or as childish, stupid, meek. There developed within the movement an attitude of toleration, an air of patronage, a feeling of condescension, and among the many invaluable contributions of the Negro abolitionists to that movement was their persistent struggle against racism.

The very first editorial of the earliest Negro newspaper (*Freedom's Journal,* N.Y., March 16, 1827) rather gently, but still firmly, remarked that "our friends . . . seem to have fallen into the current of popular feeling and are imperceptibly floating on the stream—actually living in the practice of prejudice, while they abjure it in theory. . . . Is it not very desirable that such should know more of our actual condition; and of our efforts and feelings, that in forming or advocating plans for our amelioration, they may do it more understandingly?"

Characteristic were the impassioned remarks of Reverend Theodore S. Wright before the 1837 convention of the New York Anti-Slavery Society. There, insisting upon the falseness of white superiority and the presence of its advocates within the abolitionist movement, Wright said: "I fear not all the machinations, calumny and opposition of slave holders, when contrasted with the annexation of men" with such views. "These points," he continued, "which have lain in the dark must be brought to view. . . . It is an easy thing to ask about the vileness of slavery at the South, but to call the dark man a brother . . . to treat the man of color in all circumstances as a man and brother—that is the test." He went on at length: "I am sensible I am detaining you, but feel this is an important point: for he knows that men can testify against slavery at the South, and not assail it at the North, where it is tangible. . . . What can the friends of emancipation effect while the spirit of slavery is so fearfully prevalent? Let every man take his stand, burn out this prejudice, live it down . . . and the deathblow to slavery will be struck."

One of the most persistent manifestations of white superiority within the abolitionist movement was the assumption that its white members were to do its "thinking," with the Negroes appearing as exhibits or puppets. Among certain of the whites there was a feeling that they were to do the writing and editing, formulate policy, devise strategy; the Negroes were to assist where they could, learn, improve—and keep on fleeing the patriarch paradise! Abolitionists did not fail to denounce this arrogance and to insist upon the terrible injury it was doing to the cause.

A prime example of this occurred in 1843 in connection with a Negro National Convention held in Buffalo. Here a leading abolitionist, Henry Highland Garnet, proposed that the convention urge the slaves to go on a general strike demanding freedom, and that, when the demand was rejected and the masters attempted to break the strike with violence, the slaves answer this with insurrection. After prolonged debate, the convention rejected—by one vote—the proposal.

Most of the white abolitionists were then still largely tied to the Garrisonian ideas of moral suasion as the only proper anti-slavery method and so denounced Garnet's idea. This Garnet received as an honest difference of opinion, but when certain of the whites expressed *scorn* for the thinking of the convention that was something else again. And when Mrs. Maria Weston Chapman, a well-known poet of the period and, in Garrison's absence, acting editor of *The Liberator,* organ of the American Anti-Slavery Society, took a similar position and added her fears that Mr. Garnet had "received bad counsel," she was favored with a scorching reply. Garnet, himself an escaped slave, reminded Mrs. Chapman that no one knew slavery so well as a slave and that those who had escaped came "to tell you, and others, what the monster has done and is still doing." Moreover, he went on, "You say that I 'have received bad counsel.' You are not the only person who has told your humble servant that his humble productions have been produced by the 'counsel' of some Anglo-Saxon. I have expected no more from ignorant slave holders and their apologists, but I really looked for better things from Mrs. Maria W. Chapman. . . ." For Mrs. Chapman it is to be said that Garnet's letter was published promptly in *The Liberator* and unquestionably had a salutary effect.

The patronizing attitude was also an important factor in the opposition which cropped up within the abolitionist movement to the frequent and vital, city, state, regional, and national Negro conventions and societies that played a key part in the struggle against slavery and discrimination. This, too, was a part of the hostility within anti-slavery groups to the establishment of newspapers and magazines by Negroes themselves. It is to a great degree what Frederick Douglass had in mind when, in the first number of his Rochester newspaper, *The North Star* (December 3, 1847)—the establishment of which met much hostility from the Garrisonians—he declared that he had begun the paper not from a feeling of "distrust or ungrateful want of appreciation of the zeal, integrity or ability of the noble band of white laborers in this department of our cause." Rather, he had done this because the fact "that the man who has suffered the wrong is the man to *demand redress*—that the man *struck* is the man to *cry out*—and that he who has *endured the cruel pangs of slavery is the man to advocate liberty.* It is evident," he concluded, that "we must be our own representatives and advocates, not exclusively, but peculiarly; not distinct from, but in connection with our white friends. In the grand struggle for liberty and equality now waging, it is meet, right and essential that there should arise in our ranks authors and editors, as well as orators, for it is in these capacities that the most permanent good can be rendered to our cause."

It is this same weakness, this failure to insist upon the absolute equality of the Negro, which is important in understanding the decision of the majority of those in the American Anti-Slavery Society to disband in May 1865, when the demise of chattel slavery was clear. The Negro delegates to the Society's convention of that year—like Robert Purvis and Frederick Douglass—opposed the move. They pointed out that the constitution of the organization called for the elimination of discrimination as well as slavery, and they insisted that freedom for the Negro was still very far from complete both in the North and in the South. Until, said Douglas, the Negro in the South had full political, economic, and social equality and until all Jim Crow vestiges of slavery had been abolished throughout the land, the national society dedicated to these aims should hold together and fight. Slavery, he said "has been called by a great many names, and it will call itself by yet another name; and you and I and all of us had better wait and see what new form this old monster will assume, in what new skin of this old snake will come forth."

When it realized that such an appeal did not convince a majority of even so advanced a group as the American Anti-Slavery Society, it should be clear how significant to the aborting of Reconstruction was the failure among progressive groups, to grasp the key importance of the Negro question.

The same failing has plagued the labor movement since its inception. After the Civil War, with its destruction of chattel slavery, its preservation of bourgeois democracy and the integrity of the nation and its tremendous boost to industrialization, the trade-union movement leaped forward. But from the beginning, white supremacist thinking and behavior crippled it. And from the beginning it was the Negro who most clearly saw and most persistently pointed out the necessity of unity and who, in the cause of this unity, attacked all signs of chauvinism.

A very early post–Civil War strike in the South illustrates the condition. In 1866 the white bricklayers of New Orleans, having formed a Jim Crow union, struck for higher wages. Negroes continued working and the bosses filled the places of the strikers by hiring more. As a result the strikers issued a call for a general meeting of all bricklayers, and the Negro paper, the *New Orleans Tribune,* organ of the Radical Republican Party, editorialized: "We hope that the colored bricklayers, before entering into any movement with their white companions, will demand, as a preliminary measure, to be admitted into the benevolent and other societies which are in existence among white bricklayers. As peers, they may all come to an understanding and act in common. But should the white bricklayers intend to use their colored comrades as tools, and simply remove the stumbling block they now find in their way, without guaranty for the future, we would say to our colored brethren: keep aloof, go back to your work, and insist upon being recognized as men and equals before you do anything."

This particular effort and strike failed and it failed precisely because the white workers, poisoned as they were, failed to recognize "their colored comrades . . . as men and equals."

The pattern repeated itself in the history of the first national federation of trade unions in this country, the National Labor Union, founded in 1866 under the leadership of William H. Sylvis. Indeed, Sylvis' own greatest weakness, which so tragically vitiated his fine qualities—class consciousness, enormous energy, personal honesty, and great administrative ability—was white chauvinism.[1]

What was true of Sylvis was true of the National Labor Union. In 1866, 1867, and 1868 it refused to accept Negroes though the issue was brought to the fore by the independent organizing activities of Negro workers, their calls for unity, and the awareness of the need for such unity from certain of the white leaders. Finally, with the accumulation of all these pressures, which brought Sylvis himself to call more actively for Negro-white unity, nine Negroes were seated among the total of 142 delegates to the 1869 convention of the National Labor Union. These Negroes, representing hod carriers, caulkers, molders, railroad workers, and painters, were led by the greatest pioneer figure in the history of Negro trade-union organization, Isaac Myers, a Baltimore caulker.

In Philadelphia on August 18, 1869, Isaac Myers, speaking, as he said, for all the Negro delegates, made one of the most significant addresses in American history, and while he spoke, reported the *New York Times,* he was "listened to with the most profound attention and in perfect silence."

"Gentlemen," he began, "silent but powerful and far-reaching is the revolution inaugurated by your act in taking the colored laborer by the hand and telling him that his interest is common with yours, and that he should have an equal chance in the race for life." Unity, unity on the basis of equality, was the essence of his message; that and nothing else would guarantee the potency of the American trade-union movement. "I speak today," he concluded, "for the colored men of the whole country, from the lakes to the Gulf, from the Atlantic to the Pacific—from every hill-top, valley, and plain throughout our vast domain—when I tell you that all Negroes ask for themselves is a fair chance; that you shall be no worse off by giving them that chance; that you and they will dwell in peace and harmony together, that you and they may make one steady and strong pull until the laboring men of this country shall receive such pay for time made as will secure them a comfortable living for their families, educate their children and leave a dollar for a rainy day and old age. Slavery, or slave labor, the main cause of the degradation of white labor, is no more. And it is the proud boast of my life that the slave himself had a large share in the work of striking off the fetters that bound him by the ankle, while the other end bound you by the neck."

Though this stimulated the adoption of good resolutions by the convention and the appointment of a Negro organizer, the resolutions were not implemented and the organizer was not used. Negroes shortly thereafter, again led by Myers, held their own convention of the Colored National Labor Union, in Washington from December 6–10, 1869. Over 200 delegates attended from Negro organizations and trade unions in twenty-three states including eleven in the South. In their address to the American people, they insisted they opposed "discrimination as to nationality, sex, or color." "Any labor movement," they asserted, "based upon such discrimination . . . will prove to be of very little value." Indeed it would be "suicidal" for it would encourage "dissensions and divisions which in the past have given wealth the advantage over labor." Specifically urged was a common phalanx of the Irish and German and Chinese, the Northern mechanic and the Southern poor white, men and women—all who labor and had been "so long ill taught" that their "true interest is gained by hatred and abuse of the laborer of African descent."

How pertinent for the American labor movement today is this call from the doubly-exploited, and therefore doubly-sensitive, Negro workers of eight years ago!

The immediate post–Civil War labor movement failed and among the several reasons for this is the influence of white supremacist thinking within the workers' organizations.

A somewhat similar course marks the record of the next great national labor organization in American history—the Knights of Labor. Here, however, the degree of Negro-white unity achieved was considerably greater than within the National Labor Union. The Knights, founded secretly in 1869 because of boss hostility and persecution, grew through terrible years of the "Long Depression" (1873–79) and expanded mightily in the next decade. Class conscious in its vigorous years, militant, organized along industrial lines, and welcoming women and Negro workers, it had something like 650,000 members by the middle 1880s.

However, this organization by no means made a complete break with white supremacist thinking or conduct and maintained Jim Crow, as well as some mixed locals, but it did have about 70,000 Negroes. That at least ten percent of the Knights were Negroes—when Negroes totaled about thirteen percent of the population, with the vast majority in agriculture, domestic service or other occupations largely untouched by unionization—speaks well for the degree of unity achieved and the eagerness of the Negro workers to enter unions.

Evidences of the overcoming of white chauvinism, especially when this took the form of concrete action, were hailed by the Negro people. Thus, in October 1886, a New York Negro wrote: "I had a letter sent me from Georgia by a colored man asking if colored men would be recognized in the Knights of Labor, and I have had similar questions from others of my race . . . My answer is Yes. . . . I myself belong to a local that is wholly composed of white men, with two exceptions, and I hold a very high position of trust in it. . . . I will say to my people, Help the cause of labor. I would furthermore say to colored men, Organize. . . . Let us break this race prejudice which capital likes. Let us put our shoulders to the wheel as men and victory is ours."

Ida B. Wells, a courageous Negro newspaper woman of Memphis, wrote early in 1887 of having attended a local meeting of the Knights. "I noticed," she commented, "that everyone who came was welcomed and every woman from black to white was seated with the courtesy usually extended white ladies alone in this town. It was the first assembly of the sort where color was not the criterion to recognition as ladies and gentlemen. Seeing this," she added, "I could listen to their enunciation of the principles of truth and justice and accept them with a better grace than all the sounding brass and tinkling cymbal of a minister, even though expounded in a consecrated house and over the word of God."

Nevertheless, Jim Crow locals existed and much of the top leadership, including the Grand Master Workman, Terence V. Powderly, were quite opportunist on this question. Increasingly as compromising tactics developed in the Knights in face of burgeoning monopoly capitalism the deterioration faithfully reflected itself on the Negro question.

Typical of the keen awareness of this disastrous change was the letter, written in the summer of 1887, by a Pittsburgh Negro steel worker. So significant and characteristic is this document that I will quote it as some length.

> As a strike is now in progress at the Black Diamond Steel Works, where many of our race are employed the colored people hereabouts feel a deep interest in its final outcome. As yet few colored man have taken any part in it, it having been thus far thought unwise to do so. It is true our white brothers, who joined the Knights of Labor and organized the strike without conferring with, or in any way consulting us, now invite us to join with them and help them to obtain the desired increase in wagers. . . . But as we were not taken into their scheme at its inception and as it was though by them that no trouble would be experienced in obtaining what they wanted without our assistance, we question very much the sincerity and honesty of this invitation . . . I am not opposed to organized labor. God forbid that I should be when its members are honest, just and true! But when I join any society, I want to have pretty strong assurance that I will be treated fairly . . . If white workers will take the colored man by the hand and convince him by actual fact that they will be true to him and not a traitor to their pledge, he will be found with them ever and always, for there are not under heaven men in whose breasts beat truer hearts than in the breast of the Negro.

The status of American labor in our own time demonstrates the exact truth of the words of this Negro steel worker written in 1887—"*If the white workers will take the colored man by the hand and convince him by actual fact that they will be true to him and not a traitor to their pledge, he will be found with them ever and always.*"

In concluding this brief survey of the efforts of Negroes to combat white chauvinism within two of the greatest people's movements in our history I re-emphasize that this barely touches the general subject. A history of white chauvinism would delve fully into its basic socioeconomic origins, and trace the appearance and development of its numerous stereotypes and manifestations. It would examine its impact upon the totality of American life, and would shed new light on every major facet of our past. From such a study fuller understanding would emerge of the Revolution, the Civil War, Reconstruction, the numerous third party movements (and especially the Populist movement), the fight for women's rights, the battle against imperialism, the development of socialism.

White chauvinism today is the specific tool of American imperialism. That imperialism is the main bulwark of world reaction; therefore the struggle against this chauvinism, led by the Community Party, assumes world-wide significance. During the Civil War the life of the nation depended upon Negro-white unity; today that remains true, and, in addition, the universal fight against fascism and war requires this Negro-white unity. The duty and necessity for this struggle, devolving first of all upon the American white masses is, then, crystal clear. On the success with which Negro-white unity is forged depends, quite literally, the first establishment of world peace and the progress of our country towards democracy and socialism.

Notes

1. In his "Letters from the South," published in Philadelphia Workingmen's Advocate (1869), Silvis consistently calumniated the Negro—while formally calling, within the N.L.U., for Negro-white unity!

7

The Negro Woman

Having been ruled throughout its life by the bourgeoisie, the United States has had its history interpreted, almost entirely, by servitors and members of that class. The result has been that a signal area of neglect in that history has been the aspirations and struggles of the plain people and most particularly of the working class. In addition, this capitalist class, having had as one of the bulwarks of its rule the super-exploitation of some ten to twenty percent (varying in different epochs) of those plain people—the Negro people—has seen to it that their history is "super-neglected." And this same ruling class, being responsible for the perpetuation of the especially oppressed position of the female half of humanity has seen to it that, by and large, the history of women has comprised the history of coiffures and costumes and little else.

Given this situation it is not difficult to comprehend the status of historical investigation into the past of the Negro woman, falling as she does into each area of neglect—that of the working class, the female sex, and the Negro people. This article represents an attempt to suggest something of the riches waiting here to be mined and that must be mined if the struggle against bourgeois history and the class it upholds is to succeed. We shall concentrate on the highlights of the history of the mass of Negro women. Problems which arise from class differentiation among Negro women, and various psychological phenomena require separate extended treatment.

As the minute hand moved past midnight of December 31, 1862, marking the moment when Lincoln's Emancipation Proclamation was to take effect, an aged Negro women said to 300 fellow fugitive slaves assembled half a mile north of Willard's Hotel in Washington:

> Once the time was that I cried all night. What's the matter? What's the matter? Matter enough. The next morning my child was to be sold, and she was sold, and I never expect to see her no more till the day of judgment. Now, no more that! I was going to my work, when the overseer used to whip me along. Now, no more that! No more that! When I think what the Lord's done for us, and brought us thro' the troubles, I feel that I ought go into his service. We are free now, bless the Lord! (*Amens everywhere.*) They can't sell my child anymore, bless the Lord! (*Glory! Glory! Everywhere.*) No more that! No more that! No more that, now! (*Glory!*) President Lincoln has shut the gate! That's what's the matter!
> (*Amen, Amen*).

When two-and-a-half more years of blood-shedding made real the promise of that Proclamation, time itself seemed to stand on tip-toe, straining to see the future. In the great houses of the South—the few still occupied—were despair and fear; in the slave hovels were ecstasy and wonder. Some of the Negroes sat stone-still, chewing on the wonder of it; some went shouting down the roads, needing to share the joy; some wept as though they'd never stop, as though their eyes were dams broken by the gathered gall of two hundred and fifty years of bondage.

None was so moved as the Negro woman. To her, as to the man, liberation promised the end of beatings and illiteracy, of auctions and hunting dogs. But to her, to the Negro woman slave, it promised the end of a triple enslavement and it promised the end of terrible indignities. Slavery had stolen the Negro man's labor and tried to extinguish his humanity; but from the Negro woman it also robbed *womanhood*—with the Negro man generally powerless to intervene.

The base of the Negro slave woman's super-exploitation was her position as a *slave worker,* reared upon which was the denial of her elementary rights as a mother and as a woman. This it was that made possibly the most loathsome facet of American history: not only (only!) the enslavement of an entire people, but stemming out of this, the social pattern—in the nineteenth century, not in the pre-feudal past—of what amounted to the legalized rape of the womanhood of an oppressed people

No wonder the Negro woman so often urged haste in slave plottings. Virginia, 1812: "She said they could not rise to soon for her, as she would rather be in hell than where she was." Mississippi, 1835: "She wished to God it was all over and done with; that she was tired of waiting on *white folks.*"

It is from the torrents of such torment that a Harriet Tubman found the strength to go secretly into the South nineteen different times and lead out three hundred slaves; and then to shoulder a rifle for thirty months as a scout for the Union Army. One may better understand now a Margaret Garner, fugitive slave, who, when trapped near Cincinnati, killed her own daughter, and tried to kill herself. She rejoiced that the girl was dead—"now she would never know what a woman suffers as a slave"—and pleaded to be tried for murder. "I will go singing to the gallows rather than be returned to slavery."

Negro women not only endured these unique conditions in American history; they also occupied a quite special situation which helped mold their history and that of the Negro people generally.

Up to the end of chattel slavery the American Negro's social status was inherited from the mother, not the father. A child of a slave mother was a slave; of a free Negro woman, a free person. During slavery there was no marriage per se and therefore whatever household existed revolved completely about the woman, and it was the female, not the male, who provided what little degree of stability existed for the pre–Civil War Southern Negro's home. In terms, too, of direct productive activity, the Negro female slave was as important as the male (sometimes more highly). Reinforcing this matriarchal bent was the social organization of West Africa, major source of imported slaves, where the position of women, based upon active participation in property control, was relatively higher than that of the European woman.[1]

Since emancipation—and as a manifestation of the Negro's super-exploitation—the proportion of Negro women who have been employed workers has always been much higher than that of the white, and this prevails into the present day notwithstanding the recent enormous influx of white women into industry. Thus, in 1940, while two in every eight white women were in the labor force, two in every five Negro women were in this category. And during the past two decades the decisive nature of the shift in the employment of the Negro woman (as of the man) has been from the rural to the urban area, with Negro women generally confined to the lowest paying jobs.

It is then not surprising that Negroes pioneered in the general struggle for women's rights. A Negro man, James McCrummell of Philadelphia, was the first presiding officer of that city's "Female Anti-slavery Society." The only man to associate himself publicly with the pioneer Seneca Falls Women's Rights Convention in 1848 was Frederick Douglass. And twenty-one years before that convention, the first Negro newspaper, *Freedom's Journal* (August 10, 1827), published a plea for women's rights from a Negro woman signing herself, Matilda. She deplored the "ignorance that blinds men's eyes," insisted that "we women have minds that are capable and deserving of culture" and declared that while "it is necessary to possess a knowledge of cookery," yet "something more is requisite."

In the struggle for women's rights no one could be more effective than the woman most oppressed and most closely identified with the working class. No more effective pronouncement for the rights of women has been made than that uttered in Akron, Ohio, in 1852 by Sojourner Truth. She was attending a Women's Rights Convention and had listened to sundry males decry the movement as ill-advised and absurd because of the weakness of women, the delicacy of women, etc. "What's all this here talkin' about?" demanded Sojourner Truth. "That man over there says women need to be helped into carriages, and lifted over ditches, and to have the best place everywhere. Nobody ever helped *me* into carriages, or over mud puddles, or give me any best place. And aren't I a woman?

"Look at me. Look at my arms [She bares her arm and demonstrates her muscles]. I have plowed and planted and gathered into barns and no man could head me—and aren't I a woman?

"I have born'd five children and seen 'em mos' all sold into slavery, and when I cried out with a mother's grief, none but Jesus heard . . . And aren't I a woman?"

A minister had bolstered his arguments against women's rights by referring to the difficulties one woman had brought upon the world by devouring an apple. For him Sojourner saved her concluding remarks: "If the first woman God ever made was strong enough to turn the world upside down, all alone—these together ought to be able to turn it back and get it rightside up again; and now they is asking to do it, the men better let 'em."

In the Negro people's struggles during Reconstruction to make real their freedom and to enhance the liberties of all Americans, Negro women were the most militant fighters. Here are the words of a Louisiana contemporary: "These women have followed their husbands and brothers and all who had a vote, from morning to night, around the parishes demanding that they should vote the Republican ticket. . . . They have been very active since 1868 in all the political movements; they form a large number in all the political assemblages, and they have evidenced a deep interest in all that pertains to politics." The efforts to increase the economic and political rights of women which marked the much-maligned Reconstruction legislatures were the natural results of this activity.

In the post–Reconstruction period, Negro women again were in the forefront. Thus, the Committee of Five Hundred Women formed in 1878 under the leadership of Mrs. Mary Jane Nelson, fought for complete economic, political, and social equality for *all* Negro people, men and women alike. The remarkable mass exodus movement of 1879–1880, when about 65,000 Negroes simultaneously, and as a result of years of planning, left the Mississippi-Alabama-Louisiana area for the freer soil of Kansas, Iowa, and Indiana was led and participated in, to a major degree, by Negro women.

It was a Negro woman from Virginia—and the heroine's name deserves recording, it was Mrs. Violet Keeling—who in 1884, while living in the South, engaged in the following public conversation with Zebulon B. Vance, leader of the Southern wing of the Democratic Party, then Senator from North Carolina and formerly Confederate Governor of the same state. Mrs. Keeling's husband had just been murdered for political activity and she put the blame on the Senator's party. Whereupon the following questions and answers ensued:

> Are any of the colored people in your country Democratic? *I don't know, I don't have nothing to do with that sort.*
>
> I ask if any of them are Democrats? *I am telling you just what I know; I don't have nothing to do with that sort.*
>
> Well, are any of them Democrats? *Sir?*
>
> You heard the question. *No sir; I didn't heard.*
>
> You don't speak to a Democrat? *No Sir; I don't allow him to come in my house.*
>
> Whey do you have such a dislike to a colored man that votes the Democratic ticket? *I will tell you as near as I know . . . I don't wish to see a colored man sell himself when he can do without. Of course, we all have to live, and I always like to have a man live even if he works for twenty-five cents a day, but I don't want to see him sell himself.*
>
> Now, when you find a white man voting with the colored people, don't you think he sold himself? *I will tell you what I think of him. I think he is a man who has a judgment of his own head and knows what he is doing.*
>
> Are not the white people down there good friends to the colored people? *Yes, friends to them; rather kill them.*

The remarkable Ida B. Wells, who as editor of the *Memphis Free Press* walked the streets with two pistols on her hips (to keep her press free, as she put it) and was finally forcibly driven from her home in 1892, was largely responsible for bringing the crime of lynching before the attention of the nation. Her studies first exposed the lie that lynching protected Southern white womanhood (she demonstrated that only twenty-five percent of the male suspects were even *accused* of rape) and showed lynching to be what it is—a barbaric device of the ruling class to maintain its position. She personally broadcast this message throughout the nation for some twenty years before World War I despite every attempt to silence her.

During the 1890s, too, were created the organizations which resulted, in 1896, in the formation of the National Association of Colored Women, the longest-lived of all national Negro groups. Under the leadership of women like Mrs. Marcy Church Terrell and Mrs. Josephine S. Yates, this group served as the most advanced champion of the Negro people until the formation of the Niagara Movement in 1905. The Niagara Movement itself, as well as its broader success, the National Association for the Advancement of Colored People, formed five years later, drew much of its strength from the active participation of Negro women.

Throughout these years Negro women frequently led the way, not only in organizational groundwork but also in militant resistance to oppression. The Associated Press, for example, in reporting the development of opposition to the mobs which ravaged Atlanta for several days in the summer of 1906 declared: "In the fighting the Negro women were the most warlike, urging resistance to the mob, and themselves fighting like Amazons."[2] Similar testimony has appeared since, most notably in the veritable war that gripped the nation's capital in 1919 with the white hoodlums and police acknowledging defeat—and steering clear of the ghetto—after three days and nights of bloodshed.

Union activities of Negro agricultural workers from the days of the great cotton pickers' strike of 1890 (and what a story is there!—still waiting to be told) to the heroic struggles of Arkansas Negroes in 1919 and the sharecroppers' strikes of the 1930s were led by Negro women. In factories, Negro women were outstanding the pre-C.I.O. days, playing key roles in winning industrial union recognition in several great strikes. Particularly notable was the role of Negro women in strikes against several food-processing plants in St. Louis in 1933 resulting in the recognition of the Food Workers' Industrial Union, and in garment factories of Chicago the same year leading to recognition of the Needle Trades Workers' Industrial Union. The spark-plugs in the union organizing drive launched a few years ago in the South were the Negro women, as this writer saw for himself, in Winston-Salem, Memphis, Charleston. . . .

Today, before our own eyes, the striking fact of the greatly developed militance and political maturity of the Negro people (putting them in the forefront of the American progressive battle) has owed very much to the Negro woman. Thus, for example, were one to nominate the single person who had made the greatest contribution toward the continuing fight against the lily-white Democratic party in South Carolina, he would undoubtedly select the irrepressible Mrs. Modjeska Simkins of Columbia.

Again, no segment of the American population has been more ardent and more influential supporters of the new Progressive party than Negro women, led by people like Mrs. Ada B. Jackson, Congressional candidate from Brooklyn; Frances Williams, candidate for Assembly from Los Angeles; Mrs. Charlotta A. Bass, editor of the splendid *California Eagle;* Shirley Graham, who introduced the party's platform in a magnificent address at the Philadelphia convention; and Moranda Smith, the dynamic International Vice President of the Food and Tobacco Workers Union, C.I.O. The quality of the leadership offered the Negro people and all women, as well as the Communist Party, by Claudia Jones, has been certified by the great eagerness of the government to deport her.

The Negro woman's militant history is characteristic of her sisters of other nationalities. The liberation armies of today in China, Greece, and Israel are filled with splendid female fighters whose courage and skill has won the admiration of all progressive humanity. These women fight not only against national and class humiliation, but in a profound and unique sense, as women they fight, too, against personal humiliation and outrage. The Chinese peasant woman of Tsitsihar who told Anna Louise Strong, "if I could get my hands on that—Chiang, I'd bite his throat in two with my own teeth," was expressing the desire to pay off the Shanghai gangster the very special debt of hatred his feudal-fascist regime has earned from women.

For its own liberation the American working class must have—must earn—the devotion of its staunchest ally, the Negro people. Conversely the freedom of the Negro people requires the liberation of the working class. Similarly, while the Negro woman is triply oppressed, the Negro man remains shackled. The position of the Negro woman is thus seen as a pivotal one in all democratic struggles. Appreciation of this central fact should provoke the special study and special effort that it deserves.

Notes

1. Of interest here are the revolts in Nigeria in 1929–1930 and 1947, organized and led by women—with women suffering almost all the casualties.

2. One is reminded of the remarks of the Paris Commune: "Had the French nation consisted of women alone, what a terrible nation it would have been."

8

The American Civil War: A Centenary Article

From 1861 to 1865 civil war ravaged the United States. This war has been a favorite pre-occupation with American historians—and novelists—ever since it occurred; literally thousands of volumes have been devoted to one or another aspect of the conflict. Now, with the centennial, the United States is being deluged with additional books and articles and plays dealing with the Civil War. The general weight of the literature—new and old—is to treat the war as either a senseless and needless tragedy resulting from human failure, or a mechanically determined conflict deriving from immutable and inflexible tendencies, in which human emotions, desires, plans, and activities were irrelevant. The body of the literature as whole manages to be more or less ardently pro-Confederate; almost all of it suffers from a virulent chauvinism reflected either in the omission of the Negro people from any serious consideration, or in picturing these Negro masses as indifferent to the war or, if anything, "loyal" to the master class and its Confederate states.

Since the Civil War revolves around basic issues—many of them still burning questions, in somewhat altered form, in the present United States—the literature on it is not only enormous but very tendentious and emotional. Involved is the whole question of counter-revolution and the nature of revolution, the status and rights of the Negro people and of the masses of poorer Southern white people, the "patriotism" of the rich—North and South—the active role of the masses in the making of history and their decisive role in saving the republic, the reality of international solidarity, etc. All these matters, as I have said, are not questions simply of antiquarian interest; on the contrary, they possess the most direct relevance to present-day American life and politics. With current American reality being the domination of the Government by monopolists, and therefore a sharply reactionary orientation internally and externally, the ruling tendency in historical writing is pro-Confederate, just as for World War II it is anti-Soviet.

In this paper, however, we do not wish to offer an historiographical guide; we desire, rather, to present an interpretation and analysis of certain major features of the Civil War in the United States and to do this with the brevity necessary in an article. With this purpose, and under these limitations, we shall examine the three aspects: 1) the origins of the Civil War; 2) the conduct of the War; 3) the results of the War.

I. The Origins

In origin, the Civil War in the United States was an attempted counter-revolution carried out by a desperate slaveholding class. The aggressors were the dominant elements among the slave owners, and the resort to violence was long planned, carefully prepared, and ruthlessly launched. There was not unanimity among the slave owners; some feared that the resort to violence would fail, and that its result would be the destruction of the slave system. But those who so argued were over-ruled and the richest and most powerful among the planter-slave holders carried the day for secession and war.

Why did the slaveholding class violently attack the government of the United States in 1861? It did so because it had become convinced that it had everything to gain and nothing to lose by a resort to violence, and, in the past, whenever an exploitative ruling class has reached this decision—and had the power to do so—it turned to violence. Here, specifically, the decisive elements in the slaveholding oligarchy came to the conclusion that if they acquiesced in the developments culminating in Lincoln's election in 1860, they would, in fact acquiesce in their own demise; that if, on the contrary, they did not passively yield but refused to accept this culmination, they had, at any rate, a fighting chance to reverse the course of those developments. In other words, they decided: if we yield now we shall be buried; if we do not, we may win and so bury another. But if we lose we shall be no worse off than if we did not fight—i.e., if we lose we shall then be buried. Given belief in such an alternative—and given the capacity to undertake it and carry it out—all exploitative ruling classes have chosen the path of counter-revolutionary violence. Such classes are devoid of humanistic feelings; suffering means nothing to them, since their rule is posited on human travail and their wealth and power derive from its infliction; such considerations were especially marked among the American slave owners—arrogant, ruthless, and racist to the core.

Affirming that a sense of desperation drove the slaveholding class onto the path of counter-revolutionary violence, leads at once to the question: what made this class desperate? What convinced its leaders that they had everything to gain and nothing to lose if they chose the path of civil war?

There were, I believe, four great forces producing this result; each will be examined separately, but it is vital to bear in mind that they were interpenetrating, each influencing the others.

First: the momentous socio-economic transformation of the United States north of the Mason-Dixon line and extending from the Atlantic Ocean to the Mississippi River; second: the quantitative and qualitative growth of the abolitionist movement; third: the intensification of mass unrest and class conflict within the South; fourth: the accumulating impact of certain organic contradictions within the plantation-slavery system. Let us briefly examine each of these.

A. THE SOCIO-ECONOMIC TRANSFORMATION IN THE NORTH

The basic nature of the shift in socio-economic foundations in the North appearing with the Revolutionary War, accelerating with the War in 1812 and its aftermath and accumulating speed after 1840 was the growing weight of industrialization and urbanization. It is in the decade of 1850–1860 that the value of the product of the factories approaches the value of the product of the soil for the first time in American history; that is the great watershed mark. Before that, agriculture had significantly outweighed industry in the total economy; after that the reverse was to be increasingly true. The turning point came in the decade preceding secession and marking the appearance and growth of the new Republican Party. In 1790, about five percent of the total population was urban (living in places of 2,500 inhabitants or more); in 1830 about eight percent was urban; in 1860 about twenty percent was urban—and while this urbanization did not completely skip the South, it was overwhelmingly concentrated in the North.

The population leap in the United States is remarkable in the pre–Civil War generation, rising from 12.8 million in 1830 to 31.4 million in 1860, but while half the population lived in the South in 1830, about one-third the population of the country lived there in 1860. In the 1830s immigration to the United States averaged about 50,000 per year; in the 1850s immigration averaged about 250,000 each year—and the vast majority of these newly-arrived working people settled outside the slave-ridden areas.

A rising industrial bourgeoisie was one of the results of these developments; but the predominant class in the government of the United States in the 1830s and 1840s was the slaveholding class. Its predominance was not without challenge, and increasing challenges, as the years passed and the changes accumulated, but that class did rule. It dominated Congress and its committees; it dominated the Presidency; it had a majority in the Supreme Court; apologia for slavery characterized the prevailing and respectable institutions—the press, the churches, the schools, the texts. A domestic and foreign policy to the liking of the slaveholding class characterized U.S. history during these decades. This politico-ideological superstructure became increasingly anachronistic and inhibiting as the socio-economic base was transformed in the manner indicated. Hence, political and ideological battles and recurring crises marked the period from the late 1840s and especially the 1850s; the culmination, politically, was the smashing of the two-party system, the emergence of a new, broad, coalition-type party, under the hegemony of the industrial bourgeoisie, and the ultimate victory of that Party in the 1860 elections.

Additional decisive changes were occurring in the socio-economic structure of the North. With the rise of industry and with urbanization, appeared a more and more numerous working class, and both its organization and its consciousness intensified as the Civil War approached. They found the institution of slavery more and more reprehensible—here the influx of thousands of revolutionary exiles from the Europe of 1830 and 1848 played a significant role—and found their own interests less and less considered insofar as the federal government and its policies were concerned, dominated as that government was by the slave owners. Fundamental ideological conflict appeared, especially as the challenged and distraught slavocracy began to develop a full-blown theory of the propriety and necessity—if "civilization" were to survive—of the enslavement of the laboring portion of any country's population, whether its complexion be light or dark.

Significant distinctions began to appear among the commercial bourgeoisie of the North. With the growth of factories in the North and the development of agricultural production there, slave-grown produce played a smaller and smaller part in the businesses of Northern merchants. Increasingly, these merchants were engaged in hauling and selling corn, wheat, cattle products, machinery, shoes, clothing, furniture, rather than sugar, tobacco, rice, and cotton. The merchant bourgeoisie had been the fundamental political allies of the slaveholding planters and the bulwark of the northern wing of the Democratic Party, generally the preferred party of those planters. Now, this

Northern economic and political bulwark was split; this is of basic importance in understanding the actual division that occurred in the Democratic Party with the election of 1860, so that two Democratic Party candidates ran for the Presidency (Douglas of Illinois on the Northern ticket and Breckinridge of Kentucky on the South)—without which split, Lincoln would not have been successful.

Meanwhile what was then the West—from the Ohio to the Mississippi to the Great Lakes—was being swiftly populated. Pressure mounted for a rapid and democratic land-settlement policy on the part of the Federal government, only to meet the rigid resistance of the planters; at the same time, the movement was made possible because of the tying together of the East and the West with thousands of miles of newly-laid railroads. This in turn fed the growth of industry in the northeast; it served, also, to unite the farm West and factory East, and to defeat Calhoun's grand plan of an agricultural united front of Western farmers and Southern planters and farmers which would outweigh the urbanizing East.

This socio-economic transformation showed itself, as we have indicated, in the smashing of the traditional political apparatus, and in the coming to the fore, through the new Party, of new demands appropriate to the interests of the developing classes: a protective tariff, internal improvements at federal expense, national currency and banking legislation, a homestead law, the exclusion of slavery from the federal lands, a reversal of domestic and foreign policies favoring the slave holders, including the rejection of the vitiating of the Bill of Rights which had been so prominent a part of the cost of maintaining slavery.

So much, for present purposes, by way of elucidating the first of the four forces driving the plantation oligarchy to desperation.

B. THE GROWTH OF ABOLITIONISM

Unless one sees the revolutionary nature of the abolitionist movement, he cannot understand it. This movement hitherto has been presented as either the unfortunate fruit of the labors of mischievous fanatics or some kind of liberalistic, reformist, benevolent enterprise. These views agree in ignoring the fundamental character of the movement: a Negro-white, radical effort to revolutionize America, by overthrowing its dominant class. That is, Abolitionism sought the elimination of that form of property ownership which was basic to the power of the slaveholding class, and it was that class which, as we have stated, dominated the government of the United States during the pre–Civil War generation.

The movement, being revolutionary, suffered persecution and fierce denunciation; but its members—Negro and white, men and women, Northerners and Southerners, with a large percentage of youth, and almost all of them not rich—persevered, as true revolutionaries, and finally led the nation to victory. Its great curse, early in its life, was sectarianism; it advocated courses which persistently narrowed its appeal—for instance, an extreme pacifism and anarchism. But as the classes objectively opposed to the continued domination of slavery grew, as the existence of slavery in the United States became a more and more intolerable stench in the nostrils of civilized peoples in the world, as the struggles of the slaves themselves mounted, and as the reactionary offensive of the slave owners impinged on the rights and beliefs of ever wider elements in the population, the movement itself grew. As it grew, it found the sectarianism more and more contradictory and absurd and so developed a much more rounded, flexible, and politically astute outlook; this in turn stimulated further growth. This growth was qualitative as well as quantitative; the movement turned more and more to effective political efforts and to the renunciation of a crippling kind of pacifism, especially in the face of the institutionalized violence of the shareholders.

More and more, as the 1840s gave way to the 1850s, the abolitionists became admired and respected leaders of groups decisive in both an ideological and a political sense; by the 1850s the *New York Tribune*—the newspaper with the largest circulation in the nation, whose European correspondent was Karl Marx—was decidedly anti-slavery, though not actually abolitionist.

It is not without interest that some of this sectarianism infected working-class oriented and even Marxist-inspired groups. Some tended to view the conflict between a slave-based agrarianism and a wage-labor based industrialism as merely a contest between two sets of "bosses" concerning which "real" Marxists could have no choice. Fortunately, Marx himself was then alive, and when he was appealed to for his opinion as to whether or not Marxian socialists should take a "plague-on-both-your-houses" position in this conflict, he replied that he was appalled that anyone alleging adherence to his views could possibly raise such a question. Of course, Marx insisted, Socialists were the strongest foes of chattel slavery because, in the first place, they desired the liberation of four million slaves and because, in the second place, as between industrial capitalism and agrarian slaveholding, the former was the more progressive force and the latter was completely backward and regressive.

The quantitative and qualitative growth of the abolitionist movement was seen by the slave-owning class. Its culmination in the sensational success of

Uncle Tom's Cabin early in the 1850s, the extraordinary sale and influence of the economic analysis of the backwardness of slavery produced by Hinton Rowan Helper, a non–slave holder from North Carolina, under the title *Impending Crisis* (1857), and then the noble martyrdom of immortal John Brown and his Negro and white comrades, and the intense sympathy they aroused throughout the North and the world, helped create a sense of panic and desperation in the minds of the dominant slave owners.

C. INTENSIFICATION OF CONFLICT WITHIN THE SOUTH

The dominators of the South have always sought to propagate the idea that their region is "solid," is united in support of the "way of life" characterizing the area. This effort is made today and the picture it seeks to spread is quite false; the effort was made in the days of slavery, and the picture conventionally presented of that epoch—of a monolithic South with the Negro slaves cherishing their chains and with all the whites, regardless of class position, firmly committed to slaveholding dominance in the name of white supremacy—also was thoroughly false.

The fact is that the slave South was an area torn by antagonism and basic contradictions; slaves versus slave owners, large slave owners versus the smaller slave owners, the non-slaveholding whites versus the slaveholding whites, and especially opposed to the richest among them. Far from making docile and "ideal" slaves, the Negro people created a heritage of militant and ingenious struggle during their crucifixion that has no superior among any people on earth. They resisted their oppressors in every possible way: they "slowed up" in their work; they fled by the thousands; they rose individually in rebellion; they plotted and rebelled collectively scores of times; they infused their stories and songs and music and religion—every aspect of their lives—with this central theme: resist slavery; struggle for freedom. In this sense the magnificent liberation struggles of the American Negro people today are in direct line with and represent a splendid continuation of, the profoundest traditions of their entire history.

This militancy reached its highest point in the history of American slavery during the decade from 1850 through 1860. In that period more slaves fled—singly and in groups—than ever before; more individual assaults against slave owners occurred than ever before, more numerous conspiracies and uprisings occurred than before, and many of them had a deeper political content—including the demands for the distribution of the land—than before, and characteristically in this decade, unlike the previous period, whites were involved in such plots and uprisings. The master class was keenly aware of this intensified unrest of the slaves; their private letters, diaries, and newspapers are filled with concern about it.

Class struggle between slave owners and non–slave owners characterizes all Southern politics from about 1790 on; but this reached its most intense and most widespread form in the years from 1850 to 1860. The struggle appeared in the growing cities and especially in the predominant agrarian areas. It took the form of the creation of new anti–slave owners political parties, and of significant organized efforts by the non–slave owners to overthrow the political domination of the plantation lords. The aim was the remaking of the political structure, of the taxation system, of the educational system; the aim was the achievement of something approximating an advanced bourgeois-democratic society. Its greatest weakness was that while it opposed the slave-owning class, it lost no love for the slaves. The whole system of chattel slavery made extremely difficult the forging of unity among the Negro and white victims of the plantation oligarchy, and while some advances toward such unity were made—and terrified the Bourbons—the fact is that these advances fell far short of the achievement of any real solidarity.

But, while the effort to overthrow the dominance of the slaveholding oligarchy within the South was not successful, it was serious and it worried that oligarchy very much. Many of its leaders actually feared civil war at home before they could launch their counter-revolutionary effort against Washington. This internal challenge to the continued domination of the South by the Bourbons has been relatively neglected in the literature; it is, nevertheless, one of the fundamental forces driving the slaveholding class to the desperate strategy of creating the Confederacy and attacking the United States government.

D. CONTRADICTIONS WITHIN THE PLANTATION-SLAVERY SYSTEM

In addition to the forces already described, certain contradictions organic to the nature of the plantation system, as a socio-economic system, were plaguing it and driving its masters distraught. First, the system was on that required steady and swift expansion in order to live. The system existed for the purpose of realizing a profit from the sale of commodities in a world market. The rate of profit rose in direct correlation with the increase in the number of slaves employed and in the acreage tilled, especially the tilling of virginal lands, where the crops per acre rose. The system of slavery, where mechanization was minimized and scientific farming was almost unknown, required constant expansion. Here fertilization, dry-farming, varying the crops planted, etc., either was not comprehended or was not practical, or the necessary fluid capital was not at hand—especially in view of the fact that about one thousand dollars of capital was tied up in the ownership of each slave.

Hence, the system of American slavery was very oligarchic; it moved rather quickly toward the declassing of the smaller slave owners and the concentration of the ownership of slaves and more and more land—and the best land—in the hands of the fewer and fewer great planters. So, while thirty-five percent of the white population in the South had some interest—direct or indirect, through family—in slaveholding in 1850, this figure had dropped to twenty-five percent by 1860. It is this sharp oligarchic tendency in the slave system which accounts for the intensity of the class struggle characterizing it; and it is the especially swift rate of such concentration during the pre–Civil War decade that explains the particularly sharp nature of the class struggle marking that period.

The natural tendency towards expansionism of the slave system had two other significant stimulators. One was the fact that the piling up of a slave population within a restricted area intensifies police problems. Such problems were considerable in any case; they might reach Santo Domingo proportions, with equally disastrous results for the slave holders, if they did not manage to acquire new land regularly into which the slave population could be sent and thus that "dangerous" component in the population diffused.

In addition, plantation expansion had a clear political motive. For, of course, slavery in the United States—localized in the South—faced the development of the free-labor system outside of the South. One of the meeting places of this developing conflict was the federal public lands; if these were to be settled by free farmers and workers and by a wage based bourgeoisie then the political weight of the West would fall on the anti-slavery side, and the planters' domination of the federal government would end.

For all these reasons, the expansionism of the slave-South was intense and notorious. It helped precipitate war upon Mexico in the 1840s—a rather unpopular war outside the South; it helped account for filibustering assaults against Nicaragua a little later; for the diplomatic pronouncement by three U.S. Ministers in Europe that Cuba should belong to the United States and not to Spain; and for the naval expedition financed by the U.S. government through the Amazon Valley region of Brazil, with an eye to weighing its possibilities as a base for an extended slave empire.

At the same time, this expansionism precipitated the sharpest kinds of political struggles on the national election scene; it was the Republican Party's promise that "not a foot" of federal soil would be given over to slavery—and

Lincoln's insistence, with his election, on keeping that promise—that finally decided the slave owners that whatever the Republican Party might promise as to the sanctity of slavery "where it was," the promise was useless in fact, since if slavery could not expand into where it was not, it could not last long where it was.

Here, then, are internal and external contradictions eating out of the heart of a particular form of exploitative social order; and the launching of the secessionists; attack upon Lincoln's government represents the classical reaction of a sorely threatened ruling class to the threat.

WAS SECESSION A POPULAR MOVE IN THE SOUTH?

We have characterized the Confederate assault upon Washington and the secession from the United States as a counter-revolutionary development. It was counter-revolutionary not only in its regressive motivations and its profoundly anti-democratic essence—challenging as it did the integrity of the bourgeois-democratic republic and the ideology of the Declaration of Independence; it was counter-revolutionary, too, in that it was done secretly, with malice aforethought, and *against the will of the vast majority of the Southern people.* One-third of those people—the Negro masses—abhorred the Confederacy, of course, and desired nothing so much as its destruction which, they knew, would mean their own emancipation. But, in addition, the majority of the eight million Southern white people—and there were, in 1860, only about 300,000 actual slave owners—also detested the planting oligarchy and also were opposed to secession and to the whole Confederate conspiracy.

The bulk of the literature on the Civil War assumes or asserts the contrary, I know, and insists that the Confederate movement had the overwhelming support of the masses of Southern whites, at least. But the truth is the opposite. This is why the leaders of secession made no effort to submit the question of secession to a vote of the restricted electorate in the Southern states—prior to secession—and why, in fact, they resisted all proposals for such a vote. It is for this reason, too, that this so-called popular uprising disintegrated when put to the test of a war carried to the South by the invading and—allegedly—bitterly despised foe.

In eight states of the Confederacy the question of secession was never submitted to a vote of the electorate. In the three States where the question of secession was voted upon—Virginia, Tennessee, and Texas—this was not done until after each of them had already been committed to the Confederacy, and hostilities had actually begun (except for Texas where the voting occurred on February 25, 1861). Furthermore, even the voting—held under war-time conditions, with secession an accomplished fact, and with secessionists counting the votes—showed these results: Texas, for secession, 34,794, against, 11,235; Virginia, for secession, 128,884, against, 32,134; Tennessee, for secession, 104,019, against, 47,238. Moreover, even in these three, Tennessee split in half, Virginia split in half, and the Governor of Texas (the anti-secessionist, Sam Houston) was illegally superseded.

The Southern counter-revolution knew their cause was not popular and said so. It was, for example, ex-congressman Aldrich of South Carolina who said of secession, late in 1860: "I do not believe the common people understand it but whoever waited for the common people when a great movement was to be made? We must make the move and force them to follow." It was ex-Governor Richardson of South Carolina who declared during the same period that the white people of no State in the South was for secession with the possible exception of his own. It was Edmund Ruffin, one of the richest slave owners and a leading ideologist of secession—he was given the "honor" of firing the first round against Fort Sumter—who confided to his diary on April 2, 1861, that it was communicated privately by members of each delegation [to the Confederate Constitutional Convention] that it was supposed people of every state, except South Carolina, was indisposed to the disruption of the Union—and that if the question of reconstruction of the former Union was referred to the popular vote, that there was probability of its being approved.

Only this background makes understandable the complete disintegration of the Confederacy when put to the rest of the battle. Pro-Bourbon historians, faced with this utter collapse, have no real explanations. Thus, for example, Professor E. Merton Coulter, co-editor of the multi-volumed and "definitive" *History of the South,* in the volume which he himself wrote in that series, *The Confederate States of America* (1950), "explains" the collapse by saying it resulted from a "loss of morale," that "the spirit of the people gave way" (p. 70); or "why did the Confederacy fail? . . . The people did not will hard enough and long enough to win" (p. 566).

But Coulter's explanation explains nothing; it rather poses the question in different words. Why was there a "loss of morale"; why did "the spirit of the people give way"? Because it was not a popular war; because Congressman Aldrich and Governor Richardson and Edmund Ruffin, and the members of the Confederate Constitutional Convention were correct when they feared that the Southern white people—let alone the Negroes—did not favor secession.

II. The Conduct of the War

Nowhere was Karl Marx's genius more dramatically demonstrated than in his grasp of the real nature of the Civil War and in his comprehension of the unpopular character of the Confederacy. The military experts of the world were agreed that the North would not be able to defeat the South; at best they saw a long and drawn-out war exhausting both sides with some kind of military resulting and a negotiated settlement concluding the conflict. Marx disagreed; he held that the North would defeat the South and do so rather quickly and accomplish it utterly. And Marx insisted on this exactly because he knew it was not the North versus the South, but rather the United States versus a slave-holding oligarchy. Marx, of course, paid careful attention to the class forces involved in the struggle; he followed with close attention the procedure of secession; he noted that no plebiscite on this was permitted. He insisted upon the oligarchic and unpopular character of the Confederacy.

The world's military profession agreed that the Confederacy, with its great population, its enormous area, its tremendous coastline, its numerous military cadre would never be defeated by the North (this was another reason for the failure of France and England to intervene more actively than they did on the side of the Confederacy—why do so when she *could* not lose?). Indeed, even Engels, a military expert, seriously doubted the outcome of the war, and as late as September 1862, asked Marx: "Do you still believe that the gentlemen in the North will crush the 'rebellion'?"

Marx replied that he "would wager his head" on that belief. It was based, he wrote, not only on Lincoln's supremacy in resources and men (for this alone need not be decisive—witness the American colonies versus Great Britain, Holland versus Spain, etc.), but also on the fact that the South was not in rebellion, but that rather an oligarchy of some 300,000 slave holders had engineered a counter-revolutionary *coup d'état.*

Individual monographic studies by Laura White, Georgia L. Tatum, Olive Stone, Herbert Aptheker, Albert Moore, Charles Wesley, John K. Bettersworth, Harvey Wish, Roger W. Shugg, W. E. B. Du Bois, Bell Wiley, and others have demonstrated the enormous amount of popular disaffection—among the Negro and white—which bedeviled the Confederacy, ranging from mass desertions, organized guerilla warfare (of which, by the way, there was almost none inside the South *against the Union forces*), mass flights of slaves, strikes in factories, hunger demonstrations and riots, anti-conscription outbreaks, etc.

When one remembers the degree of treason among the officer caste in the United States Army—with almost none among the enlisted men—the pro-Confederate activities of Buchanan's Administration in the days before Lincoln took office, the Copperheadism in the North, the white chauvinism there, the graft and corruption with which the bourgeoisie always conducts government and especially government faced with war, the hostility of most western European governments to Lincoln's government and the assistance given the Confederacy, I think one must conclude that there were grounds, apparently, for the belief that the North would lose. In the face of all these sources of weakness, Lincoln's victory—and within four years, little enough time, as nineteenth century wars were conducted, especially in the vast distances of the United States—could not have transpired without the active opposition to the Confederacy by the overwhelming majority of Southern people.

In the result of the War, that the sympathy for the cause of the Union was felt by the common people of all Europe, of Canada, and of Mexico was important. The role of the First International, under the personal leadership of Karl Marx, in helping to organize and focus this popular opposition, especially in Great Britain, is well known. Less well-known is the important contribution to the Union cause made by the Mexican revolutionary masses, led by the great Benito Juarez, in resisting the efforts of France to conquer Mexico. Had this conquest been complete and not seriously contested, the Confederacy would have had a long land border with a friendly French power, and this would have added difficulties to the imposition of an effective blockade of the Confederacy. It is somewhat ironic that the Mexican masses helped preserve the integrity of the United States, less than twenty years after the United States had stolen from Mexico, through war, one-third of its own territory.

In the actual fighting of the Civil War, it was the common people—the working men and the farming masses—who bore the brunt of the battle, made the sacrifices in blood, crushed the Confederacy, and saved the American republic. The basic patriotism of these masses—in the South and in the North—came to the fore and with it grew an understanding of the stakes of the conflict so far as the cause of democracy was concerned.

THE NEGRO PEOPLE IN THE WAR

By now a considerable literature depicting in truthful and realistic terms the absolutely decisive role of the Negro people in the Civil War has made its appearance. It was to maintain and extend the system of their enslavement that the counter-revolution was launched; here one has a classical example of the profound involvement of the general fate of the United States, and especially of the democratic advancement of the United States with the specific condition of the Negro people. Here one sees how the system of the Negro's special oppression almost caused the suicide of the entire American republic.

The Negro leadership was at the forefront of the effort to make clear the decisive nature of the slave system to the power of the Confederacy; it therefore led in advancing the necessity to revolutionize the conduct of the war. The war, if conducted passively, defensively, if conducted only to "defend the Union" with an insistence that the institution of slavery was irrelevant to the conflict, would not terminate happily for the Union. No, to defend the Union it was necessary to destroy the power base of those who attacked it; to defend the Union it was necessary to add to its resources the mighty power and passion of the Negro millions. To defend the Union it was necessary to destroy slavery. The salvation of the Union required the emancipation of the slaves; the emancipation of the slaves required the salvation of the Union. Thus did the dialectics of history manifest itself in specific form in the great Civil War.

The process of revolutionizing the conduct of the war was a relatively prolonged one; and it was one that required agitation, organization, and struggle. In this, the Negro masses were in the front ranks. And when success was achieved in the basic change of strategy, to implement the change, the Negro fighter would have to stop forward and show his mettle. The Negro people did so and did so with decisive results for the course of the War. About 220,000 Negro men fought as soldiers; about 25,000 battled as seamen. Another 250,000 Negro men and women served Lincoln's forces as teamsters, scouts, pioneers (what are now called engineer troops), cooks, nurses, fortification and railroad builders, etc. And in the South, the Negro masses were the eyes and ears of the advancing Union forces; without effective military intelligence, battles and wars cannot be won. The best source of such intelligence for Lincoln's army and navy came from the Negro masses who knew—and know—the South better than anyone else. Meanwhile, the Negro slaves fled by the thousands—probably half a million succeeded in fleeing during the four years of War—and in doing this withdrew their labor power from the despised Confederacy and brought it to the side of the Union. Dr. Du Bois once characterized this phenomenon of mass flight as kind of "mobile general strike" and the observation is highly illuminating.

Conventional American historiography—deeply chauvinist as it is—presents the Civil War as a white man's quarrel as a result of which, rather absent-mindedly, the Negro people were *given* their freedom. Nothing could be further from the truth; the basic connection between the institution of slavery and the source and nature of the Civil War is clear, and the active role of the Negro people in fighting for their own emancipation—and for the integrity of the Republic—is established by the evidence. Rather than declaring that the American Negro people were given their freedom as an incident of the War for the Union, it would be more accurate to say that the Negro people contributed decisively towards the salvation of the Union as part of their heroic battle to achieve emancipation.

This whole matter shows again the deep interpenetration of the history and struggles of the Negro people with the struggles of the mass of the American people altogether to advance the cause of progress and democracy; it shows, too, that in this organic connection no one is doing anyone else any favors. This matter of Negro-white unity is a question not of benevolence but of alliance.

III. The Results of the War

The basic structure of modern America is laid down with the Civil War and its outcome. The unity of the republic is confirmed; the preservation of the bourgeois-democratic form is achieved. Industrial capitalism emerges triumphant and dominant; it fastens its grip upon the State, and it leaps forward mightily as an economic force. Organization of this bourgeoisie on a national scale is achieved, and it moves swiftly ahead toward achieving complete hegemony over the national market. At the same time, with the leap ahead of industrial capitalism, its necessary antagonist leaps forward too; the working class multiplies in a short period and becomes very much more highly organized—also upon a national scale—by 1866 than it had been in 1860.

By constitutional amendments—the 13th and 14th—the institution of the chattel slavery is prohibited and efforts at compensation by some of the former slave owners thwarted. Here appeared an extremely significant precedent; these Amendments consummated a revolutionary transformation. With the 13th Amendment, several billion dollars worth of private property—hitherto perfectly legal—were confiscated and by this blow a basic element in an entire social fabric was eliminated. This was done on the basis of the reactionary and truly subversive character of such property ownership; it is a revolutionary precedent that the present ruling class prefers be forgotten.

In preserving the bourgeois democratic form, in the leap forward of industrial capitalism, in its achieving governmental domination, in the destruction of the system of chattel slavery, in the emancipation of four million Negro men and women, in the advance of the labor movement, the American Civil War, which begins as a counter-revolutionary effort, terminates as the second American Revolution.

That the industrial bourgeoisie, swiftly moving towards monopoly status, coveting the enormous resources of the South, desiring the retention in the country of a large mass of especially exploited working people, and wanting the political support of the former slave owners, fail to complete this Revolution is another question. They are a leading element in the coalition of forces which hurls back the threat of the slave owners, but when that common foe is defeated, the bourgeoisie betrays the coalition—and especially the Negro people. It allows the former slave owners to remain the dominant plantation owners; it makes of them straps—"little foxes," in the worlds of Lillian Hellman's incisive drama—and the basis of the Republican-Dixiecrat reactionary alliance is laid back in the 1870s betrayal of the hopes of the masses.

Much unfinished business remains from the Civil War, and much more unfinished business has accumulated for the forces of democracy and peace in the century since that was fought. The "handling" of these questions creates every day's headlines in the American press; they remain fundamental social questions, on a new level, for the United States of the 1960s.

Their nature cannot be understood, however, without a comprehension of the great struggle waged in the United States from 1861 to 1865. That struggle was a momentous landmark in the effort to secure a "government of the people, by the people, for the people." The struggle continues, on new and higher levels, in our time. The American people have not been found wanting in the decisive struggle in the past, and they will not be found wanting in our own new and challenging epoch.

9

Black-White Unity: A Basic Theme and Need in United States History

At the time of the Revolution which gave birth to the United States of America, people of African derivation made up over twenty percent of the total population; from then to the present, African American people have never constituted less than some eleven percent of the inhabitants of this country. Since the African American people have been overwhelmingly working people—including women and children—the percentage of the total producing population in the United States which has been black has averaged probably some twenty-five to thirty-five percent. The rate of exploitation of black people having been greater than that of others, one may understand the consequences of their labor in terms of the production of wealth and the accumulation of capital in the United States.

These constitute basic socio-economic data in the history of the African American people and therefore in the history of the United States. Additionally, black people made up the overwhelming bulk of the enslaved population in the United States, and the institution of slavery was a basic economic-political-historical reality from about 1700 to the end of the Civil War. Furthermore, in the eleven decades since the end of that war, black people, as sharecroppers, tenant farmers, peons, and workers—skilled and unskilled, in agriculture, mining, shipping, and industry—have been systematically and significantly discriminated against and underpaid, as compared with other workers; this system of super-exploitation and special oppression has spawned and been sustained by racism—a poisonous form of thought and practice which, more than any other single evil in U.S.

experience, has divided and therefore weakened democratic and working-class forces.

Those who, in the history of the United States, have fought against tyranny, monarchy, slavery, peonage—let alone those whose development made it possible for them to fight against capitalism—have understood, generally, that such struggles, to be successful, required black-white unity. The understanding, particularly among white people, has varied greatly in degree and has had different sources. In some cases, the main source seems to have been religious, with influence deriving from the egalitarian teachings present in all the great religions; in other cases, the main source was secular, drawing on the libertarian thread running through the heart of the Enlightenment and the Age of Reason. Most recently—that is, in the past century and a quarter—a basic source has been Marxism and then Marxism-Leninism, infused as that science is with the liberating essence of the working class and all allies of that fundamental class, especially the nationally and racially oppressed peoples of the earth.

Decisive among white people in terms of the history of the battle for black-white unity and against racism has been the objective reality that their own well-being, their own advances, their own struggles are not in fact "their own." That is, democratic progress, the advancement of the labor movement, the women's movement, the struggle for education, for health, for housing, for an end to war and preparations for war—for what, in a phrase the immortal Du Bois once called "the Joy of Living"—all of this requires black-white unity; none of this can be achieved unless racism is fought as an integral part of the battle itself because racism is the main weapon of reaction and the negation of humanism itself.

If a democratic movement, in the United States, does not fight racism, it is not democratic; if a progressive movement in the United States does not fight racism it is not progressive. This is not a matter of sentiment or rhetoric; it is a matter of cold and hard fact, and its truth is proven by the history of the United States. Indeed, one might almost say that the demonstrations of that truth make up the history of the United States. Furthermore, we repeat, if a democratic movement does not fight racism, it not only is not democratic but it also will not be and cannot be successful and, of course, it does not deserve success! Fundamental to the very definition of "democracy" is anti-racism.

Three aspects of the history of the United States will be commented upon, briefly, to illustrate the truth of the principles just stated: the Revolution; the Civil War; the labor movement.

The Revolution

Capital comes into the world, as Marx told us, dripping with the blood and sweat of the Africans: observe that the name of the first English slave-trading ship to reach Africa was "Jesus"! All men are created equal, said the revolutionary manifesto drafted by a Virginia slave owner; and Abigail Adams pointed out that women also existed, and black people in Massachusetts reminded the legislature of that then-revolutionary state, in January 1777, that "They cannot but express their astonishment that it has never been considered that every principle from which America has acted in the course of her unhappy difficulties with Great Britain pleads stronger than a thousand arguments in favor" of those black people petitioning for an act of emancipation.

To a degree the democratic stimulus of the Revolution—*and the military needs of that Revolution*—did lead to some advances north of the Mason-Dixon line in the struggle against chattel slavery; and even south of that line both forces induced the manumission of several thousand black people and the employment of thousands as soldiers and sailors in the revolutionary forces. This was something, but it was terribly partial, and especially partial in the South where, then, ninety percent of the black people toiled.

The failure of the bourgeois-democratic revolution, infected as it was with chattel slavery and racism, to terminate slavery left a cancer in the bowels of the new Republic. Black people at the time warned that if it were not excised it would grow with the expansion of the Republic and in time threaten the very life of the country—as, of course, it did within ninety years.

Let it be added that British officers in the field in the South suggested to the War Command in London that if the British troops could raise the standard of an end to slavery this would guarantee an end to the colonial rebellion. This was seriously debated in England but the ruling class there rejected it—though partial and false promises were actually made—and they rejected it because Britain possessed colonies in the West Indies wherein were exploited some 750,000 slaves; because many of the richest slave owners in Georgia, South Carolina, and even Virginia, were themselves Tories; and a declaration of freedom would be highly contagious and could not be limited to the slaves of rebels only!

The British rulers, then, faced with growing European opposition, finally admitted defeat in the New World and sued for peace; but the cancer of slavery and racism was not excised and therefore—as black people had warned—it grew and attacked the vitals of the nation and soon tore the very country apart.

The Civil War

There is no more dramatic and clear illustration of the need for and the reality of black-white unity in the history of the United States than is afforded by the Civil War. The slave owners not only dominated the South; they also were the ruling force in national politics from about 1820 to the election of Lincoln. The transformation in the economy of the non-slaveholding portion of the United States was *one* of the basic forces challenging the slave holders' grip on Washington. The development of industry, of a free-labor-based agriculture, of a commercial bourgeoisie which increasingly was engaged in business other than that connected with the slave economy, afforded the base for the appearance of an effective new political party—the Republican Party—to challenge the two-party system of slaveocratic domination which had prevailed for over a generation.

The forces behind that transformation wanted and needed tariff policies, money policies, banking policies, and policies for the development of the vast middle section of the nation (especially in terms of transportation and land-use) which were in direct conflict with the traditional policies and programs of the slaveholding class. This made possible increasing influence of and alliance with components of the great and growing abolitionist movement; it pointed the way toward increasing support of anti-slavery politics by the growing urban working class and by the farmers of the non-slaveholding areas. Simultaneously, opposition to Bourbon domination inside the South among those not owning slaves there and a significant rise in the resistance movements of slaves themselves combined finally to drive the Bourbon oligarchy to the desperate expedient of attempting a counter-revolutionary coup. Thus commenced the Civil War, with the military assault upon the Republic by that desperate slave-holding oligarchy.

To suppress that counter-revolution, only revolutionary conduct would be successful. The Republican party—dominated as it was, even at birth, by the bourgeoisie—was significantly racist and opportunist and moved to the necessary revolutionary policies only with great vacillation and hesitation; but it did move and it did so because if it had not so moved it would not have been able to defeat the Confederacy and establish its own hegemony over the nation. That is, as the abolitionists kept on insisting—and foremost among them the black abolitionists—only a policy of emancipation was capable of saving the Union; at the same time as Frederick Douglass in particular insisted, only a policy of saving the Union would make not only necessary but also realizable the emancipation of the slaves. Here the dialectical unity of the enhancement of democracy, of the salvation of the Republic and the struggle against slavery and racism became crystal-clear.

Hence, there came the enlisting of black men into the U.S. Army and Navy, arming them and using them (finally with equalized pay!) to fight shoulder-to-shoulder with white men against an army of white men fighting for the retention and extension of slavery and the destruction of the United States.

Abroad, Marx, in his leadership role in the First International, threw himself into the effort to enlist the support of the workers in England, France, and Germany behind the Lincoln government and the effort to help move that government to the Left; above all, Marx saw the need to develop working-class political and social power in Europe to keep London's Tory government and France of Napoleon the Little (who was seeking the acquisition of Mexico) from fully supporting the Confederacy.

The unity of the Republic and the destruction of slavery made possible the swift development of the productive capacity of the United States and the rapid growth within the United States of the proletariat. Thereafter, the central necessity was the completion of the bourgeois-democratic revolution in the South and the rise of an organized trade union movement and politically conscious working class, allied with the farming masses. The first required the destruction not only of slavery but of the plantation system, and the distribution of the land to those who tilled it; it required also, in the words of Douglass, that the working people, white and black, have the "ballot-box, the jury-box and the cartridge box"—that is, the right to vote and be voted for, the cleansing of the judicial system of elitism and racism, and the establishment of a militia and police system that would be fully democratic—i.e., that would not favor the rich and the white.

And the second required, in the never-to-be-forgotten words of Marx himself, an understanding that "while labor in a black skin is branded, labor in a white skin cannot be free." It required, then, the achievement of real proletarian unity which would understand that racism was a poison concocted by the boss and used by the boss to divide and to fatally weaken working people.

But the bourgeoisie, now in full power and thirsting to take over the resources of the South, were not about to permit all this to develop. Hence, that bourgeoisie, in the guise of the Republican party, betrayed its promises as soon as it could, turned the Southern masses over to the tender mercies of the Bourbons and their KKK lackeys, crushed the smaller farmers in the nation and mounted a fierce legal, extra-legal, illegal, and sheer-murder assault upon the labor movement. But all such efforts, if successful, are successful only for a limited time; masses remain for they are immortal and their needs remain also and therefore reassert themselves, under new conditions and at new levels, in new periods.

The Labor Movement

An embryonic trade-union and labor movement existed in the nation—even in the slave-South—by the late eighteenth century and continued to grow with the growth of the working class, so that by the time of the Civil War, trade unions were able to play a role of some importance in the winning of the battle against slavery. Thereafter, the creation and growth of a trade union movement depended upon resistance to the boss attack, and a comprehension of the fact that discrimination against workers who were female and against workers who were black would guarantee that the bosses would win and that the working class in the United States would be weak, unorganized, and politically without influence.

The history of the labor movement since the Civil War is a history of fierce and often bloody resistance to a brutal bourgeoisie. It is a history of the struggle to overcome various forms of national prejudices, to understand the absolute necessity of creating real unity among men and women who work and, as a central test and task in the United States, to realize in practice the slogan originated by the Communist Party: "Black and white, unite and fight."

Where unity was achieved, or to the degree it was achieved by the Knights of Labor, the IWW, the UMW, and above all in the 1930s by the CIO and in the great struggles of the unemployed, then the entire trade-union and labor movements were invigorated, strengthened, and relatively successful.

The highest form of unity in the labor movement, in both theory and practice, has appeared in the Communist movement. Marx, in his writing and struggling, emphasized the need—for example—of unity of Irish and English if both peoples were to achieve real freedom, of the liberation of India if England was to progress, of the liberation of black people if the white workers were ever to be liberated. And a basic point in Lenin—an essential component of the very meaning of Marxism–Leninism—is the comprehension of the nature of imperialism, of the significance of its main ideological façade, racism, and of the necessity of unity of the struggle against imperialism and against racism with the struggle against capitalism; indeed, Leninism *means* a comprehension of the fact that the struggles for national liberation, for full equality and for socialism are absolutely intertwined and that no one may be successful while another is neglected.

This black-white unity—the fact that the Communist Party is the party of black and white unity—has been symbolized also by its leadership throughout its history; from Foster and Ford to Dennis and Davis to Hall and Winston. This has come about naturally, logically, inevitably because of the nature of our country, of its working class and because of the nature of Marxism–Leninism, and a Party based upon that science.

Within the history of black people in the United States, an awareness of the need for black-white unity—the *mutual* need—forms a central thread. There have been aberrations on this question in that history, but these have been only aberrations—induced basically by persistent white chauvinism. The fact is that one of the greatest contributions made by black people to the history of the United States, and particularly to the working class in the United States, has been the leadership offered by black people on this question of the vital need for black-white unity.

In the final analysis, however, the responsibility for giving leadership on this question must come from the white working people; they constitute the majority, and it is white chauvinism which is the main obstacle to that unity; without it the working class of the United States simply cannot achieve liberation.

On this need for black-white unity, no one is doing anyone any favors. This is not a question of philanthropy; it is a question of mutual self-interest, of absolute necessity. When that is really understood and acted upon, the speed with which the working class of the United States will march forward and will affirm its political power and will achieve its historical goal of socialism—of human liberation—will astonish the world.

10

Mississippi Reconstruction and the Negro Leader, Charles Caldwell

Charles Caldwell's story deserves to be known. In telling it one must tell the story of the post–Civil War decade in Mississippi because his career is inextricably interwoven within the rich fabric of Reconstruction history. His name has appeared but rarely in books and then only in terms of execration: "a Negro of desperate character"; "one of the most daring and desperate negroes of the day"; "a notorious and turbulent Negro."

Charles Caldwell lived all the days of his life—except his last ten years—as a slave, and the anonymity that covered most such lives covered his, too. We know not even when or where he born, but as an adult he lived in the village of Clinton, some dozen miles from Jackson, in Hinds County, Mississippi, worked as a blacksmith, and had a son whom he called Charles, Jr.

There is no direct evidence as to what this particular Negro did or thought or said in the years 1865 and 1866. But what years those were for Mississippi's half million Negroes! In May 1865, the last of the disheartened and whipped troops of the defunct Confederacy had surrendered. In the big houses—those not abandoned and empty—were foreboding and deep despair; in the huts were rejoicing and ecstatic hope.

As a consequence of the war over two billion dollars of capital—of constitutionally recognized private property—had been wiped out (some $300 million in Mississippi alone) and with it went the traditional foundation of the Old South's social order. What was to replace it? Who was to determine and dominate the new order, and how new was it to be?

Those who had ruled were determined that the changes would be as few and as superficial as possible. One of the most astute among them, James

Lusk Alcorn—who had owned some one hundred slaves and estate worth $250,000, had been a state representative and senator for a decade, and a Confederate brigadier-general, and was to be, in his role of vitiating radicalism by attaching himself to it, a Reconstruction governor and United States senator—wrote to his wife as early as May 16, 1865:

> We will now take the oath to support the Constitution and laws of the United States; elect our senators and representatives; claim that we have our slaves until slavery is abolished and upon the question of amending the constitution for its prohibition Mississippi has a vote.[1]

And the President was with them. As Provisional Governor of Mississippi he appointed, on June 13, 1865, the former slaveholding anti-secessionist, William L. Sharkey, who from the start of his political career in 1828 had been one of the most important cogs in the apparatus of slavocratic rules, serving for nineteen years (1832–1851) as chief justice of the state's highest court. This individual did the following: First, he provided for the election, early in August, of delegates to a Constitutional Convention, with the electorate restricted to those who had had the vote in January 1861, and had taken the President's loyalty oath. Second, he reappointed all local officials who had been functioning under the Confederacy, requiring again only the taking of the same oath. Third, he urged President Johnson to remove all Federal troops—the vast majority, Negroes—from the state. And lastly, he ordered—without even informing the Federal Commander—the formation of a state militia to be made up of white men only and "particularly," said Governor Sharkey, "of those young men of the State who have so distinguished themselves for gallantry," i.e., in the war against the United States, then but three months terminated![2]

The election was held as scheduled, and the political complexion of the approximately one hundred delegates was what one would expect: Seventy were old-line Whigs; eighteen were Democrats, that is, somewhat to the right of the majority; and nine were Conservatives—so much to the right of the majority as to deny the termination of secession. This Constitutional Convention, with the haste typical of the entire reactionary maneuver, met August 14 and adjourned ten days later. In that time it accomplished this: After prolonged debate it was agreed that simply announcing Mississippi's ordinance of secession as null and void would cast the least aspersions upon those responsible for it. Following considerable argument it was decided to acknowledge the end of slavery in the State by merely asserting that "the institution . . . was destroyed" thus once again permitting no derogatory remarks (even though, this found eleven members in opposition); and, finally, provision was made for the election of local officers and a state legislature in October, the electorate being identical with that which had created the convention. Just in case anyone was so dull as not to have comprehended the essential function of this coming legislature that was spelled out for all the world to see: " . . .the Legislature at its next session . . . shall provide by law for the protection and security of the person and property of the freedmen of this State, and guard them and the State against any evils that may arise from their sudden emancipation."

It has been observed that no direct evidence has been found as to Charles Caldwell's feelings and actions while all this was going on, but some record does exist concerning the Negro people as a whole. Thus, on June 19, 1865, a mass meeting of Negroes assembled in Vicksburg denounced Johnson's Provisional Government, protested against the meeting of a Constitutional Convention in the election of whose delegates they would have no voice, and called upon Congress to refuse to restore Mississippi to the Union until she had enfranchised "her loyal colored citizens." And following the Constitutional Convention but preceding the elections of October, the Negro people gathered again in Vicksburg, reiterated their denunciation of Johnsonian Reconstruction, or, better, restoration, excoriated police brutality and peonage, and warned the nation that real liberation was being thwarted. And with perfect prescience they concluded:

> That is our firm conviction and we hereby put it on record, that should Mississippi be restored to her status in the Union under her amended constitution as it now stands, that her Legislature, under pretext of guarding the interests of the State from the evils of sudden emancipation, will pass such proscriptive class laws against the freedmen as will result in their expatriation from the State or their practical re-enslavement.

Under the gratuitous prodding of an over-eager press demanding "a well devised legislative system . . . so stringent in character as to compel the Negroes to work as formerly, upon the plantations . . . willingly if possible, but forcibly if need be" and that the Negro "should remain a servant [and must not] have the right to hold real estate conferred upon him," the legislature of October–December 1865 met. With an ex-Confederate general as Speaker of the House and an ex-Confederate colonel as president of the Senate, the press's explicit directions were hardly needed for the actions of these gentlemen were so blatantly reactionary as to be somewhat embarrassing to their most astute friends, including President Johnson.

The legislature refused to ratify the Thirteenth Amendment; it refused to even consider suffrage for the Negro no matter how circumscribed or limited, and among its acts were a memorial to the president begging him to free Jefferson Davis—"our blood . . . our treasure"—and a joint resolution calling upon the same official to remove all federal troops from Mississippi.

And for the majority of Mississippi's inhabitants, for the Negro people, came their "practical re-enslavement" in a law entitled "An Act to Confer Civil Rights on Freedmen, and for other purposes"! The civil rights are quickly enumerated: Negroes might marry—among themselves; they might sue and be sued; they might possess personal property. But enumerating the "other purposes" takes a little longer. Negroes were forbidden to own land, nor might they even "rent or lease lands or tenements except in incorporated towns or cities." Negroes were required to carry written evidence of a lawful home and to have a contract for labor. From this labor they were not to leave "without good cause" under penalty of forfeiture of pay, a fine of $100 as a vagrant, and the necessity of working out this fine in the employ of anyone who should pay it. No Negro might carry arms, and the militia as previously organized by Governor Sharkey was now provided for by law. Negro children, without means of support, were to be apprenticed to white employers (former masters being given priority) until reaching the age of eighteen.

Once again the Negro people responded militantly. A delegation was appointed to go to Washington and to present a petition to Congress explaining precisely what was happening in Mississippi. In January, Senator Sumner of Massachusetts presented their document, demanding immediate enfranchisement so that, said the Negroes, we might "protect ourselves in the enjoyment of those sacred rights which were pledged to us by the emancipation proclamation." Shortly thereafter Senator Wade of Ohio presented another petition, "very numerously signed," from Negro soldiers in Mississippi demanding the same right for themselves and all of their people.

And the masses of the plantation responded too, for law or no law, the planters, though possessing the land and thus having the final word in terms of food—in terms of life and death—found it very difficult to get Negroes to sign contracts. They could not buy land, they could not rent land, yet many of them insisted that they would not work except for wages—stipulated regular monthly payments in cash.[3] Such a wage system made possible some degree of independence, some degree of effective struggle, and therefore many refused—let the planters do their worst—to acquiesce in a sharecropping regime of semi-slavery. This is the significant feature of the following passage from the report of the Untied States Commissioner of Agriculture for 1867:

> The payment of wages—a plan tried extensively in 1866—generally proved unprofitable, the freedmen being inclined to use too freely their newly-found liberty, and planters were generally quite as little at home in the management of free labor. Much of the labor was inefficient, and idleness became contagious, *of a more malignant type in proportion to increase of numbers working together,* crops were neglected, upbraiding and threats sometimes followed, *and the cotton-fields were in many cases left in the lurch at the critical season of picking.*

Things had indeed come to a sorry state when Negro washerwomen in Mississippi's capital had the audacity, in June 1866, of actually threatening to strike unless higher pay were forthcoming!

The planters, moreover, had moved too far, too fast, and too brazenly. The North, still burying its dead, with Republican supremacy by no means assured, with an economic *modus vivendi* still to be formulated vis-à-vis the South, with the prodding of the Negro people and their radical allies, called a halt. In November 1865, the military disallowed those acts of the legislature forbidding Negroes to lease lands or bear arms. In March 1866, Congress decided to seat no senator or representative from an insurrectionary state until it had declared that the state entitled to representation, with the result that the individuals sent as senators from Mississippi, William L. Sharkey and James L. Alcorn, were rejected. The next month the Civil Rights law was passed, over Johnson's veto, and this declared the freedmen to be citizens and specifically endowed them with the civil rights adhering to citizens, including the right to possess all kinds of real and personal property. In June, Congress passed the Fourteenth Amendment and started it on its way through the state legislatures. That autumn the electorate presented the left wing of the Republican Party with an overwhelming majority for the ensuing Congress.[4]

Thus it came about that the new Congress enacted, in March 1867, its Reconstruction legislation, the essential feature of which was that ten of the Southern states were to hold Constitutional Conventions, the delegates to which were to be elected "by the male citizens . . . of whatever race, color, or previous condition." The registration of these voters and the conduct of the polling was to be administered and regulated under the supervision of the United States Army.

In Mississippi registration continued for five months with a total of almost 140,000 potential voters as the final result, of whom 75,000 to 80,000 were Negro and 55,000 to 60,000 were white. These figures, which dismayed the Bourbons, were reached despite some intimidation, and the enunciation of a policy of boycott—"masterly inactivity"—on the part of most of the planters. The vote itself, cast November 5, 1867, was overwhelmingly pro-radical and pro-convention; out of a total of about 76,000 voters, 69,739 favored a convention and 6,277 opposed.

We have already indicated that no direct evidence had been found as to the opinions and activities of Charles Caldwell whose career we proposed using as a space with which to unearth something of Mississippi's—and the South's—history. But it is not possible to doubt what those opinions and activities were for he was among the sixteen Negro Republicans sent to the much maligned "Black and Tan" Constitutional Convention of 1868. Of the remaining eighty-four delegates—all of whom were white—twenty-nine were Conservatives and fifty-five were Republicans, of whom, incidentally, thirty-three were native-born Southerners.

Ignoring provocations, the delegates assembled in Jackson on January 7, 1868, and upon their deliberations there promptly descended from the press a thick veil of silence which today is almost impenetrable. Yet the convention's journal exists and, while it is bare and formal, it does record the proposals, amendments, votes, and results. And it does preserve the brief speech of greeting delivered at the convention's opening by its temporary president, a property-less white man named Alson Mygatt of Warren County. He said, with an over-optimism born of fervent desire:

> This hour brings to a final end that system that enriches the few at the expense of the many—that system that hindered the growth of towns and cities, and built up large landed aristocracies—that system that discouraged agricultural improvements, and mechanic[al] arts—that destroyed free schools, and demoralized church and State, has come to an end.

He concluded that in spite of opposition from the president, the planters, and the press they would continue to labor for justice and equality for all, and they would not fail.

After a hundred and fourteen days of deliberation—prolonged in part by the obstructionist tactics of the reactionary minority—the delegates completed their constitution, an instrument aimed at creating a non-oligarchic bourgeois democracy. Property rights of women were recognized; imprisonment for debt was forbidden; a non-segregating public school system was provided for; local governmental organs were democratized; the judiciary was overhauled; the vote was given all men over twenty-one; and any and all discrimination by governmental units or private corporations, especially vested with public functions, on the basis of religion, color, or previous condition of servitude, was illegalized. Included, too, after lengthy debate, were rather drastic disfranchising provisions aimed at all who had held office under the Confederacy or had voluntarily assisted her. As for Caldwell, during all this, the record makes it possible to assert only that he faithfully attended practically all meetings, was a member of one committee, and generally voted with the radical majority.

An event occurred involving Caldwell, however, in 1868, after the convention had adjourned, which vividly demonstrates that while Alson Mygatt was premature in hailing the end of "that system that enriches the few at the expense of the many," fundamental changes had indeed come to Mississippi. For in that year, in broad daylight and on a street of Jackson, Charles Caldwell shot and killed a white man, the son of a Judge Johnston, and was tried and acquitted, the verdict being based on the fact that the act had been committed in self-defense after the victim had attempted to shoot the defendant. It would appear safe to say that Caldwell was the first—perhaps the only—Negro to kill a white man in Mississippi, be tried for the act, win an acquittal, and go unscathed.

Caldwell was a leader in the bitter, and, at first unsuccessful, effort to obtain the Constitution's ratification. Terror and intimidation and a federal military command generally sympathetic to the planters largely account for the initial setback suffered in the voting late in June 1868, when, by a majority of under 8,000 in a total of over 12,000 the constitution was rejected.

Grant, however, finally removed General Gillem and replaced him with General Adelbert Ames. In April 1869, Grant received authorization from Congress to order the submission of the constitution of Mississippi (and those of Virginia and Texas) without such provisions as he might deem it best to omit.

When, therefore, the Mississippi constitution was voted upon in December 1869, along with a slate of state officers, it was shorn of the disfranchisement clauses and was supported even by the Democrats. The latter, in an effort at deception equaling Hitler's National Socialist label, called themselves National Union Republicans, spoke up for the constitution, and nominated President Grant's brother-in-law, Judge Lewis Dent, for the governor's seat (together with several Negroes for other positions). The maneuver had a sad denouement, for while it resulted in the almost unanimous adoption of the constitution (113,7735 to 955), the Republican ticket scored a smashing victory with Alcorn, the gubernatorial candidate, beating Mrs. Grant's brother by almost 40,000 votes.

The legislature that was then elected and which convened in January 1870, contained one hundred and seven representatives and thirty-three senators. In the House, there were eighty-two Republicans, of whom thirty were Negroes and in the Senate there were twenty-eight Republicans, of whom five were Negroes. Among the five was Charles Caldwell who had had to resign his position as a member of the powerful Hinds County Board of Police to accept this new assignment. And in this new position Caldwell remained until the counter-revolutionary *coup d'état* of 1875.

Once again these men are known by their fruits alone, for little remains of their work, in terms of record, other than the legislative journals and the session laws. These may be summarized for the years from 1870 to 1874.

The Fourteenth and Fifteenth Amendments were ratified; a uniform system of public education and many institutions of public welfare were established; the vagrancy laws were abolished; tax rates on the tools and implements of mechanics and artisans were lowered; and all acts having special and invidious reference to the Negro were repealed with this explanation appended:

> That it is hereby declared to be the true intent, meaning and purpose of this Act, to remove from the records of the laws of this State all laws of whatever character, which in any manner recognize any natural difference or distinction between citizens or inhabitants of this State, or which in any manner or in any degree, discriminate between citizens or inhabitants of this State, founded on race, color or previous condition of servitude.

To put teeth behind this enactment another law provided a fine of $5,000 to be assessed against any officer or agent of any railroad or vessel guilty of Jim Crowism.

Two laws enhancing the rights of women were passed. One provided:

> That the wages and compensation of married women for service and labor done and performed by them, shall be free from the debt and control of their husbands, and their employers are allowed to pay such wages and compensation directly to such married women, and payment to them shall be a full discharge and acquittance of the employer.

The other declared:

> That it shall not be lawful for a married man to sell or otherwise dispose of his homestead without the consent of his wife, and no deed of conveyance

> from the husband for the homestead shall be valid unless the wife shall join in such conveyance....

Scores, perhaps hundreds, of incorporation charters were granted by the Reconstruction legislatures of Mississippi during their very short period of existence. Railroad, banking, public utility, mining, and manufacturing concerns were established as the state officers consciously strove to break the stranglehold of an agrarian, one-crop, semi-feudal economy whose controllers were, of course, their political enemies. A most interesting law was passed to encourage industrialization providing a refund of all taxes for a period of ten years to manufacturing establishments earning a profit under four percent.

For the planters the situation was an impermissible one. With such laws and such legislators, with courts, juries, police, city and county governments, and schools falling more and more under the influence of the radicals and with the latter gaining experience, competence, and confidence with every passing month how long would their monopoly of the land remain decisive? How long before the political events and the economic developments they fostered and in turn mirrored and the developing class of Negro officials and entrepreneurs would decisively challenge that monopoly itself?

More and more, too, the forms by which that monopoly expressed itself were being challenged. Thus, in 1869 and again in 1870, Negro mass meetings and organizations, particularly their Loyal Leagues, in Caldwell's county of Hinds and elsewhere, denounced sharecropping and even urged Negroes to refuse to work on plantations for wage pittances but to insist upon the status of renters and to pay, as rent, no more than $1.50 an acre. The planters were, of course, hysterical in their fury at such ideas and their press could hardly contain itself in hurling invectives at the "impudent and impertinent niggers," while even the leading Republican organ, edited and controlled by whites, thought these were the proposals of madmen. Still, might not the insane propositions of today become the realities of tomorrow? Comparing 1860 with 1870 who was to say what 1880 might bring? There was no time to lose.

The ranks of the Democrats had to be purged and closed; ruthless, coordinated and sustained terror needed to be employed upon the radical rank and file as well as the leadership; and splits in the Republican Party needed to be fostered and developed. Thus, the *Columbus Mississippi Democrat* was calling, in December 1870, for a revitalized party whose "leading ideas [should be] that white men shall govern, that niggers are not rightly entitled to vote. . . . There are professed Democrats who do not understand Democratic principles, that want the party mongrelized . . . [such] unprincipled men . . . will sink lower in the social scale than the niggers themselves."

The knout, the rope, the club, the torch, the gun, and the white hood are the instruments, stuffed ballot boxes, the burned schoolhouses and churches, the heaped corpses are the results. And behind it all, wealth—corrupting, devastating wealth. Give up your dreams or starve: come over to us and prosper.

It is not possible to count the victims of this terror; it is very much easier to count the numbers punished for there are none. Reported the United States Attorney for the Northern District of Mississippi in April 1872, on his execution of the Federal anti-KKK act passed the preceding year: two hundred arrests, no convictions except of twenty-eight men who confessed their guilt, but even for these "the sentence was suspended." The report of the Attorney for the Southern District of the state was similar: one hundred and fifty-two indictments, twelve confessions, no one punished. Teachers, Negro and white, were the particular objects of this terror, and in Winston County, in 1871, *all* Negro schoolhouses and churches used as schools were burned.

It was largely on the question of the suppression of this terror that the sought-for split in the Republican Party occurred, for the conservative element in that party, notably the planter-governor himself, James L. Alcorn, helped frustrate all suggestions of vigorous counter-action. And even when, at the height of the terror, in March 1871, President Grant informed Congress that neither life nor property was secure in much of the South and especially in Mississippi, and that body moved to the consideration of an anti-Klan law, Alcorn vehemently opposed such action. On April 2, he wired the Mississippi congressional delegation urging them to defeat the proposed legislation and declaring that doing nothing "will lead to absolute repose."

Learning of this, several members of the state legislature wired to Mississippi's Senator Ames the next day that "the auditor's books show 54 killed from March 1, 1869 to March 1, 1870, and 83 killed from March 1, 1870 to February 17, 1871. Report of inquests on many known to have been killed since January 1, 1871 not yet received by the auditor." On April 4th, Ames was told by the same people: "Auditor's books show killed last three months, January, 11; Feburary, 14, March, 23. Auditor states at least 15 more killed in March not reported." In the ensuing months the division between the Alcorn, or moderate, Republicans, and the Ames, or radical, Republicans, grew.[5]

In 1873 this split reached the point worked for and dreamed of by the Bourbons for both Alcorn and Ames announced themselves as gubernatorial candidates. When the regular party nomination went to Ames, Alcorn bolted and ran as a so-called Independent Republican, whereupon the Democrats made no nomination and threw their support behind him. This tactic and the terrorism that had preceded it cut the radical majority, but, to the intense chagrin of the planters, Alcorn was beaten by almost 20,000 in a total of some 126,000.

But one decision was possible for the Bourbons: the time for maneuvers and deals was passed. Nightly visits to annoying individuals, spies, and stool pigeons to reveal the names of leaders, remained useful. More important now, however, was to be the technique of mass assault and mass terrorization, the technique of the "riot" accomplished and followed by the slaughter of impertinent ones, in groups of five, ten, a score. And all of this was to be in preparation for the supreme effort, the attempt at actually seizing the reins of government, to come during the elections of 1875.

This had worked elsewhere—Tennessee, Louisiana, Alabama—it might be made to work in Mississippi. There had been tentative stabs at it, as a matter of fact. Thus, at Meridian, in March 1871, about thirty Negroes were killed and the local Republican government was overthrown, but this had not resulted too happily for it had been the direct inspiration of a Presidential message to Congress calling for protective measures which in turn led to the anti-K.K.K. act.

But when a country distraught by the panic of 1873 and disgusted by the colossal corruption of the nouveaux riches industrial bourgeoisie and their political henchmen inflicted a resounding defeat upon the Republicans in the congressional elections of 1874, Southern Democrats, and particularly those in Mississippi, flung aside all restraint. In November and December 1874, a systematic massacre of Negro leaders began with the killing of about half a dozen in Austin and anywhere from about forty to eighty in Vicksburg. The latter event was so horrible that it resulted in the dispatching of some Federal troops in order to call a halt, after the legislature, meeting in special session, had appealed to the President.

In the election year of 1875 the butchery went on with regularity—though not without resistance and occasional fatalities among the assassins—Water Valley, Louisville, Macon (here some dozen Negroes were killed by strong-arm squads coming in from Alabama), Vicksburg again, and, on September 1, Yazoo City where the radical white sheriff, A. T. Morgan, a former Union colonel was driven out and the usurpers continued their reign of terror under the guise of a self-imposed martial law.

The climax, however, came on September 4 near Caldwell's home village of

Clinton at the so-called Moss Hill riot. The occasion was a Republican political celebration, parade, and barbecue, to be accompanied by speeches. At the suggestion of Caldwell, himself a candidate for re-election to the state senate and chairman of the Hinds County Executive Committee of the Republican Party, a Democrat was invited to debate the issues at this meeting.

In the midst of the Republican's speech, loud cursing and heckling began. Caldwell himself, as he stated:

> proceed[ed] to the spot indicated. When I got there I asked what is the matter. A policeman said this man Thompson has drawn a pistol on one of the colored men who was marching in the procession, using certain opprobrious epithets. I remarked, my young friend, for God's sake don't disturb the meeting. I soon saw that the feeling was so strong and so determined that I called upon some of the other white men to assist me in preserving the peace. No one responded. I saw Neil Wharton and Thompson [white] draw their pistols and I slipped up to Neil telling him that would not do. I did the same with Thompson and they put their weapons back in their pockets. In a few minutes they had drawn again; then the shooting began. I saw Thompson shoot the first shot that was fired, pouring some four or five shots into the crowd of which he had formed a part. At this time the firing had become general. The colored people soon concentrated at this point, when the white lines dispersed, and the firing ceased.

The casualties at the scene were approximately two whites killed, four wounded, two Negroes killed, five wounded. There followed, in and around Clinton, four days of unbridled, systematic slaughter of Negro and white radical leaders, the total murdered coming to somewhere between thirty-five and fifty. This was accomplished by about two hundred local "citizen soldiery" as they were called, reinforced by a trainload of expertly trained and fully armed men, known as Modocs, sent from Vicksburg at the request of Clinton's mayor. In the words of the Democratic leader of Hinds county, "throughout the county for several days the Negro leaders, some white and some black were hunted down and killed . . . ." but not all were captured for several hundred, including Caldwell, escaped to the capital.

The Modocs did not fail to visit Caldwell's home, where his wife was busy nursing two Negro victims of the riot. "About fifty came to my house that night [Sept. 4]," Mrs. Caldwell tells us, where they "plundered and robbed." They stayed until daybreak when, before leaving, their leader told her to inform the senator that they were "going to kill him if it is two years, or one year, or six; no difference; we are going to kill him anyhow. We have orders to kill him, and we are going to do it, because he belongs to this Republican party, and sticks up for these negroes." Then, leaving her,

> They went to a house where there was an old black man, a feeble old man, named Bob Beasly, and they shot him all to pieces. And they went to Mr. Willis's and took out a man, named Gamaliel Brown, and they shot him all to pieces . . . and they goes out to Sam Jackson's, president of the [Republican] club, and they shot him all to pieces . . . and they went out to Alfred Hastings . . . and they shot Alfred Hastings all to pieces . . . every man they found they killed that morning . . .

So it went for three more days, the Negroes meanwhile vainly beseeching the authorities for arms with which they might defend themselves.

In Clinton, through all this a small detachment of federal troops bestirred itself not at all, though on the fourth day, "An arrangement was made . . . that if they would stop the killing of the negroes, the United States officers would not assume command but leave matters in charge of the [self-imposed] civil authorities." At a dinner for these officers and gentlemen the guests all "arose, saluted and loudly cheered until the whole building resounded with their tokens of good will" when the genial guest of honor, Major Allen, the Federal commander, entered.

On September 6 the leader of these usurpers, one S. M. Shelton, wired J. Z. George, head of the state Democratic Party:

> There can be no peace in Hinds County while the radical leaders are at large. We are fully prepared to meet the issue and accept no terms which do not assure their surrender or removal from the county. We do not recognize the Ames government but will have no conflict with the Federal authorities.

The next day Governor Ames issued a proclamation taking note officially of the violence and terrorism and of the forceful overthrow of legal county governments in Yazoo and Hinds, and, calling upon all extra-legal armed bodies, into which most of the Democratic clubs had by now transformed themselves, to disband.

This was greeted by defiance and ridicule. "Ha! Ha! Ha!!!" said the *Mississippi Weekly Pilot* the next day, "'Command.' 'Disband,' That's good." And the *Yazoo City Herald* snorted, on September 10:

> What impudence. Our dapper little Governor Ames comes to the front with a proclamation ordering the disbandment of all the military companies now organized in the State. If he had brains enough to know his right hand from his left, he ought to know that no more attention will be paid to his procla-

mation than the moon is popularly supposed to pay to the baying of a sheep-killing dog.

And behind it all, the bitterness, the derision, the terror, as the Yazoo City Banner admitted in a moment of frankness on September 23, was this: " . . .wenches wedded to carpetbaggers, and can't work out—young Negroes ain't worth a damn. No cotton pickers to be found for the big crop. Ain't we in a hell of a fix?"

The day after his proclamation, Ames appealed to Grant for Federal assistance, but on September 11 George wired to the Attorney General, Edwards Pierrepont, that "perfect peace prevails throughout the State, and there is no danger of disturbance unless invited by the State authorities, which I hope they will not do." The two Mississippi Senators split on their advice to the President, the recently elected Negro, Blanche K. Bruce, urging Federal aid, while James L. Alcorn, true to his role, condemned such a course. President Grant, through Pierrepont, informed Ames, on September 14, that "The whole public are tired of these annual autumnal outbreaks in the South," that he, himself, was not convinced federal aid was really needed, and that therefore he was sending none. Meanwhile, Pierrepont secretly sent a personal agent to Mississippi to observe, report back, and to do his best to keep the disorder below the surface.[6]

With the handful of Federal troops in the state officered by men being dined and applauded by the planters, with legally elected county governments overthrown and the usurpers publicly asserting their defiance, with the press greeting appeals for the terror to cease as "impudence" and announcing that, "The people of this State are now fully armed, equipped, and drilled," with hundreds of refugees crowding Jackson and with the federal government announcing itself as "tired" of reports of disturbances, Ames turned to enrolling and activating a state militia.

State officers, both Negro and white, were appointed and the enlistment of companies begun. In September and early October seven companies were formed (five Negro, two white), and the first of these to be mustered and armed—being the first to offer itself—was Company A, 2nd Regiment of Mississippi Infantry, commanded by Captain Charles Caldwell and 1st Lieutenant Eugene B. Welborn.

The first mission considered for Caldwell's company was that of spearheading a drive to overthrow the violently imposed reactionary regime in Yazoo county and to reinstate in the sheriff's office Colonel Morgan. When this proposition was put to the latter he rejected it on the ground that one or even two militia companies (*i.e.*, about two hundred men) would never succeed in such a task but would simply be wiped out, and so the attempt was not made. "It was certainly not the fault of the colored company that he did not try," Morgan wrote later, "My old friend, Charles Caldwell, was its captain. They were at all times ready to go." That Morgan's estimate of the situation was correct is apparent from a contemporary account of the preparations made to greet him in Yazoo when his coming was rumored—nine hundred mounted, armed men were waiting.

But the governor did entrust Caldwell with a mission. It was possible to enroll men in the militia, but how to get arms to them? Some that had been sent from Jackson unprotected had been captured and appropriated by the "civilian army." Now arms would be delivered under guard. There was a company formed at Edwards' Depot, some thirty miles due west of Jackson; it needed guns and Caldwell's company would see that it got them.

In the morning of October 9, 1875, Captain Caldwell and his one hundred and two Negro men, carrying four days' rations, and one hundred extra guns plus ammunition, set out—flags flying, drums beating, bayonets fixed—for a march of a day a half via public road in the heart of Mississippi. They bivouacked overnight just outside Clinton—from which many of the men were refugees—sleeping lightly, it may be believed. Then, the next morning, on to Bolton and into Edwards' Depot before noon. Back they went, the same day, Caldwell leading two hundred men now. On the return trip they picked up another company—this from Brownsville, a town ten miles north of Bolton—and thus did Caldwell come marching into Jackson with three hundred Negro militiamen, two-thirds of them armed, completing a truly amazing feat of courage, and, above, all, leadership.

While Caldwell and his men were marching, the Democratic managers were frantically telegraphing and visiting key personnel and begging them to offer no resistance to the Negro. For, as they pointed out, he would fight to the death, the battle could not be hidden from view, he was the Governor's official representative, and violence might lead to real Federal intervention, a supervised election and defeat.

Desperately late as this action was—the election but three weeks away—had it been energetically pursued, through the state, the result might possible have been different. But late in September the Democratic command filed suit for a warrant restraining the state auditor from issuing any funds for military purposes (since the state was not at war!) and this was granted by the Chief Justice, E. G. Peyton, another one of the wealthy old-line Whigs who, like Alcorn, had joined the Republican Party. On October 12 Governor

Ames, apparently deciding all was lost, ordered the disbanding of the militia companies and the disarming of their members, although the latter command does not appear to have been obeyed with alacrity or completeness.

Three days later, at the prodding of the Democratic leaders and the agent of the attorney general, the governor entered into a formal peace treaty with the former. This, while on its face an armistice, actually represented Ames' capitulation. It pledged both parties to abstain from violence, fraud, and intimidation, while Ames agreed to maintain the demobilization of the militia, to complete its disarming, and to take no new step without first consulting George, leader of the forces engineering the *coup d'état.*

Meanwhile in the same month another "riot" occurred at Friar's Point resulting in the death of six Negroes and two whites, whereupon Senator Alcorn urged the attorney general not to be unduly upset; " . . .there need be no alarm for the peace of this country . . . A community of planters may be relied on for kind treatment of laborers." Thereupon the sheriff of Alcorn's own county of Coahoma was driven out two weeks before the voting to assure its result and to guarantee the "kind treatment."

Newspapers bore upon their mastheads the slogan, "Carry the election peaceably if we can, forcibly if we must," bribery flourished, employers fired known radicals, physicians refused to treat them, and their names were published "for future reference" with the whites among them marked for special vituperation. And if, said the planters, it should be some miracle happen that we lose, "all landowners will resist payment of all taxes. Legal resistance will, when exhausted without giving results, be succeeded by such protection as that afforded by Winchester rifles and other peace-makers."

On October 29, Caldwell wrote the governor that the peace treaty was a farce:

> The intimidation and threatening of colored voters continues uninterrupted, and with as much system, determined purpose, and combination of effort as if it were a legitimate means of canvassing . . . the peace agreement is held in utter contempt, and only serves as a cover for perpetrating the very wrongs . . . it was intended to prevent. In behalf of he people whom I represent [he concluded] I appeal to your excellency for the protection which the laws of the State guarantee to every citizen regardless of party or race.

The day before the election a Negro wrote the governor from Yazoo City:

> I beg you most fulley to send the United soldiers here; they have hung six more men . . . now they are going to have war here to-morrow; send help; they told Mr. Richardson if he went to the telegraph office to-morrow they would

> hang him; help, help, help, help; soon as you can . . . fighting commence just as I were closing; 2 two killed; we would of carred this election, but you keep listen at the white people; pleas send troops and test the election; help; send troops and arms, pleas. . . .

Meanwhile *The Nation* was informing its cultured and liberal clientele that "peace and harmony reign" throughout Mississippi where "arrangements have been made by which fairness and spirit of concord will prevail in the future." This happy result eventuated because of the wise refusal to send troops into the area and despite the "large and ignorant black population, and among the whites a considerable number of lawless fellows fond of knifing and shooting . . ."

As for the voting the leader of the Democratic Party for Hinds County tells us what happened. First, the Republican registrar was bribed to stay away. And, as for the Negroes, there was "individual effort . . . persuasive, but if necessary, intimidation"; as for the ballots, "destruction of Republican tickets when they could be gotten," or "substitution of Democratic for Republican tickets." Precisely what was "intimidation"? Nine days after the election, the *Aberdeen Examiner,* published in the seat of Monroe County, explaining that though a bridge had been torn down and pickets posted to prevent the appearance of Negro voters, still they came. As a result, "the man in charge of the Democratic war department" {!} surrounded them with cavalry imported from Alabama and with native infantry, kept the Negroes covered with an artillery piece "and then sent a strong arm squad into the crowd to beat the Negroes over the head."

But, for *The Nation,* "The election passed off quietly," there had been "a fair vote" and Mississippi was "emancipated."[7]

Charles Caldwell voted. Eugene Welborne, who had been Caldwell's militia lieutenant, tells about it. On election day he said to Caldwell:

"Senator, I think we might just as well give up; I don't see any use trying to stay here any longer; we can't do anything there. Here these men are riding all about the country with their sixteen shooters and cutting up in this manner."

Caldwell replied: "No; we are going to stay right here; you must just come right along, and keep your mouth shut. I don't care what they say to you, don't you say a word." And they voted.

The Bourbons won the election. In Coahoma County while there had been 1,300 Republican votes in 1873, there were 230 in 1875; in Yazoo County where 2,500 Republican votes were cast in 1873, there were 7 in 1875. Yes they won. But the remarkable thing is that there were tens of thousands of radicals who voted.

In Caldwell's own county over 2,300 Republican votes were cast—true, over a thousand below that of two years before, but there were the votes. And in the state as a whole, while the Democrats won by over 30,000 nevertheless there were 67,171 Republican votes counted. And twenty-two our of seventy-four counties were won by Republicans, a Negro Republican, John R. Lynch, was re-elected to Congress (with considerable white support), and sixteen Negroes were returned to the state House of Representatives, in spite of everything.[8]

Clearly, from the Bourbon's viewpoint, the victory of 1875 was much too uncertain to permit them to dispense with terror. No, the leaders whose names had been ostentatiously entered on "death lists" during the election and who still survived must be eliminated. High on that list was such a one as Charles Caldwell, and his murder came quickly.

It happened on Christmas Day 1875, and this is how it was:

Living with the Caldwells was a nephew named David Washington. Early that Christmas David was in a Clinton blacksmith shop when several white men, whom he knew, entered. They wanted to know how many he, David, had killed on the day of the Moss Hill Riot, and did he come to town now to kill more, and if not what was he doing in town anyway? David hurried home and told his aunt about this, and she said, "Don't go out anymore. Probably they are trying to get up a fuss here."

Late in the afternoon Caldwell came home from work, learned of the conversation and went into town "to see about it." He returned shortly, had his dinner, and just before sundown went back to the village.

There was a friend (white or Negro does not appear in the evidence—a Judas, in any case), named Buck Cabell, greeted him and this was returned, for Caldwell "never knowed nothing against him." Cabell insisted that Caldwell go with him to Chilton's store and let himself be treated, on this holiday, to a drink. The two men went to the store's basement, poured their drinks, lifted their glasses, and then " . . .at the tap of the glasses . . . as they struck their glasses, that was the signal to shoot." And he was shot in the back of the head by someone "from the outside of the gate window, and he fell to the ground."

In the streets stood the assassins—many of them. But Caldwell was not yet dead. He called for Judge Cabaniss, "a particular friend," but the judge did not come, and he called for the storeowner, but he did not come, and he called for "I don't know who else. They were all around, and nobody went to his relief; all of them men standing around with their guns." Finally one Preacher Nelson went to the cellar door and called in to Caldwell not to shoot him and he'd just come to him. Caldwell said he would not harm him, just "take me out of the cellar" for he "wanted to die in the open air, and did not want to die like a dog closed up."

Preacher Nelson carried him to the street and Caldwell asked that they "take him home and let him see his wife before he died; that he could not live long." But they would not do it; instead "they all cried, 'We'll save him while we got him; dead men tell no tales'." Caldwell "never begged them" and he stood up and then "taking both sides of his coat and bringing them up so, he said, 'remember when you kill me you kill a gentleman and a brave man. Never say you killed a coward. I want you to remember it when I am gone.'" Then "they riddled him with thirty or forty of their loads" and he was dead. And Preacher Nelson told his widow that "a braver man never died than Charles Caldwell."

Just then up the streets of Clinton rode Caldwell's brother, Sam, a man quite unlike Charles, a mild man, "never known to shoot a gun or pistol in his life never know how," but they killed him, too, for fear he would spread the alarm.

Yes, the alarm did reach the Negro community; it was still early—"the moon was quite young, and the chapel bell rang" and this was the signal of danger. "When the bell tolled [the Negro men] rushed right out; they went through the door and some slid down the window and over they sprang; some went over the fence. They all ran to the chapel and got their guns"—one hundred and fifty guns and then they stood guard over their homes.

Later that evening the bodies of Charles and Sam Caldwell—Sam's wife now alone with three young ones—were brought home and laid out and the widows mourned. But not in peace did they mourn, for Caldwell's murder had so enraged the Negro people that the planters felt a need for reinforcements, and in from Vicksburg once again came the Modocs. And once again they called on Mrs. Caldwell. It was now one o'clock in the morning of the 26th.

"They all marched up to my house," said Mrs. Caldwell, "and went into where the two dead bodies laid, and they cursed them, those dead bodies, there, and they danced and threw open the window, and sung all their songs, and challenged the dead body to get up and meet them." "Get up and fight," they said to Charles Caldwell, and then they struck him, but this time, for the first and only time, Caldwell did not meet their challenge and did not answer blow for blow.

With such blood fertilizing its soil, the *Commercial and Financial Chronicle* of New York could well tell its subscribers that the South "now presents a more hopeful condition than any other portion of the country. She is virtually out of debt; her people have learned to economize . . . labor is under control for the first time since the war, and next year will be more entirely so, permitting of further economies . . ."

So perished, as the chroniclers of Mississippi have asserted, "a notorious and turbulent Negro." Those having different values may find other adjectives.

It is altogether likely that one day Mississippi school children, Negro and white, will be taught to revere the name and to hold precious the memory of Charles Caldwell.

Notes

1. Alcorn topped a devious career by serving as one of the two Republicans in the 1890 Bourbon constitutional convention and voting there to disfranchise the Negro people. He was typical of many wealthy Southern planters—mostly pre–Civil War Whigs—who joined the Reconstruction Republicans or advocated cooperation with the Negroes in order to prevent fundamental change. See D. H. Donald, "The Scalawag in Mississippi Reconstruction," in the *Journal of Southern History* (1944), 10, pp. 447–60; and note the testimony of Josiah A. Campbell, a top Bourbon politician and one of the forty-nine signers of the Confederate constitution, in the *Boutwell Report*, p. 937, where he admitted his object in forming "an alliance with the negroes politically . . . [was to] acquire ascendancy over them, and become their teachers and controllers. . . ."

2. This militia order was too much even for the federal commander, Major-General Slocum, politically sympathetic though he was to Johnson and to Sharkey. He therefore countermanded it, but told General Sherman: "I did not like to take this step; but Sharkey should have consulted me before issuing an order arming the rebels—and placing them on duty with the darkies in every county of the State. I hope the U.S. Military will soon be removed from the State, but until this is done it would certainly be bad policy to arm the militia."—dated August 27, 1865—*In Memoriam Henry Warner Slocum* (Albany, 1904), p. 105. President Johnson ordered the general to rescind his own order and to allow Gov. Sharkey to proceed with the forming of the militia, an act Carl Schurz believed "the most unwarranted trick yet perpetrated at Washington."—letter to his wife, Sept. 2, 1865, in F. Bancroft, ed., *Speeches, Correspondence and Political Papers of Carl Schurz* (6 vols., N.Y., 1913), 1, p. 267. General Slocum resigned in September to head the Democratic ticket in the 1865 elections in New York. Before departing he was dined by the gentry of Vicksburg and there toasted Sharkey as "a sound statesman and true patriot. May he long be spared to the state he has served so well." An analysis of the class allegiance and political affiliations of Army administrators after the Civil War—indeed, throughout American history—has been almost completely ignored and with great damage to realistic historiography.

3. In Mississippi, as throughout the South, the Negro's desire for the land was acute

and his belief in an impending land distribution was widespread. Contemporary sources are filled with this. To cite one witness referring to this state in the summer of 1865, " . . .they ardently desire to become freeholders. In the independent possession of landed property they see the consummation of their deliverance . . . it must be admitted that this instinct is correct."—Carl Schurz's Report to the President, *Senate Ex. Doc. No. 2*, 59th Cong, 1st Sess., p. 31.

4. There is, frequently, a profound distinction between the enunciation of policy from the top and its actual execution in practice, especially when the top levels themselves are split. Congress might legislate on Reconstruction policy, the president appointed most of the administrators of that policy. Thus, for example, in Mississippi, the military commanders, Generals Ord and Gillen—Johnson's appointees—were not radical Reconstructionists, the latter in particular being a personal friend of the president. We find, then, that the 1865 legislature is allowed to reassemble late in 1866 and early in 1867. In accord with congressional legislation it repealed the anti-landowning provisions of the Black Code and allowed Negroes to testify but not to serve as jurors. Most of the Apprenticeship Law of 1865 was repealed, but a convict-leasing system was instituted. *Laws of the State of Mississippi at a Called Session . . . Oct., 1866 and Jan. and Feb. 1867* (Jackson, 1867) pp. 252, 554, 736. Perhaps the crowning act of these individuals was that in which they adopted the report of one of their joint committees recommending that the legislature decline to ratify the 14th Amendment, while "an expression in the report that it was beneath the dignity of the State to hold any communication with Secretary of State Seward on the subject received special applause." J. L. Power, "The Black and Tan Convention" in *Proceedings of Mississippi Hist. Soc.* (1900), 3, p. 76.

5. Alcorn resigned his governorship in November 1871, and took his seat in the Senate to which the legislature had earlier elected him. While there he opposed in December 1871, Sumner's Civil Rights Bill, demanding: "Give us the removal of our disabilities (*i.e.*, disfranchisement of top Confederate figures and officials] and I will go with him who goes farthest to demand of the southern people obedience to the law. Down, then, with the Klu Klux, and I will go with you in all that is necessary to enforce that demand."—*Cong. Globe,* 42nd Cong., 2nd sess., p. 247 (in 1872 the disabilities were removed). In a speech on the floor of the Senate Alcorn broke completely, and bitterly, with Ames. The later, a native of Massachusetts, had risen to the rank of general in the Union Army (as an artillery lieutenant he had won the Congressional Medal of Honor) and was prominent in military affairs in Mississippi prior to aligning himself with the left-wing of the Republican Party. Benjamin F. Butler was his father-in-law. A biography of Ames is needed.

6. This was a New York businessman, George K. Chase. It clear that while Chase's own agents reported violence almost everywhere so that he himself told Pierrepont on October 28, 1875—rather late!—"It is impossible to have a fair election on November 2 without the aid of U.S. Troop," his central function was to help maintain a resemblance of order—*Boutwell Report,* 2, pp. 1801–19.

7. Nov. 4, 1875, 21, p. 285. Somewhat belatedly—on July 26, 1876—President Grant confessed to Governor Chamberlain of South Carolina, that, "Mississippi is governed today by officials chosen through fraud and violence such as would scarcely be credited to savages, much less to a civilized and Christian people." *The Nation,* Aug. 10, 1876, 23, p. 81. A Federal Grand Jury reported from Oxford, July 8, 1876, " . . .we must say that the fraud, intimidation and violence at the late election is without a parallel in the annals of history . . ." *Boutwell Report,* 2, Doc. Evid., pp. 105f. The findings of the Senate committee were the same, but, as *The Nation* declared: "Senator Boutwell's report seems to meet with universal condemnation from the Republican press . . ."—Aug. 17, 1876, 23, p. 97. Reconstruction was old stuff, the Hayes-Tilden bargain was soon to be struck—let's get on with the Lord's work, getting rich. Was not Bishop William Lawrence of Massachusetts to usher in the twentieth century by remarking, "Godliness is in league with riches"?

8. Statistics from official figures in the *Boutwell Report,* 2, Doc. Evid., pp. 144–45. Mechanically comparing the Republican vote of 1875 with the Ames vote of 1873, as does Donald, "The Scalawag in Mississippi Reconstruction," in the *Journal of Southern History* (1944), 10, p. 459, and concluding that the Republicans polled only 3,000 less in the former year than in the latter is completely unrealistic and ignores the fact that the 1873 election saw both candidates running, nominally, as Republicans, thus splitting the vote. The idea that Negro political activity and struggle simply and immediately ceased with the overthrow of Reconstruction, while very widespread, is quite erroneous. In Mississippi, for example, the pattern of 1875 was repeated at each election until 1890, when the illegal disfranchisement of the Negro was put into the constitution—a constitution, by the way, never ratified by the people. But that requires a separate study.

11

Literacy: The Negro and World War II

Modern educational and social psychologists, interested in the question of the comparative intelligence of peoples varying in class status, cultural pattern, and ethnic origins, or combinations of these differences, have long dreamed of a particular type of experiment. This dream experiment was one which would involve scores of thousands of subjects of all groups, classes, and backgrounds. These subjects would be carefully tested and sorted, and would all be about equally deficient in a common skill or aptitude. They would then be put through a learning process—not a mere test—and that process would be conducted by carefully selected teachers who would be provided with all the equipment that they needed and desired. The motivation of the subjects would be nurtured, and the rapport between teachers and learners would be good. The learning process would be continual for the period of the experiment, and it would not be broken by subjecting the examinees to other and extraneous environments while it was being conducted. And the living conditions of the subjects would be excellent and as uniform as could be established. Finally, having achieved these ideal conditions and situations, the experiment would climax with an objective test to discover whether or not the common deficiency had indeed been eliminated.

Exigencies of the Second World War made possible, as we shall show, the realization, in very large part, of this dream. But to appreciate the full significance of this, it is necessary that one understand the reality that called it forth.

The fact is that educational and social psychology has been and still is plagued by what is termed the nature-nurture controversy as concerns the comparative intelligence of peoples. Starting some fifty years ago, so-called "intelligence tests" were developed in America and in Europe as the result of social needs. Their purpose was to provide a measuring rod of the learning capabilities (as deduced from past accomplishment) of individuals for obvious uses in educational, vocational, and industrial fields.

Very soon after the formulation of these tests their function was distorted, and vicious conclusions based upon this distortion were announced. The view was expounded that these tests did not demonstrate merely the level of learning capabilities attained under given conditions and as ascertained by specific questions; but rather that they were instruments measuring an innate, unchangeable quality of human beings—labeled intelligence—and that, therefore, where particular groups did poorly on these tests those results scientifically proved the innate inferiority of those groups. Using these tests uncritically, and applying them as indicated, one was able to assert that science had demonstrated the innate inferiority of the rural folk as compared to the urban, of the poor as compared to the rich, and of the Negro (predominantly rural and poor, anyway) as compared to the white.

It did not matter to these mythologists masquerading as scientists that the pioneers in testing, the creators of the tests, had themselves denounced these tests, had themselves denounced these interpretations. Thus, for example, the greatest of these pioneers, the Frenchman, Binet, had explicitly denounced "some recent philosophers" who supported "the deplorable verdict that the intelligence of an individual is a fixed quantity . . .,"[1] and had, himself, experimentally increased some scores made on his tests by the same individuals by changing conditions affecting them. And, again, an American pioneer in this field had been careful to point out that the tests could have validity in terms of ascertaining native ability, only "when we compare individuals in a group who have had common experiences," and that, "tests are valid only within a group who have had identical or very similar opportunities for gaining familiarity with the materials of the test, and who have not only the same opportunity to learn, but the same desire to learn."[2]

And these mythologists persist in promulgating their notions—which, being attuned to and derived from the demands of the socio-economic status quo and functioning as props for that status quo, retain a widespread popular acceptance[3]—notwithstanding the series of devastating blows dealt them in recent years.

Let us summarize these blows. First, is the fact that the median score of Negroes on intelligence tests is practically identical with (indeed, slightly higher) than that recorded for some white groups, such as Portuguese, Italians, and Mexicans.[4] Second is the fact that in several tests, where environmental conditions were approximately the same, the scores of Negroes matched, and at times surpassed, those made by whites.[5] Third is the fact that where environmental conditions for Negroes may be assumed to be better than that for whites, the former scores have been higher than the latter.[6] Fourth, studies have demonstrated, as a rule, that improving environmental conditions improves scores obtained in tests. This has been true, of course, not only of Negroes, but of all other peoples. The cumulative effect of environment—good or bad—upon scores has also been demonstrated. Fifth, the intimate connection among such things as formal education, rapport, and motivation, in all of which Negroes are, generally, at a disadvantage, and scores obtained on intelligence tests is established without any question.[7]

Of even more importance than all of the previous, however, and that phase of reality which has been most decisively responsible for evoking the dream that has been described, is the fact that the validity of the intelligence tests as scientific instruments for measuring any and all population groups, has been seriously, and successfully challenged.

Otto Klineberg has demonstrated and insisted upon the importance of cultural and environmental factors in explaining and accounting for differences in scores. Another has shown, specifically, that one particular cultural distinction—that between urban and rural groups—is important, and that, since the intelligence tests generally in use were standardized by using examples, it is to be expected that their results would favor urban folk. In addition, it has been demonstrated that a test standardized on rural individuals resulted in lower scores for urban examinees.[8] The importance of this for the Negro—so largely rural—is obvious.

Moreover, application of the tests now in use have uniformly resulted in lower scores for the poor and higher scores for the middle class and the rich. An essential reason for this, in addition to the data presented above, is that *the intelligence tests were standardized using white, urban, middle- and upper-class subjects.* Employing the tests, therefore, as measures of some absolute quality labeled "intelligence" is not merely unfair, but is absolutely invalid, absolutely unscientific. Such a procedure is analogous to using a linear standard to measure a liquid and speaking of a gallon of wood, for example.

This is why a psychologist recently wrote, after surveying the literature on this question: " . . .that these tests cannot be used for measuring the capacity of different social levels within our own society . . . [and that] the mean difference in IQ found to exist between children of the lowest and highest status may be accounted for entirely in environmental terms."[9]

A final point bearing on the validity of the results obtained from these tests must be mentioned. This is the fact that these results are expressed in terms of quotient (IQ) in which the mental score age is divided by a chronological score age. But this mathematical process presupposes that the two scores possess a constant relationship. This basic presupposition "in point of fact does not exist" as a leading psychologist has written very recently.[10]

Thus, we have a situation where mathematical figures derived from a nonexistent relationship and based upon measuring instruments standardized upon particular sets of subjects, are used to describe levels allegedly attained by different sets of subjects! And, to confound confusion, these levels are then put forth as marking the innate intellectual capabilities of the individuals concerned, which is contrary to the avowed intent of the inventors of the very instruments from which the levels were derived!

With this as the situation one can readily understand the origin of the dream delineated in the beginning of this paper,[11] and the crucial character of the results of the realization of that dream becomes readily apparent.

As has been remarked, the necessities of war accounted for this realization. In the First Report of the Director of Selective Service, he quite frankly remarked that he had believed, upon assuming his task, that he was dealing with a "literate America."[12] The result of this assumption was that the first regulation of Selective Service on literacy, promulgated in the winter of 1940, stated that those registrants "who passed the physical examination and could understand orders given in the English language" were acceptable.

What immediately followed disillusioned General Hershey as to the literate quality of large masses of the American population. In the first place, it was found that in the two registrations prior to Pearl Harbor there were over 347,000 men who made their marks on cards because they were unable to write their names, and that of these over 125,000 were white and over 220,000 were Negro.[13] Secondly, and as a consequence of the practical absence of literacy requirements for induction, about 60,000 illiterate men entered the Army in the half-year prior to the onset of war.[14]

These illiterates, thrust into the midst of desperate efforts to mold a modern war machine, were, generally, "useless to commanders,"[15] and, though some feeble efforts were undertaken "to make them more literate" even these were largely abandoned, for "under the circumstances of peacetime . . . the Army felt its facilities and personnel could be more profitably used."[16]

Thus it came about that, on May 14, 1941, the Army, by regulation, announced that no registrant possessing an education less than that attained by one who had completed the fourth grade in an American elementary school was to be inducted. This, it was believed, "was certainly a low enough minimum," but facts and necessities were to prove the contrary.[17] Within six weeks after the promulgation of this regulation about 55,000 registrants were deferred because of it, and by September 15, 1941, this number had increased to over 140,000 men, of whom about 60,000 were white and the remainder Negro.[18]

The situation was critical. Thus, during the three months from April through June 1942, it was found that of every thousand whites rejected, illiteracy, as defined by the regulation of May 1941, accounted for over thirty-eight, and of every thousand Negroes rejected, it accounted for one hundred twelve. Moreover, figures compiled at about that time showed that of all men then registered, except those with dependent children, approximately three-quarters of a million (about half million white, quarter million Negro), though physically fit, might be lost to the armed forces because of insufficient schooling.[19] When it is remembered that the United States, at the conclusion of the war, had put into the field no more than eighty-nine combat divisions (i.e., about one million men) the meaning of this educational failing, in terms of the very life of the nation, becomes clear.

Remedial action was vital. New Army regulations announced that, effective August 1, 1941, "any registrant who is able to understand simple orders in English and who possesses sufficient intelligence to absorb military training rapidly is eligible for induction into the military service."[20] To prevent wholesale swamping, however, it was added that the number of men unable to read and write English in a fourth grade standard accepted for induction on any one day at any station was not to exceed ten percent of the white and ten percent of the Negro registrants.

Nevertheless, General McNary informed the Senate Committee on Military Affairs on October 14, 1942, that "The Army has inducted 135,000 illiterates."[21] Thus, the situation remained unsatisfactory.

On December 5, 1942, a Presidential Executive Order stopped all voluntary enlistments, and also placed upon the Selective Service Administration the responsibility of supplying men for the Navy. This, together with the impending decision of the Navy to accept Negroes provoked a restudy of the entire problem of the induction of illiterates. The decision (taken February 1, 1943) was to revert to the fourth-grade educational test for induction into both services, but "the Army would not accept educationally deficient selectees not to exceed five percent of the total number of men accepted and assigned to the Army by color at each induction center on each day."[22]

This makeshift [solution] for an intolerable condition lasted but four months, and on June 1, 1943, both the Army and the Navy began to accept all registrants who passed certain intelligence tests, with no limitation on percentage of illiterates. This, however, was no improvement in terms of solving the manpower problem. Indeed, as might have been foreseen, under this arrangement the rate of rejection was even greater than before, particularly for Negroes. This was so, because to the "educational and cultural background" that had accounted for the high rate of rejection under the illiteracy requirement, were now added, since tests were given, the conditions under which this was done, and "attitudes of the tests" plus the "resulting non-cooperative attitudes on the part of the registrants."[23] Indicative of the consequence is the fact that as of September 1, 1943, it has been estimated that over 340,000 men were placed in class IV-F because of educational deficiency.[24]

The problem, resulting from generations of chronic and inexcusable social injustice, was insoluble, in any immediate sense. Remedial action was possible and necessary, however, and this was introduced in earnest by the Army in June 1943. At that time, Special Training Units were created with the purpose of giving those illiterates who had survived the so-called intelligence tests, an intensive thirteen-week course (later reduced to eight to twelve weeks) aimed at the specific task of raising them to a minimum literacy level equivalent to that obtained as the result of successfully completing the fourth grade in an "average" elementary school.[25]

Here, then, one had men from many walks of life, of all colors, creeds, and nationalities, from all sections of the country, from urban and rural backgrounds, identified only by a common intellectual failing—illiteracy. The theoretical value of the experiment in terms of the question of comparative intelligence is enhanced, too, by the fact that these men were to be subjected not to a mere test of brief duration, but were to be put through a learning process of appreciable duration, the results of which had a relatively well-defined and objective base—namely, have the subjects overcome their illiteracy to the indicated level? When it is remembered that fundamental to all definitions of intelligence is the idea of "ability to learn," or "ability to meet new situations quickly and successfully"[26] the significance of this effort becomes clearer.

The plan of the experiment was as follows:[27] Illiterates accepted for training in the Special Training Units were to receive psychological interviews, and careful medical tests. They were then to be given placement tests designed to reveal their degree of functional literacy, as a result of which they were to be placed in classes of appropriate levels. In addition, periodic achievement tests were to be administered and men reassigned, if necessary, as a result of these findings, thus permitting them to advance as quickly as possible, and assuring an homogeneous content (in terms of learning standards) to the classes.

The classes were to be small (not over about eighteen members was the desideratum), and the teachers were to be carefully selected for ability and eagerness. The content of the material presented to the students was to be alive and functionally useful, and related to their own experiences, both past and present. Expense was not to be spared, and physical facilities and training aids were to be excellent, practical, and helpful. Negro teachers were to be employed extensively for Negro students. Special attention was to be given to motivation and morale of the students. Not all the work was to be academic, but rather physical exercises and some military training were to be included. Of course, the living conditions of the subjects (food, clothing, medical service, etc.) were to be the equal of the average domestic army post.

This was the plan and, of course, as in all plans made by and for human beings, there was no identity between the concept and the execution. It is certain that not all the teachers and administrators (company commanders) were of equal quality, and it is likely that some were poor. Certain it is, too, that in different units there existed varying levels of motivation and morale, and that even physical conditions varied somewhat throughout the experiment.

It is likewise a fact that the plan itself envisaged no breaking away from the Jim Crow pattern of the Army. In the words of the Acting Deputy Director of Military Training of the Army Service Forces: "There were some Negro special training units as such. The majority of the units contained both Negroes and whites, who were organized into separate companies and instructed separately."[28] It is true, too, that while Negro instructors were used in Negro units, many Negro classes in general units were taught by white instructors, and the latter were not always entirely free of that bigotry which plagues our nation.

Yet the great fact remains that the plan was carried out substantially as envisaged, and that scores of thousands of American received, finally, a fraction of that education which is supposed to be their birthright.

Specifically, one is able to present these data: From June 1943 through October 1944 approximately 180,000 men were placed in Army Special Training Units as functional illiterates. Of this number about 150,000 (85%) successfully completed their training and attained—or were said to have attained—a basic degree of literacy.[29] Among the 150,000 men just mentioned, 86,670 were Negroes.[30]

Of particular importance is the fact that of the whites who entered these units during the aforesaid period 84.2 percent successfully completed it, while 15.8 percent failed and were discharged from the army. Of the Negroes who entered these units during the same period 87.1 percent successfully completed it, and 12.9 percent failed and were discharged. "In other words," as General Trudeau has stated, "experience in the Army indicates that a slightly higher percentage of Negroes than the whites successfully complete the Special Training Program, i.e., achieve fourth grade standards in reading, language, and arithmetic and demonstrate sufficient mastery of pre-basic military subjects to warrant their being forwarded for regular training."[31] It may further be remarked that no great difference between Negro and white appeared in the speed with which this learning process was accomplished, for while 71.7 percent of the Negroes completed the training in less than sixty days, the comparable figure for the whites was 75.6 percent.

The conclusion is clear. The learning accomplishment of scores of thousands of Negroes from all sections of the country over an extended period of time compares quite favorably with that attained by scores of thousands of similarly diversified whites, in this greatest experiment of its kind ever conducted by the American government. And the other striking characteristic of this experiment is the fact that the conditions to which Negroes and whites were subjected were fairly similar—certainly more nearly similar than are the conditions under which Negroes and whites live, work, and study in the conventional American civilian pattern.

These data not only constitute a shattering blow to racists, but present a challenge to their opponents to urge and to demand that their government do in peacetime what it felt had to be done and what it at least began to do in wartime—namely, conduct an all-out, scientific, and democratic assault upon the twin disgraces of illiteracy and educational integrity that remain as huge blights upon the lives of untold millions of its citizens.

Notes

1. A. Binet, *Les Ideés Modernes sur les Enfants* (Paris, 1909), pp. 141–46.

2. Stephen S. Colvin, "Principles underlying the construction and use of intelligence tests," in *The 21st Yearbook of the National Society for the Study of Education* (Bloomington, 1922), pp. 19, 20, 23. Emphases in original.

3. For an example showing this popular acceptance see E. L. Horowitz, "'Race' Attitudes," in O. Klineberg, *Characteristics of the American Negro* (N.Y., 1944), p. 226.

4. *Ibid.*, p. 35.

5. Thus, early tests by Stetson (1897), Ferguson (1916), and Bunne (1917) found Negroes getting equal or higher scores in the entire tests or in critical sections thereof. Tests by Peterson and Lanier (*Mental Measurement Monographs*, 1929, 5, pp. 1–156)

showed higher scores for whites in Nashville, very slightly higher in Chicago, and identical in New York. Practically identical scores were found by McAlpin in Washinton in 1932 (*Journal of Negro Education*, 1, pp. 44ff.) and Long had the same result there in 1934 (*ibid.*, 3, pp. 805ff.). Note, too, the well-known test of five hundred Negro youngsters in the Los Angeles (1925) by Clark, where the scores achieved by them (median of 104.7) was slightly higher than that of the whites (*Education Research Bulletin*, Los Angeles City Schools, 1925).

6. An outstanding example of this is, of course, the result of the Army Intelligence tests during the First World War, in which Negroes from Pennsylvania, New York, Illinois, and Ohio achieved higher median scores than whites from Mississippi, Kentucky, Arkansas, and Georgia.

7. Specific documentation of these facts would cover almost the entire literature of educational psychology for the past twenty years. As examples, see W. C. Ragley, *Determinism in education* (Baltimore, 1925); Clark Foreman, *Environmental factors in Negro elementary education* (N.Y., 1832); O. Klineberg, *Race Differences* (N.Y., 1935); and *The 39th Yearbook of the National Society for the Study of Fducation* (Bloomington, 1940), Part 1.

8. M. F. Shimberg, "An investigation into the validity of norms with special reference to urban and rural groups," *Archives of Psychology* (1929), No. 104. For an awareness of this problem of standardization see David Wechsler, *The Measurement of Adult Intelligence* (3rd edit., Baltimore, 1944), chapter 8. Of his own devices, the Wechsler-Bellevue Seale, he writes (p. 107): "We have eliminated the 'colored' vs. 'white' factor by admitting at the onset that our norms cannot be used for the colored populations of the United States."

9. Walter S. Neff, "Socio-economic status and intelligence," in *Pyschological Bulletin* (1938), 25, pp. 727–56. Emphases in original. For a critique of Neff, which does not refute his basic point, see Hollingworth, Terman, and Oden, "The significance of deviates," in *The 39th Yearbook of the National Society for the Study of Education* (Bloomington, 1940), Part 1, p. 48.

10. Wechsler, *The Measurement of Adult Intelligence* (3rd edit., Baltimore, 1944), p. 12.

11. For lamentations over the fact that experiments such as the one described in this paper were impractical for they would be "so difficult and expensive," see Hollingworth, Terman, and Oden, "The significance of deviates," in *The 39th Yearbook of the National Society for the Study of Education* (Bloomington, 1940), Part 1, p. 49.

12. *Selective Service in Peacetime: First Report of the Director of Selective Service 1940–41* (Washington, 1942), p. 174.

13. *Selective Service in Wartime Second Report of the Director of Selective Service 1941–42* (Washington, 1943), p. 230.

14. *Selective Service in Peacetime* . . . p. 174.

15. *Selective Service as the Tide of War Turns: The Third Report of the Director of Selective Service 1942–44* (Washington, 1945), p. 207.

16. *Selective Service in Peacetime* . . . p. 174.

17. *Idem.*

18. It may, perhaps, be unnecessary to remark, as does General Hershey (*Selective Service in Peacetime* . . . p. 259), that this very much higher rate of illiteracy for Negroes as compared to whites exists "not because Negroes resist education or for any other reason than that 'educational opportunities just are not available to them.'" It is of particular interest to note that while the percentage of Negroes rejected from May 15–September 15, 1941, because of illiteracy (12.3%) is about eleven times that of the white rate (1.1%), in fifteen states the rejection rate for Negroes was less than the total percentage of white rejections and that in twenty-six states the rejection rate for Negroes was less than that for whites in ten Southern states. See *The Black and White of Rejections for Military Service* (American Teachers Assn., Montgomery, Ala., 1944), p.3.

19. *Selective Service in Peacetime* . . . p. 174, *Selective Service in Wartime* . . . p. 231.

20. *Selective Service in Wartime* . . . p. 232.

21. *Selective Service in Wartime* . . . p. 231.

22. *Selective Service as the Tide of War Turns* . . . pp. 207–8.

23. *Idem.*

24. *Black and White of Military Rejections* . . . p. 5.

25. *Selective Service as the Tide of War Turns* . . . p. 208.

26. H. C. Warren, ed., *Dictionary of Psychology* (Boston, 1934), p. 140; Colvin, "Principles underlying the construction and use of intelligence tests," in *The 21st Yearbook of the National Society for the Study of Education* (Bloomington, 1922), p. 154; F. N. Freeman, "The meaning of intelligence," in *The 39th Yearbook* . . . p. 18; P. Witty, "New evidence on the learning ability of the Negro," in *Journal of Abnormal and Social Psychology,* pp. 401–404 (1945).

27. For descriptions of the work of the Special Training Units, see: A. G. Trudeau, "Army experiences and problems of Negro education," in *Education for Victory* 3: pp. 13, 16 (1945); P. Witty, "New evidence on the learning ability of the Negro," in *Journal of Abnormal and Social Psychology*, (1945), pp. 401–4; S. Goldberg, "Psychological Procedures Employed in the Army's Special Training Units," in *Journal of Clinical Psychology,* 1: pp. 118–25 (1945); P. Witty and S. Goldberg, "The use of visual aids in Special Training Units in the Army," in *The Journal of Educational Psychology* 35: pp. 82–90 (1944); Witty and Goldberg, "Evolution in education through Army experience," *ibid.*, pp. 338–46; Witty and Goldberg, "The Army's training program for illiterate, non-English speaking and educationally retarded men" in *Elementary English Review,* 20: pp. 306–311 (1943); N. Kaplan, "Salvaging illiterates in the Army," in *Occupations,* 6: pp. 23–74 (1944); J. C. Evans, "Adult education for Negroes in the Armed forces" in *Journal of Negro Education* 14: pp. 438–39 (1945). None of these articles is in any sense critical, and all are in reality more descriptive of the plan than its execution.

28. Letter from Colonel R. M. Prouty to the present writer, dated Washington, March 5, 1946.

29. Figures created by men and dealing with men are subject to error. The writer has heard, from people whose opinions he respects, of men who completed STU work but remained illiterate. Pressure did exist, it may be believed, on administrators to make as good records—on paper if necessary—as possible. Yet these figures are official, nothing else exists, and the numbers involved are so vast that individual irregularities probably would not materially affect the percentages.

30. Figures from letter from Col. S. M. Prouty to present writer, dated Washington, March 18, 1946.

31. A. G. Trudeau, "Army experiences and problems of Negro education," in *Education for Victory* 3: p. 14.

12

The Negro People in America: A Critique of Gunnar Myrdal's "An American Dilemma"

I. What is a Dilemma?

The annual report for 1938 of the president of the Carnegie Corporation announced that it had "for some time felt the need of a general study of the Negro in the United States." And it was thought to be essential that the "study be made under the direction of a person who would be free [from] presuppositions and emotional charges." Accordingly, the corporation's eyes turned to Sweden and discovered there "a distinguished student," a member of both the faculty of the University of Sweden and of the Senate of Sweden, and an official economic advisor for that government. Thus is it was that, commencing in October 1939, and continuing for a period of about five years, Dr. Gunnar Myrdal, with the help of scores of other learned individuals, conducted the Carnegie study of the American Negro.

The ultimate result appeared in 1944 when Harper issued a two-volume, fifteen-hundred-page, three-quarter-of-a-million-word analysis of the Negro people in America under the title, *An American Dilemma: The Negro Problem and American Democracy.* This work has been hailed, almost universally, and quite uncritically, as "undoubtedly the best study of the problem of the Negro in America which has ever been made," "exhaustive and objective analysis," "the most penetrating and important book on our contemporary civilization that has been written." The somewhat ambiguous term "monumental" has been pinned upon it frequently, and quite recently it has been announced that it "is accepted as definitive." It has, moreover, been pointed out that men like Otto Klineberg, Franz Boas, and W. E. B. Du Bois were consulted in connection with it so it is felt certain "that the facts are authentic and the study of the highest calibre." The study has had and continues to have great influence and wide circulation. It has been condensed and issued in pamphlet form by the Public Affairs Committee and by others, and serves as an allegedly authoritative text for innumerable interracial and intercultural clubs, councils, committees, and groups. From all this praise it is necessary to make vigorous dissent. Not only is it true, as shall be shown, that the work contains numerous and serious misstatements of fact, but it is also true, and this is of crucial importance, that the work—which is meant to be, as Myrdal states, "an analysis, not a description" (p. li)—is based upon a fallacious philosophic concept. This fact vitiates the entire book, and leads one to assert not only that it is not definitive, but that it is vicious.

While it is true that many eminent experts were called upon to assist in the Carnegie study—like Boas, Klineberg, and Du Bois—it is not true that they, in their own writings and thinking, tend to agree with the analysis and interpretation of Myrdal. The contrary is the fact, for the distinguished late anthropologist, the social psychologist, and the historian maintain positions on the Negro question directly contrary to that adopted by him whom they advised.

It may be asked whether there is anything of value in the two volumes. The answer is yes, there are some things of value. The book contains interesting and keen insights into the minds of—significantly—middle- and upper-class whites and Negroes, and apt material on the vested interests in segregation that lead some of the latter to adopt reactionary attitudes generally and even specifically towards the aspirations of their own people (pp. 38–43, 767, 795–97, 1395). Statistical data, as obtained from the census and other official or semi-official sources, on numerous socio-economic aspects of Negro life, are conveniently (though, at times, as shown below, inaccurately) presented (chapters 7, 14, 15, 16, and appendix 6). Even here, however, a reader would do better to go to the work on which this material is based, namely Richard Sternber's *The Negro's Share.* Again, the *description* of the *mechanics* of discrimination is valuable (chapters 24–27) if one cannot find the time to go through Charles S. Johnson's *Patterns of Segregation* upon which it is based. But this job of summarization and condensation (marred as it is by too frequent errors) certainly does not warrant hailing the word as definitive, particularly since it forms but a minor portion of the total book, and since it is ensconced in the midst of weak and dubious interpretation.

Pertinent to a critique of the Myrdal work is the question: what is a dilemma? Webster tells us that a dilemma is "a situation involving choice, especially in actions, between equally unsatisfactory alternatives." It is perhaps understandable how an advisor to and an official of the government of Sweden, which treated the late war against fascism as a dilemma and preferred neutrality (especially a neutrality made lucrative by "necessary" trading with Nazi Germany) might decide to christen the fact of the exploitation and oppression of the American Negro people dilemma—"a situation involving choice . . . between equally unsatisfactory alternatives." Nor is it surprising to find such an individual clearly in error in his own thinking about fascism, so that he writes (p. 1311): "modern fascism and Nazism . . . are no more like conservatism than radicalism but could, perhaps, best be characterized as a peculiar blend of reactionism and radicalism." Let it not be believed that this choice of a title, this label of dilemma, is fortuitous or the result of the misapprehension of a common enough word. In the first place, a title is carefully selected. In the second place, the same word recurs throughout the work (pp. 390, 507, 629, 749, 795, 809, 1003, 1319) and is used to characterize the entire ninth and last part of the second volume. And, finally, the philosophy motivating the study leads inevitably to the conclusion that the Negro question is an insoluble problem, and does, indeed, represent a dilemma.

II. Myrdal's Philosophy

Myrdal explicitly repudiates a materialistic concept of society and adopts that of an idealist. For him, therefore, the status of the American Negro represents a moral problem. The work's introduction is entitled, "The Negro Problem as Moral Issue." We are told, in italics that (xliii):

> *The American Negro problem is a problem in the heart of the American. . . . This is the central viewpoint of this treatise."* It follows from this that: "*What we usually call 'social trends' have their main significance for the Negro's status because of what is in white people's minds. . . . The important changes in the Negro problem do not consist of or have close relations with 'social trends' in the narrower meaning of the term but are made up of changes in people's beliefs and valuations* (990).

How delightfully nebulous are these phrases, "heart," "mind"! Indeed, Myrdal devotes an entire page to a discussion of the "totally irrational, actually magical belief" (100) behind anti-Negro prejudice. Time after time he refers to "this magical sphere of the white man's mind . . . deep and mystical sense," and finds that he can only lament "the difficulties in expressing it in rational language and explaining it in such a way that it makes sense."

How quickly the commercial press pounded upon these fundamental conclusions! *The New Republic* hastened to agree that, "The American Negro problem is a problem in the heart of every American." *Time,* putting it somewhat more pathetically, confesses that "America is continuously struggling for its soul," while David L. Cohn, borrowing the very words of Nazism, says, "it is at bottom a blood or sexual problem." The haste ill-concealed the joy to find so pretentious and academically respectable a source fortifying their own circumlocutions. For surely, if the status of the Negro is a problem, and if it is a problem in the hearts and minds of every American, and if it is moral in origin, then can there be no solution? And, obviously, there is none, for has it not been labeled a dilemma?

Loud have been the wailings against the dangers of materialism. One who very clearly expressed this bemoaned the alleged fact that in the eighteenth and nineteenth centuries the purposes of social studies "included the appreciation of culture, training in moral values, and the inspiring love of country." But, in our present degraded era, "we tend to look on an understanding of the political, social, and economic world in which we live as the primary aim of the social studies program." And this leads to a belief in "the need for change. . . . A materialist interpretation of past and present problems presupposes a materialist solution. . . . The door is thus directly opened to the 'isms'" and no longer is there full reliance on "inner authority . . . moral and spiritual principles [and] Divine authority."

Having decided that some unaccountably created morality is fundamental to the American Negro's condition, Myrdal does not fail to present his opinion that the dilemma springs from innumerable, interwoven, interdependent, painfully complicated, equally important "causes." This is inevitable for if the disease is incurable, its origins must be unknown, if not—as Myrdal states some of them are—unknowable. And here we are introduced to the "vicious circle," the "principle of cumulation" theory. As the author remarks (1065), this theory "reappears in every part of the book." Since it does, and since it is so important to an understanding of the work, it is given in full. Myrdal states that "the best formulation of our hypothesis (1069n.) is that given by E. R. Embree of the Julius Rosenwald Fund, as follows: There is a vicious circle in caste. At the outset, the despised group is usually inferior in certain of the accepted standards of the controlling class. Being inferior, members of the degraded caste are denied the privileges and opportunities of their fellows and so are more rigorously denied advantages, and so around and around the vicious circle. Even when the movement starts to reverse itself—as it most certainly has in the case of the Negro—there is a desperately long unwinding as a slight increase in good-will gives a little greater chance and this leads to a little higher accomplishment and that to increased respect and so slowly upward toward equality of opportunity, or regard and of status.

There we have a classic statement of the reformist, liberal bourgeois school of moderation pleaders. The entire paragraph is keyed to gradualness: "desperately long unwinding," "slight increase," "a little greater chance," "a little higher accomplishment," "slowly upward." The theory presupposes an identity of interests and values as between the Negro people and the "accepted standards of the controlling class," and there is no doubt that these standards are the standards not only of the "controlling class," but also of Embree—and of Myrdal. The confusion of the concepts of class and caste is also noteworthy. Observe, too, in terms of bourgeois values, how the exploitation and oppression of the "inferior" group are explained on the basis of the latter's so-called inferiority. It is because of their own inferiority that they are "denied the privileges" and this denial accentuates their inferiority, which leads to their being "more rigorously denied advantages." Clear, too, is the mystical quality of the passage, for the crux of the matter, in its own terms, the original "inferiority," and the "desperately long unwinding," the "reversal," are both left unexplained, though these are exactly the items which—assuming for a moment the validity of the analysis—would require explanation. Observe, finally, the absence of "leaps" from this interpretation, the absence of transforming events—mass movements, great and basic alterations, wars, revolutions—an absence which exposes the utter superficiality of the diagnosis.

Each of these characteristics is developed by Myrdal; he does not rest content with merely quoting Embree and with referring about a dozen times to the "vicious circle."

We have referred to the gradualness that is an integral part of the "vicious circle" theory and to the denial of a solution which is implicit in the choice of the word dilemma. These ideas are explicit in Myrdal's work. Thus, at one point, in speaking of his system of multiple causation, in which "there is no 'primary cause' but everything is cause *to* everything else" (78), he finds that "the scientific solution of the Negro problem should thus be given in the form of an interconnected series of quantitative equations, describing the movement of the actual system under various influences. *That this complete, quantitative and truly scientific solution is far beyond the horizon does not need to be pointed out.*" (1069) (My emphasis—H. A.)

The bourgeois values of Myrdal are also given quite explicitly. He states (929n) that to him the terms good and bad are "defined according to our value premise of placing the general American culture 'higher.'" The same bias is apparent in Myrdal's choice of the "friends" of the Negro. To him, "the Negro's friend—or the one who is least unfriendly—is still rather the upper class of white people, the people with economic and social security." (60) And in another place Myrdal names one of these upper class people, Edgar G. Murphy, "who is distinguished as one of the most sincere friends of the Negro among the conservative-minded old Southerners." (1318) This individual, a leader in the Alabama movement to overthrow Reconstruction government and constitution, felt that so far as the Negro is concerned, "the spirit of the South has been the spirit of kindliness and helpfulness. . . . The South gives to him the best gift of a civilization to an individual, the opportunity to live industriously and honestly. . . . The South, must, of course, secure the supremacy of intelligence and property." Such, to Myrdal, is "one of the most sincere friends of the Negro."

The same type of thinking is evident from his political dynamics. Impulses come from and should come from the upper classes, the so-called enlightened. Thus, Myrdal has the audacity to explain "why the Negroes in the South are getting so much [!], and are gradually getting even more, education" (461), on the basis of the presence somewhere within the marrow of the conservative Southerner of the equalitarian American creed! The facts—that only as a result of a Civil War was the Negro's legal right to an education fully established, that the Reconstruction governments fought tooth and nail against these white conservative Southerners in order to realize that right, that these same individuals are responsible for the throttling of Southern education, and that the considerable advances which have been made have been due to organized mass pressure (Negro and white, directed against these same gentlemen) are here ignored and the dynamic cause is ascribed to some progressive kernel seen by Myrdal within the ossified brains of Southern Bourbons! But then, is this not perfectly in line with a philosophy which dismisses "social trends" as inconsequential and ascribes all power to "what is in white people's minds" from some unexplained origin? Again, he asserts that the problem for liberals "appears to be first to lift the masses to security and education and then to work to make them liberal." (73) Ignoring for the moment the materialist conditions here declared by Myrdal himself to be necessary in order to accomplish certain mental innovations, which contradicts his own main thesis (a contradiction that recurs frequently), attention is called to the passivity and clay-like quality ascribed to the "masses." This idea is repeated many times and is typical of the prejudices of the author. Thus, he finds the masses marked by "relative inertia and inarticulateness" and characterizes them as "powerless" and believes an alleged "lack of . . . organized people's movements in America" is "a significant historical fact usually overlooked by American histories." (712–14) Precisely the opposite condition is true. American history consists of demonstrations of the people's efforts, of "organized people's movements," of anything but "inertia" on the part of the masses, and of the efforts of the propertied interests to repress, weather, divert, or vitiate the demands of those masses; while American historiography, at least until the last generation, consisted very largely of works devoted to describing anything but those same mass movements and impulses. Myrdal's caricature of the masses in general prepares us for his opinion of the Negro masses in particular. To him (731) "the Negro masses in the South . . . often become . . . so utterly passive that they simply do not care very much about anything except their animal demands and personal security" while elsewhere the reader is told that "a large portion of the Negro masses is utterly apathetic." (632) This slander, and it is but a small part of the vilification flung at the Negro in this work, as we shall see, represents ignorance, if nothing more, so profound as to be amazing. In this connection, while Myrdal does not hesitate to tell us in detail of the desires of the Negro masses, it is significant that he frequently refers to interviews with upper and middle class whites and Negroes, but in not a single instance throughout the two volumes is there mention of any sort of individualized personal contact—let alone interview—with the poor, either Negro or white!

The class bias of Myrdal is so insistent that he does not refrain from making it explicit by pointing out that his position—that of a liberal reformer—is functionally useful, if not vital, to the maintenance of the basic *status quo.* He asserts that it is "urgent . . . from a conservative point of view *to begin allowing the higher strata of the Negro population to participate in the political process as soon as possible, and to push the movement down gradually.*" (518–19, italics in original) This he rationalizes by slander again, asserting that the masses are "less intelligent . . . and most likely to constitute the corrupt" voters. But he warns that "political conservatives, who have been successful for any length of time, have always foreseen impending changes and have put through the needed reforms themselves in time. *By following this tactic they have been able to guard fundamental conservative interests even in the framing of reforms. They have thereby also succeeded in slowing them up; changes have not overwhelmed them as avalanches. They have kept the control and preserved a basis for the retention of their political power.*" (My emphasis—H. A.) Is it not amusing—and revealing—how when the distinguished doctor recommends action he relaxes his grip upon his philosophical idealism? Here it may be noted that Myrdal's final and most emphasized bit of advice for Negro leaders is the insulting and petty reformist one of "be honest" and his meaning of honesty is strictly monetary. (857) This reminds one, in its superficiality and inane quality, of Oswald Garrison Villard's recent serious admonition to the Negro people in which he said that the most important message he had for them, after his fifty years of service, was—be courteous! To such insipidness does one descend when one decides that the all-important item in the Negro question is the state of mind of the white man, and of the propertied white man in particular!

This study contains two theoretical positions, one dealing with the past, the other with the future, and both highly revealing. Myrdal finds the revolutionary liberation of the slaves to have been rather unfortunate, and believes the demands of the Southern masses after the Civil War for the confiscation and redistribution of the land to have been utopian. He regrets (225) that slaveowners were not fully remunerated from Federal funds for their loss of property in Negroes, since preserving "individual property rights to the maximum" is "always of the greatest importance for a smooth readjustment" (note the assumed desideratum—"readjustment"), and believes that much of the land might have been purchased by the government and distributed in small lots (with the state holding the mortgage), and then careful supervision maintained (again by the state) over the new occupiers of the land, who might, in addition, receive *vocational* education.

This proposal—of giving the rebellious slaveholders several billions of dollars (the four million slaves would have brought about three billion dollars at current prices, to say nothing of the value of the land) from the treasury of the government which they had assaulted, and of turning the Negro people into state peons (with the state controlled, unquestionably, by their "best friends," the conservative white Southerners)—bears a striking resemblance to an actual piece of legislation enacted by another liberal during the period of the American Civil War. We refer to the emancipation of the Russian serfs, by Tsar Alexander II, in 1861, as a result, largely, of mass pressure and unrest. That act, drafted by the Tsar and the gentry, munificently and immediately reimbursed the owners for all serfs (except domestics) and provided for state-controlled and limited distribution of the land to the peasants, again with full remuneration to the property holders. The result of all this is well known—the peasants were put "at the mercy" of a greatly enriched moneyed class, and this resulted in "a rural-industrial crisis which, vast of dimensions, and momentous of historical import, waxed, ultimately, to a political crisis through the fact that every branch of popular labor had come to stand more or less fettered and paralyzed with poverty. . . ." The parallel between the proposals of Myrdal and the enactments of the Tsar are certainly striking!

The other proposal—and the only far-reaching one to be found in the work—is put in the form of a "reflection" which this "outside observer of the irrational, inefficient, and cruel American caste system" would not help making. (798–800) Myrdal expresses surprise that no Negro, and amazement that no white, had put forth a demand for full, complete, legalized, outright segregation.

See what a vista would open up for a "Negro leader, who really accepted segregation and stopped criticizing it." How boldly he "could face the dominant whites with a number of far-reaching demands!" True, the right to the suffrage would be relinquished, but then one could demand separate representatives and while they would not have a vote in the legislature, they could discuss and petition. And perhaps even separate lower courts might be established, and a "nationally planned policy" of residential segregation might be instituted, and certain "Negro jobs," of the poorest sort, of course, might legally be provided, and—well, what did the ghettos of the tsars and of Hitler have that we might not have! But, Myrdal concludes, it is an "extraordinary thing . . . how the national ethos works, in the short run, as a bar [is there no more concrete bar than the "ethos"?] against clear and constructive thinking toward mitigating the inequalities which, contrary to the American Creed, are inflicted upon a weak group. In the long run, this same Creed might come to save, not only, as now, America's face, but perhaps also its soul." How stupid of the "apathetic masses" to refuse to accept such "clear and constructive thinking" when instead all they retain is a Creed that "might, perhaps," save so ethereal an item as the nation's "soul."

SUBJECTIVISM

An integral part of Myrdal's rejection of materialism is his subjectivism, his denial of reality except as it is recognized and felt by individuals. This idea is used, too, to assist in an attempted refutation of one of the basic postulates of Marxism, namely, the reality of the class struggle, and so it may be fittingly examined at this point.

Myrdal denies the existence of class interest, because he says for this to exist, "the assumption must be that they [workers] actually care about each other's welfare, that they all feel as a group." (790) Again: "if white and black workers do not feel united as a group, there is, of course, no 'common interest.'" (791) And, in an earlier work he had written concerning this point, "the truth of the statement [of the reality of class interest] is entirely dependent on the subjective factor." Is there, then, no distinction between class interest and class consciousness? Is there no reality in societal organization itself, but only in how people "feel" about such organization? Is not a vast proportion of all sociological literature for the past fifty years filled with studies of the class content and divisions of our civilization? Has not this been a main concern of psychologists, anthropologists, economists, and historians for the same half century?

And we ask this question: did, or did not, an anti-fascist interest exist in the non-fascist world once that scourge appeared? The enemy was there, very real. The institutions of fascism were in existence and their victims could testify and did testify to their reality. The common enemy of the non-fascist world existed and was very real before an anti-fascist coalition came into being. The anti-fascist interest preceded the anti-fascist consciousness. Consciousness always follows interest. First is the reality, the fact, then the idea appears. He who denies the existence of class interest in the face of the class-consciousness that does already exist and in the face of the record of modern history—a record of class struggle—is worshipping the long decomposed corpse of Bishop Berkeley and is denying the world.

It is of some interest to remark, at this point, upon the contradictions in Myrdal's own work on this position of subjectivism. The contradictions appear when he deals with concrete situations, as they generally do in the work of any idealist when he leaves his dream and returns to actuality. Thus, at one point he notes that economic inequality is maintained "for it is the barrier against social equality."(216) Again, he permits himself to say that "discrimination against Negroes is thus rooted in this tradition of economic exploitation" (208), and that the beliefs associated with racism function so as to "defend interests." (111) And, in a truly amazing passage, Myrdal remarks that if the Negro and organized labor should become firmly united, "if this were once accomplished and an identification reached with the white laboring masses, it would mean the beginning of liberation of the Negro soul." (794) While the metaphysical language here is obscure and unfortunate, what stands out as perfectly clear is the utterly contradictory quality of this remark—and it remains but a remark, it is not developed or repeated—to the entire superstructure of "cumulative causation," "vicious circle," denial of the basic significance of material, actual conditions and social forces, and of the existence of class interest.

Having denied the reality of class interest on subjective grounds, it is natural for Myrdal to minimize what class solidarity, particularly as between Negro and white, has existed and does exist. He declares that "much has been made of even the faintest demonstration of such solidarity" (68), though he does not tell us where or when this exaggeration has occurred. Certainly, he does not intend to "make much" of this, and though he writes that he "has seen how a quick and radical change in racial attitudes has been brought about in some places where the tie of a common organization has materialized" (598–99), and though one should think that such developments would be particularly pertinent to an investigation of an alleged dilemma in the face of exactly that "problem"—the creation of unit—and ought to be described at length, such is not the case, and one is left with the bare and intriguing single sentence.

Precious little space, too, is devoted to the question of whether or not the propertied class recognizes the existence of a working-class interest (independent of a consciousness) and deliberately attempts to stifle and prevent displays of solidarity. On this crucial point Myrdal finds that he has room for only this very carefully worded remark: "Plantation owners and employers . . . have at times been observed to tolerate, or even co-operate in, the periodic aggressions of poor whites against Negroes." (598) Is one being unkind by daring to suggest that history would allow us to make a somewhat bolder characterization, and that if one declared that plantation owners and employers almost always tolerate, frequently co-operate in, and often themselves instigate and provoke "periodic aggressions of poor [and rich] whites against Negroes" he would be very much nearer the truth? And may one point out that these owners and employers have ruled the South for three hundred years and with very short interruptions, and that they rule it today and that such social patterns as aggressions against Negroes do exist and *can* exist only with the consent and co-operation of those rulers.

In addition to the preceding, Myrdal positively distorts the facts concerning the attitudes of the laboring class. Thus, he insists that the workers rather than the rich are conservative (33, 398–99), though not only is this contrary to universal observation, but it is also contrary to the findings of scientific inquiries into the actual opinions of American and other workers. These have uniformly shown that the bulk of the Left strength, of all progressive movements, is composed of the poorer classes, while the opposite is true of the well-to-do.

In line with this he also repeatedly asserts that the most violent and pervasive hatred of the Negro is found in the working class, in the poor, while it is the rich and secure who are the least unfriendly. (Pp. 69, 583, 597–98) This idea, which is assiduously spread by the propertied groups and has wide currency, is false. And it was declared to be false in a study made by Eugene L. Horowitz *specifically for the Myrdal work.* Horowitz, in surveying the rather scanty scientific studies of the subject, concluded, and so informed Myrdal, that no significant relation had been found between income and attitude toward the Negro. And of even greater significance is the fact that the single large-scale attempt to obtain data on this question, undertaken as a *Fortune* survey in 1939, *at the request of the Carnegie Corporation for the Myrdal study,* found that those with low incomes had considerably less prejudice than those with high incomes.

Specifically, this study, based upon interviews with about five thousand people from every section of the country, showed that the people with the lowest incomes were those possessing the least prejudice, and that, in terms of percentage, about three times as many of the poor as of the rich had a high regard for the intelligence of the Negro, and about fifty percent more among the poor than the rich were opposed to segregation.

A varied miscellany of facts tends to confirm this finding. Thus, the good will displayed by the white people of Detroit who actually lived in the same neighborhoods with the Negroes during the rioting of 1943 is well known. Again, studies of public housing projects have shown that real friendship regularly develops among the poorest tenants—Negro and white—and that this good will decreases as the income rises, reaching antagonism where the whites are prosperous. And of greatest importance is the whole record of the great success of progressive labor organizations, particularly the C.I.O., in developing comradeship between Negro and white members both in the North and in the South. Especially striking has been the solidarity displayed in recent strikes in the auto, steel, shipping, meat, tobacco, and other industries.

Yet Myrdal chose to ignore the advice of his own expert on this question, to ignore the finds of his own opinion survey and the other facts here cited, and to repeat an ancient cliché founded upon the casual observations of uninformed and generally bigoted individuals. It seems fair to remark that this choice was made because that cliché more aptly fits his own presuppositions concerning mass interest and solidarity and the behavior of the masses.

III. Conclusion

In summary, we find Myrdal's philosophy to be superficial and erroneous, his historiography demonstrably false, his ethics vicious and, therefore, his analysis weak, mystical, and dangerous. And we affirm two things: (1) the Negro question is basically a material one, not a moral one. The oppression and super-exploitation of the American Negro—and the prejudice based thereon—exist and are maintained because they were and are profitable and useful to America's propertied interests; and (2) there is no American dilemma for believers in, and fighters for, democracy and full rights for all people.

We do have a situation involving choice, but the alternatives are not equally satisfactory. The choice lies between the attempted preservation of our existing exploiting system, which nurtures the oppression of minority peoples, or the introduction of fundamental and vital changes now, and the consequent hastening of the transformations of our society into a pattern of socialism. The choice lies between, on the one hand, bolstering the status quo, whether by blood or iron, or the perversion and watering down of the people's demands, and, on the other hand, assisting in the organized struggle of the labor movement, the farmers, segments of the harassed middle class, and the vast majority of the Negro people for the acquisition by the latter of complete and absolute social, political, and economic equality.

Specifically, there must be developed a people's mass movement for the immediate outlawing of Jim Crowism and all other manifestations of bigotry. It is necessary that there be enacted a potent national Fair Employment Practice Law, and that this law be enforced. It is necessary that barriers to the full exercise of the right of suffrage be removed, and that all people, regardless of color, creed, or national origin, possess the right to be elected or appointed to any office or position in the country. Inequalities in education, and in the use of any and all facilities and institutions, must be abolished. The struggle against the ghetto and restrictive covenants must be intensified. A serious and uncompromising campaign must be undertaken to force the use of all the resources of the national government to guarantee the Negro people against violence and to insure them full judicial rights. Every vestige of peonage must be thoroughly exposed and extirpated by the concerted effort of all law enforcement agencies in the country and, particularly, by the Federal Department of Justice.

These reforms are on today's order of business. They can be accomplished and they must be accomplished if the forces of reaction are to be met and overcome.

The oppression of the American Negro has served as a stumbling block to the forces of progress and freedom for the entire nation throughout its history. It must no longer be tolerated or permitted. In fighting it we fight not only for the Negro, but for all Americans. And in the fires of this struggle will be forged a comradeship and a unity whose drive towards a peaceful, fruitful, and creative life for humanity will be irresistible.

13

The Suppression of the African Slave Trade

Introduction

Having graduated in June 1884 from the high school in Great Barrington, Massachusetts, the sixteen-year-old W. E. B. Du Bois, with the support and encouragement of relatives and townsfolk, shortly thereafter went South to study at Fisk University in Nashville, Tennessee. He graduated with four classmates (three of them, women) in 1888 and then realized his bold dream of entering Harvard as a junior that fall. Two years later, at a commencement where he was one of the orators, Harvard conferred an A.B. upon him.

Scholarships had made this possible and further grants allowed the Black orphan to go on to graduate studies at Harvard, which contained probably the most remarkable aggregation of scholars ever to grace one United States faculty: William James, Albert Bushnell Hart, Edward Channing, Frank Taussig, Justin Winsor, Josiah Royce, George Palmer, Nathaniel Shaler, Barrett Wendell, Charles Eliot Norton, Francis Peabody, and George Santayana were among them. Of these, most influential in Du Bois' development were Peabody, Royce, Wendell, Channing, and—in particular—James and Hart. Indeed, the last two became friends; Du Bois visited their homes, knew their families, and exchanged letters for years. In history, it was Hart above all who guided the young student: for him and with him, Du Bois studied especially the institution of slavery in the United States, the struggle to abolish it, the uprising of Nat Turner, and—at Hart's direct suggestion—an examination of the African slave trade to the United Sates and efforts to suppress that abomination.

Du Bois spent about thirty months—through part of 1889, all of 1890, and most of 1891—in a thorough examination of contemporary sources and then the few secondary accounts treating the African slave trade and the history of the efforts to suppress it so far as the United States was concerned. In 1891, Harvard conferred upon Du Bois an A.M. degree: early in December he presented to the Hart-conducted seminar in history the results of his findings. With Hart's encouragement and support, young Du Bois was on the program of the 1891 Annual Meeting of the American Historical Association, which met in Washington in December.[1] Here he presented a paper entitled, "The Enforcement of the Slave-Trade Laws,"[2] which anticipated and, in a way, outlined the book.

For a young Black man, in the city of Washington in the year 1891, to report on any subject before a gathering of (all-white) scholars was unusual; to have that Black man describe something of the realities of the African slave trade, the complicity of the highest officials of the United States in violation of law and to conclude in the manner that follows certainly was extraordinary:

> If slave labor was an economic god, then the slave trade was its strong right arm; and with Southern planters recognizing this and Northern capital unfettered by a conscience it was almost like legislating against economic laws to attempt to abolish the slave trade by statutes. Northern greed joined to Southern credulity was a combination calculated to circumvent any law, human or divine.

The response among the auditors was polite, and two among them published appreciative accounts of the occasion and the paper for periodicals then of national importance. Professor Herbert Baxter Adams, of Johns Hopkins University (then Secretary of the Association), devoted a straight-forward paragraph in his account of the meeting to summarizing the "scholarly" paper presented by Mr. W. E. B. Du Bois, A.M. Fellow of Harvard University. He made no mention of Du Bois' color. Edward G. Bourne—then a professor at Adelbert College in Michigan—published a column on the "American Historical Association" in which he emphasized the "harmonious gathering together" of Northern and Southern scholars for the discussion of subjects ordinarily considered "inflammable." Further, he added:

> What would Southern teachers of history within the lifetime of many readers . . . have thought of going to Washington to listen, among other things, to a paper on the Enforcement of the Slave Trade Laws by a colored man, the holder of a fellowship at Harvard University? It will surprise many to learn

> that Mr. Du Bois estimated that from 1808 to 1861 over 300,000 slaves were smuggled into the United States.[3]

On the basis of a grant from the Slater Fund—then headed by former President Rutherford B. Hayes—graduate student Du Bois received a total of $1,500 (half of this a loan, at five percent interest) for two years of study at the University of Berlin. He worked under Gustav Schmoller, Adolf Wagner, and Henrich von Treitschke, heard Max Weber lecture, and—probably most important—traveled widely through Europe. All this while he was maturing his scholarship: upon his return to the United States in 1894 he not only at once sought employment (and found it as a teacher of "classics"—meaning Greek and Latin—at Wilberforce University in Ohio) but also completed the preparation of his dissertation for the degree of doctor of philosophy granted him by Harvard in 1895.

In that same year Harvard's department of history had decided to commence the publication of an Historical Series; not then having its own press, the early volumes were published by Longman, Green & Co. in New York City, and the first in this series, issued in 1896, was the present book (its preface is dated March, 1896).[4]

The book was widely reviewed and well received. *The Nation* (December 31, 1896; 63:498–500) in a six-column review—published without signature, as was then its custom—accurately summarized its contents. In a notable closing paragraph, the reviewer observed that Du Bois was a black man, that his book was written with great clarity "and in an interesting style rarely found in monographs." While pedantry was absent, the reviewer continued, the scholarship was sound; it was confidently, and accurately, predicted "that this study will long remain the authoritative work on the subject." Furthermore:

> Amid all the discussion over the probable future of the Negro in this county, it is a matter of profound significance and great encouragement that a member of the race which, scarcely more than a generation ago, was openly bought and sold and hunted in our streets, should have traced, out of abundant knowledge and with unbiased mind, the course of our national connection with that unholy traffic, from its beginning to its close, in a volume which is an honor alike to be its author, to the university whose approval it has received, and to American historical scholarship.

A four-page, unsigned review in *The American Historical Review* (April, 1897:II, 550–559) also is largely devoted to a summary of its contents, illustrated with rather lengthy quotations.[5] There are three gently critical suggestions. The reviewer thought that Du Bois presented the development of a more commercialized slavery in the nineteenth century, as contrasted with an allegedly "patriarchal serfdom [at the time] of the founders of the republic" in "perhaps" an exaggerated form; he did not sufficiently observe the existence of opposition to reopening the slave trade among some slave-owners within "the cotton states" nor the arguments they offered; and the author permitted himself "the use of a few adjectives here and there that characterize the advocate rather than the historian." Overall, however, the reviewer found the book "an immense amount of faithful and diligent work."

Of the three criticisms, the first would seem to be unwarranted by the facts; if anything, indeed, Du Bois displays a tendency to exaggerate the "patriarchal" nature of the eighteenth-century slavery in areas like Maryland and Virginia and to accept somewhat uncritically the then very widely held belief that in those areas at that time the institution was in decay and was widely expected to more or less automatically disappear in the fairly near future. This is related to the highly dubious concept, also then universally held as valid, and present in this work, of a "Cavalier" origin to the ruling circles of Virginia in particular as contrasted to rather ruder beginnings for the inhabitants of both New England and the deeper South.

The second point is well-taken, and documented in the review; though it might well have been added that Du Bois' work was the first extended examination of the movement within considerable sections of the slaveholding class to reopen the African slave trade—one of the many areas wherein Du Bois pioneered.

The third point, of "advocacy" as allegedly in contradiction to history writing, raises a matter still very much in dispute, of course. On this question, Du Bois' attitude was clear and unchanging: history writing was inseparable from advocacy but by no means the same as advocacy. In applying for his fellowships at Harvard in 1890 he made plain that he sought to master scholarship the better to serve his people; while studying in Berlin he told his diary, in 1893, that this was his purpose and that though it cost him his life he would serve it. From time to time, Du Bois put this in print: a good example comes from the paragraphs he devoted to *The Rise of Black American Civilization* by Charles A. and Mary R. Beard in his *Black Reconstruction.*[6]

Reading their book, wrote Du Bois, one had "the comfortable feeling that nothing right or wrong is involved." Two differing systems develop in the North and the South, Du Bois continued, and "they clash, as winds and waters strive." The "mechanistic interpretation" failed because human experience was not mechanistic. Furthermore, in such a presentation

> There is no room for the real plot of the story, for the clear mistake and guilt of building a new slavery of the working class in the midst of a fateful experiment in democracy; for the triumph of sheer moral courage and sacrifice in the abolition crusade; and for the hurt and struggle of degraded black millions in their fight for freedom and their attempt to enter democracy. Can all this be omitted or half suppressed in a treatise that calls itself scientific?

The reader, then, will find in this book—and in all of Du Bois' writings—no doubt as to what was right and was wrong in his opinion and the bringing forward of "the hurt and struggle" of his people was his fundamental and towering contribution to human knowledge. Indeed, in this very book, in its preface, the reader is told of the author's hope that it will represent "a small contribution to the scientific study of slavery and the American Negro." Du Bois never doubted that the absence of such study reflected, as it bulwarked, racism and that providing it was part of the "struggle" to overcome the "hurt."

Another unnamed reviewer gave the book some five hundred words; he found it "thorough" and characterized by "great clearness and fairness" and even "brilliance." Still, half the review was taken up with an effort at refuting Du Bois' reiteration (on p. 21) of what was then a "general tradition"—namely, that the Germantown, Pennsylvania protest of 1688 against slavery emanated from the Quakers; not so, wrote the reviewer: "it was the work of Mennonites." The reviewer was terribly long-winded about this, the more so since he seems to have been wrong.[7]

The most critical review appeared in the magazine which later in the same year was to publish one of Du Bois' seminary essays: this was *The Atlantic Monthly.* Two pages in an unsigned section, "Comment on Recent Books in American History," treated the book. The tone was patronizing; it noted that Dr. Du Bois taught at "an institution devoted to the higher education of the colored race." The reviewer felt that Du Bois had "shown good judgment" in choice of subject and that he had been "most industrious" though the book's "substance" might be "reached more succinctly" in an encyclopedia! Still his "reasoning" was weak and "what we may call his hortatory application seems to disclose a lack of appreciation of the subject in its historical proportions." Those "proportions" were the realities of racism so that "the suppression of slavery and the slave-trade was not such a simple matter as he [Du Bois] considers it." The reader will search in vain for any evidence that Dr. Du Bois thought this a "simple matter"; on the contrary one of the fundamental points of his book is that it was far from a simple matter since both slavery and the slave-trade had become basic components of the socio-economic system in the pre–Civil War United States and that, therefore, the government of the United States was in fact subservient to both the system of enslavement and the trade. One feels that it is these findings and the unequivocal nature with which the Black scholar was asserting and proving them that made *The Atlantic Monthly* reviewer uncomfortable—and untruthful.[8]

One of the better of the contemporary reviews was that by Bernard C. Steiner, then on the faculty of Johns Hopkins. No biographical data concerning Du Bois is offered: Professor Steiner writes only of the book and reports it to be "a thoroughly good piece of work" whose "research has been exhaustive and accurate."[9] A brief but astute summary is offered and particular attention is called to the fact that Du Bois' work had documented "the influence which the Haytian revolt, under Toussaint L'Ouverture" had had upon United States history—another of the pioneering contributions in Du Bois' first book.

Professor Steiner did wonder "whether Mr. Du Bois is not too severe in his condemnation of the founders of our national constitution for their compromise on the slave trade," but he seems to conclude that he was not for he wrote: "Some circumstances may be urged by way of pallation, none by way of excuse. This indictment is not made with passionate invective, but through the careful statement of well-ascertained facts."

He did note that "the papers on slavery in the Johns Hopkins University Studies are not mentioned" and this is a legitimate criticism. How or why this omission occurred is not easily explained: at least two of those studies were quite germane to Du Bois' effort. Certain other omissions mentioned by Professor Steiner are less significant, for the works involved barely touch Du Bois' subject and Steiner's suggested "correction" of Du Bois concerning slavery in Vermont seems to be mistaken.[10]

One of the most discerning reviews of this book came from the pen of H. T. Kealing of Philadelphia, the editor of the *A.M.E. Church Review*[11] and a man with whom Du Bois had a fairly close relationship for several years. This calls particular attention not only to the role of Toussaint in Du Bois' book but also that work's emphasis upon reality and the fear of slave militancy and rebellion as affecting questions by the slave trade—still another of the pioneering insights offered by Du Bois. Keenly, Kealing estimated the book as "epochal" and urged that its author "must write more" since all that he would produce, Kealing was certain, would help bury "the almost antediluvian conceit of exclusive Caucasian scholarship."[12]

For some fifty years after its first printing, Du Bois' book was out of print. It was cited thousands of times; but this seems most often to have been merely ritual as so often happens with a "standard" work. The illuminations and suggestions and openings it offered—and offers—certainly were not assimilated by the historical profession in the United States, overwhelmingly racist as it was and to a degree remains.

So far as Du Bois was concerned, quite out of the blue he received a letter, dated March 30, 1954, from a just-established organization, Social Science Press, located in New York City and headed by a then-graduate student at Columbia named Eugene D. Genovese.[13] This informed the Doctor that one of its hoped-for accomplishments was the reprinting of the Suppression volume. Du Bois was delighted and responded favorably at once: he suggested that "a preface, 'sixty years after' might be needed."[14] Preparations continued: by the end of August Du Bois envisioned not a preface but what he then called a "postlude." "I want it," he wrote on August 25, "at the end of the book instead of at the beginning, and to be a short explanation of the omissions in that book."

The reprint appeared at the close of 1954: one thousand copies were produced. The book was photo-offset from the 1896 edition and contained a three-page "Apologia"—updated but written in October 1954. In those three pages Du Bois made four points. He thought that the concentration on a specific and limited topic—necessary to the monograph—did tend toward some distortion: he added, however, that the particular subject of this book produced a minimum of such imbalance. Something of this criticism had appeared in the review of the original edition in *The Atlantic Monthly* to which reference has been made:[15] it may be that Du Bois recalled that when he went on to comment on two other failings which he wrote he had not seen discussed.

These were a certain naiveté in terms of the realities of human motivation and psychology which reflected, he felt, the pre-Freudian epoch of the book's production; and another omission to which he gave greater weight, namely, that of the Marxian analysis. Here Du Bois carefully distinguished between the economic emphasis, which, as he quite correctly points out, is in his book, and the struggle of class domination of the State and class interest and struggle as basic in the process of history, which is not in the book. At any rate, and this was the Apologia's final point, the book was a good one: it did represent conscientious effort and on the whole it was accurate and complete.

Two reviews of this 1954 edition were published—and both appeared in scholarly journals issued by predominantly black organizations. One was especially pleased with the fact that Du Bois had not hidden his partisanship in writing of the slave trade; indeed, "this moral indignation adds to the worth of the study." But this reviewer, as also John Hope Franklin—who similarly felt the 1896 work to be indeed classical—regretted Du Bois' emphasis in his Apologia on the failure to apply the Marxian insight to his material. Professor Franklin, in particular, though that Du Bois had underplayed the economic emphasis in his original work by this lament; but here Professor Franklin is himself repeating the common mistake of identifying economic determinism with Marxism. Of course, the economics of slavery and the slave trade are in Du Bois' study, and its emphasis helps make the study quite remarkable for its time; and in the Apologia, Du Bois comments on this presence. But he also observes that it is not economic interest itself which makes a study Marxian, but rather its appreciation of the class interests and class struggle aspects of history which are decisive to the Marxian vision. As Du Bois writes quite explicitly in his Apologia: "What I needed was to add to my terribly conscientious search into the facts of the slave trade the clear concept of Marx on the class struggle for income and power, beneath which all considerations of rights or morals were twisted or utterly crushed."[16]

Certainly this is the plain judgment of the fully mature author of this work first produced by a budding scholar at the age of twenty-seven.

Du Bois' *Suppression of the African Slave Trade* is the first treatment of a significant subject and one which has not been supplanted. It is also the first full-length product of African American scientific scholarship; as such it is the seed, just as Du Bois is himself the Father, of the African American intelligentsia.

In addition to its pioneering emphasis upon the economics of slavery and the slave trade, its observation of the central role both in the militancy of the slaves, and the significance for United States history of Toussaint and the revolution he led—to which attention has been called earlier—there are additional investigations in this work which, at the time, were quite new.

Thus, the Suppression volume contains a detailed examination of the relationship of slavery and the slave trade to the national politics of the United States, and especially to the politics (including the international ramifications) of the Revolutionary period and the years of the formation and adoption of the Constitution. In the latter, for example, Du Bois' work is in no way superseded by that of Staughton Lynd, published in 1967,[17] though Dr. Lynd does not cite Du Bois at all in this connection.

Similarly, Du Bois' book contains the first discussion of the movement in the South for the legalization of the slave trade, of the reasons for this, of the arguments offered against it and of the politics associated with it up to the Civil War. Again, a very recent book finally treating this important subject at length, does not render obsolete Du Bois' work though it very nearly completely ignores it.[18]

The historical profession has yet to produce a work analyzing the roots of the Civil War in the United States that is superior to that Du Bois offers in chapter ten of this book. His concept of the War's origins as being an attempted "political coup d'état" by a desperate slaveholding oligarchy (pp. 153–54) remains years ahead of most in the historical profession and it forms a significant element in post-Beard, not to speak of post-Rhodes thinking.

The book is a blistering attack upon the practice of the United States government in helping to maintain the oppression of Black people either through positive action or through deliberate failure to enforce its own laws where such enforcement would challenge that oppression. Thus, Du Bois shows repeatedly and courageously that acts inhibiting or outlawing the slave trade "came very near being a dead letter" (p. 109); or that "The execution of the laws within the country exhibits grave defects and even criminal negligence" (p. 127); or "The efforts of the executive during this period (the 1850s) were criminally lax and negligent" (p. 184).

One must recall that Du Bois was publishing in 1896 when George Bancroft's concept of the divinity of the Fathers and the Constitution held sway to appreciate the full impact and daring of such observations as these:

> No American can study the connection of slavery with United States history, and not devoutly pray that his country may never have a similar social problem to solve, until it shows more capacity for such work than it has shown in the past. It is neither profitable nor in accordance with scientific truth to consider that whatever the constitutional fathers did was right, or that slavery was a plague sent from God and fated to be eliminated in due time. (pp. 197–98)

While the moralistic conclusion, with its non-class approach and its generalized reproach was the kind of weakness Du Bois had in mind in his 1954 Apologia, altogether valid is a theme of the book: the enslavement of Black people vitiates the quality of life in the United States as a whole. That enslavement finally resulted in a war that threatened the very existence of the Republic and took half a million lives; the practices surrounding and bulwarking that slavery have not been extirpated and the question of their elimination "sometime must be fully answered" as the young Du Bois warned on the last page of this 1896 book and as he continued to warn until his last breath almost seventy years later.

What the young Du Bois hoped when he penned the preface to this book back in Ohio in 1896, he accomplished—to make a "contribution to the scientific study of slavery and the American Negro."

Notes

1. The Association was then in its infancy; it had been formed in 1884 but only incorporated by act of Congress in January 1889; its organ, *The American Historical Review,* did not appear until 1895.

2. In *Annual Report of the American Historical Association for the Year 1891* (Washington, 1892, Government Printing Office), pp. 163–74; in his posthumously published *Autobiography* (N.Y., 1968, International Publishers, p. 149) this is erroneously dated in 1892.

3. Professor Bourne was inexact. Du Bois had said: " . . .from 1807–1862 . . . the total number thus brought in contravention alike of humanity and law was not less than 250,000." (Cited article, p. 173). The Bourne piece was in *The Congregationalist* (Boston), January 4, 1892, 57, p. 2; that by Adams in *The Independent* (N.Y.), January 7, 1892, 44, pp. 10–11.

4. Not quite accurately, Professor John Hope Franklin, in reviewing the 1954 re-issue of the book, wrote: "as the first book in the Harvard Historical Studies it set the stage for university sponsorship of the publication of learned manuscripts" (*Journal of Negro History,* April 1955, 40, p. 182); and in his introduction to a 1969 reprint, Professor Franklin referred to the Harvard Historical Studies as "the first series of scholarly works to be published by an American university" (edition published by Louisiana State University Press, Baton Rouge, p. vi). The Johns Hopkins University Studies commenced in 1882; under Albert Bushnell Hart's direction there had commenced what were called Fay House Monographs, being Publication of the Society for the Collegiate Instruction of Women and in 1891 through Ginn & Co. it published Marion G. McDougall's pioneering *Fugitive Slaves, 1619–1865* cited herein by Du Bois. Also, through G. P. Putnam's Sons, the history and economics department of the University of Nebraska commenced publication of scholarly work in 1891, while J. Franklin Jameson edited *Papers from the Historical Seminary of Brown University,* which commenced in 1894.

5. This unsigned review was written by Stephen B. Weeks, as is noted in the index to the volume. I am obliged to Professor John Hope Franklin for calling my attention to this.

6. Du Bois, *Black Reconstruction* (N.Y., 1935, Harcourt, Brace), pp. 714–15; on this point see my *Afro-American History: The Modern Era* (N.Y., 1971, Citadel Press), pp. 51–55.

7. For the evidence on this, see especially Thomas E. Drake in *Bulletin of the Friends Historical Association* (1934), 22, pp. 96ff. The review referred to appeared in *The Critic,* August 21, 1897, 31, p. 100. Du Bois mentions this review and the question it raises and affirms the probability that the reviewer is wrong, in his *The Philadelphia Negro* (1899), p. 11, note 3.

8. *The Atlantic Monthly,* April 1897, 79, pp. 560–62. Du Bois' essay, "Strivings of the Negro People," appeared in this magazine in August 1897, 80, pp. 194–98; this was his first publication in a nationally circulated periodical.

9. In *Annals of the American Academy of Political and Social Science,* May 1897, 9, pp. 432–34.

10. See Jeffrey R. Brackett, *The Negro in Maryland: A Study of the Institution of Slavery* (Baltimore, 1889, Johns Hopkins Univ. Press); Bernard C. Steiner, *History of Slavery in Connecticut* (Baltimore, 1893, Johns Hopkins Univ. Press). On Vermont, the question revolves around the existence of slavery; the source Steiner cites tends to substantiate Du Bois rather than Steiner—see Isaac Jennings, *Memorials of a Century . . .* (Boston, 1869, Gould & Lincoln), pp. 63–64.

11. This is in 13, pp. 357–39 (1896/97); for an indication of the Du Bois-Kealing relationship, see my *Afro-American History: The Modern Era* (cited work), pp. 149, 290.

12. Of other contemporary notices and reviews, three may be mentioned: in *The Dial,* August 16, 1897, p. 90; *Athenaeum,* August 13, 1898, p. 224; and highly favorable and rather long, signed by C. P. Lucas, in *English Historical Review,* July 1897, 12, pp. 572–74.

13. This is the now well-known historian who heads the department of history at the University of Rochester at the present time.

14. Du Bois to Genovese, April 2, 1954, replying to a letter from Genovese dated March 30. The letters are in the Du Bois Papers at the University of Massachusetts in Amherst.

15. The words in that review read: "We suspect that he has failed in a satisfactory answer to the historical problem involved in his thesis by trying to isolate it too completely . . ." (cited work, p. 562).

16. The two reviews were by William H. Lofton in *Phylon* (1955), 16, pp. 105–106; John Hope Franklin in *The Journal of Negro History* (1955), 40, pp. 182–84. Professor Franklin repeats this point in his introduction to the 1969 reprint of *The Suppression* book, issued by Louisiana State University Press and containing the Apologia. There have been two other reprints: one is by Dover Publication (N.Y., 1970); this does not contain the Apologia of 1954 and has a four-page preface by Philip S. Foner. The other was issued in 1969 by Schocken Books (N.Y.) and prints the Apologia in the beginning of the work; it contains a nineteen-page introduction marked by a high incidence of misinformation from A. Norman Klein. Among other astonishing errors is Professor Klein's statement (p. xxi) that Du Bois "overlooked the African slave-trade with Brazil and Cuba," an allegation important to a major point Klein is

making. The reader is invited simply to inspect the index of this book to judge the accuracy of this criticism.

17. See Lynd's *Class Conflict, Slavery and the United States Constitution* (Indianapolis, 1967, Bobbs-Merrill), especially chapters 6, 7, 8.

18. Ronald Takaki, *Pro-Slavery Crusade* (Urbana, 1971, University of Illinois Press).

Note: A typographical feature of the book deserves notice. In the 1896 edition the word "Negro" is spelled throughout with the uppercase N. This was not general practice at the time and it did not become general practice in the non-Black press until about 1930. The Harvard Historical Series volumes, after Du Bois', all used a lowercase n for Negro as late as its Number 37, by Roland D. Hussey, *The Caracas Company* (1934). Du Bois battled over this question for a generation; just how he managed this particular victory in 1896 is not clear from his Papers.

14

Personal Reflections on W. E. B. Du Bois: The Person, Scholar, and Activist

HERBERT APTHEKER AND FAY APTHEKER

Recorded and edited by
Benjamin Bowser and Deborah Whittle

Introduction

There are some very good biographies of Dr. Du Bois which outline in great detail the life of this extraordinary man. One should read David Lewis's *Du Bois: Biography of a Race, 1868–1919* (1993); Manning Marable's *W. E. B. Du Bois: Black Radical Democrat* (1986); Herbert Aptheker's *The Literary Legacy of W. E. B. Du Bois* (1989); and Arnold Rampersad's *The Art and Imagination of W. E. B. Du Bois* (1976). And then, of course, there is Dr. Du Bois' own biography—*The Autobiography of W. E. B. Du Bois: A Soliloquy On Viewing My Life From The Late Decade of Its First Century* (1968). What we hope to do in this paper is not substitute for any of these works but rather we will attempt to answer a number of essential questions that emerge out of a careful reading of the Du Bois biographies and autobiography. His later years are especially important to look at. Who was W. E. B. Du Bois as a person; how did he produce such extraordinary work; why did he work so hard and so long; what were his goals and intentions; why did he return to the NAACP a second time and why did he eventually leave; how did he attain his physical longevity; why was it necessary for the U.S. Government to persecute him; and did he really give up on the United States when he left the country? In responding to these questions, Fay and I will draw from our personal knowledge of Dr. Du Bois and from four decades of immersion in editing the Du

Bois works. There are also a few good points that the biographers missed that will give the reader a good sense of the man.

I first met Dr. Du Bois personally in the spring of 1945. He had a small office at the National Association for the Advancement of Colored People's (NAACP) headquarters on 41st Street and Fifth Avenue across the street from the New York Public Library's main building. He was Director of Special Research and was kind enough to offer a corner of his already cramped office to me to work on my *Documentary History of the Negro People in the United States,* volumes 1–2 (1951). Dr. Du Bois frequently complained about his lack of space to the NAACP president, Walter White, but it was to no avail. My family and I became very close to Dr. and Shirley Graham Du Bois. We frequently spent time together with him, admired him, and it was an honor for me to see to it that his later works were published. Dr. Du Bois was a father to me and his late wife, Shirley Graham Du Bois, told others that he regarded me as a son. As one of the greatest figures of this century, it has been a great privilege to have spent the past four decades editing his work and making certain that his extraordinary contributions are available for all to read. Our reflections on W. E. B. Du Bois are based on both the written record and of Fay's and my memories of our many occasions with him.

Du Bois' Early Years

Du Bois was especially devoted to his mother, Mary Du Bois, and during his early years in Great Barrington, Massachusetts, he could not be separated from her. They were very poor, but he never felt poverty. He used to help out by performing various chores for the neighbors such as delivering newspapers and coal. His friends consisted primarily of other black children who lived in the area. He spoke of playing with them in the hills, of sled-riding in the winter, and of generally having a very happy childhood. His father had left the family quite early. Du Bois did not know his father, but he knew that his father was a Civil War veteran. Apparently, his father left the family in Great Barrington for some unknown reason. Du Bois suspected that it might have been because he had difficulty finding work. Great Barrington was a predominantly white town with a small black community there and in the surrounding villages. Opportunities for work were very limited. Some years later he was incensed that Arna Bontemps wrote that he was born illegitimate. Dr. Du Bois corrected Dr. Bontemps by explaining that his mother and father indeed were married.

We knew very little else about his family. He had a grandfather, Alexander

Du Bois, who lived in New Bedford, Massachusetts, whom he occasionally visited. Apparently his grandfather was very stern and went to great length to affirm his worth as a man, not simply as a Negro. He was also a real task-maker whom the young Du Bois came to appreciate. On one of his trips to visit his grandfather, when he was about fourteen years old, he went to the Connecticut State capitol building in Hartford. He took great pride in signing the capitol visitors' book. He was so excited about signing that he wrote to his mother and told her that by signing this book "his name would last." I believe that Du Bois' grandfather was buried in the Yale University cemetery during the late 1880s. It came up in the conversation with Du Bois in reference to a debate then as to whether or not a black man should be buried there. Du Bois also had a half-brother of which he was not aware until the Great Depression. This alleged half-brother was destitute, and a social service agency tried to get Du Bois to take financial responsibility for this half-brother. I remember that Du Bois was irate over this matter, refused to make payments, and was very troubled by it.

Du Bois' extraordinary talents were very apparent early in his schooling. It was all the more uncommon for a black child to complete elementary school and go on to the local high school. He was the only black student in the high school and was at the head of his class. At the age of fifteen he wrote local newspaper articles, some of which appeared in T. Thomas Fortune's *New York Globe*. He wrote some articles for the *Springfield (Mass.) Daily Republican*. He was very conscious of his abilities early in his life. In fact the whole town knew of this, especially when he graduated from high school as their youngest graduate and with high honors.

There was another extraordinary event in young Du Bois' early years. The people in the town, both black and white, got together and raised money so that young Du Bois could go to college. There were several people responsible for this—his mother, who died shortly after he graduated from high school, Frank Hosmer, the high school principal, Edward Van Lennep, superintendent of the Congregational church's Sunday schools, and Rev. C. C. Painter, a retired federal Indian agent and former pastor of several Congregational churches (Marable 1986, p. 7). Mary Du Bois had been a member of the local Congregational church and had undoubtedly approached Frank Hosmer. She was also a member of a new African Methodist Episcopal Zion Church in Great Barrington.

But even with the extraordinary talent and backing of the town and several prominent citizens, racism did not go unnoticed in young Du Bois' life. The reality of race became very clear to him as a teen. Young Du Bois loved to dance, and, of course, went to his first high school dance expecting to enjoy himself. The girls used to have dance cards where they had the names of prospective dance partners. Since he was the only black student in the school, he was also the only black student at this dance. So he went to a white student and asked her to dance. She refused. He did not press the matter, but he knew that she refused because of his race. Also after graduation from high school, Du Bois wanted to go to Harvard University. But despite his clear talent, Rev. Painter dismissed young Du Bois' interest in Harvard and insisted that his place was at Fisk University in Nashville, Tennessee, among his own kind. Since Rev. Painter and his churches were providing most of the money for Will Du Bois' college education, his decision stood. Du Bois did not object. While he wanted to go to Harvard, he also wanted to be in the company of other black people. Fisk would give him that opportunity.

The Student Years

Du Bois arrived in Nashville in the fall of 1885 and described Fisk as a small college built after the New England tradition, wherein Latin, Greek, mathematics, and history were taught. There were then twenty-five students in the college department; the school was very small and had very good teachers. At Fisk, one went to bed at 10:00 P.M. sharp. Du Bois was to maintain this practice as a life-long habit to which he partly attributed his longevity. Here as in Great Barrington, Du Bois was also a leading student. He wrote again for the newspaper, the *Fisk Herald,* and became an active member of the larger Nashville community as he had been in Great Barrington. His professors recognized his talent, but his strong interest in the community and in the average and generally uneducated blacks went against the advice his professors gave. This interest found expression in his service as a summer-school teacher in the Tennessee countryside. He plunged into this new activity which would expose him to his people. He also went to dances in Nashville against which his classmates and teachers had warned him; and, during one of his teaching summers, he had his first sexual experience with his landlady who seduced him. He spoke in amazement many years afterward of the beauty of black women at Fisk.

As in Great Barrington, not all of his experiences in Nashville at Fisk were without crises. There were two incidents that had a profound, long-lasting affect on him. In the first, he agreed to manage a small glee club that would make money during the latter part of August with singing engagements in the Midwest. But in order to get there and support themselves the club members had to work as waiters at a summer resort hotel in Lake Minnetonka, Minnesota. The job exposed Du Bois to the worst of white bourgeois culture—husbands with their girlfriends, lavish spending, women looking for sexual encounters, waiters competing with one another by clowning for guests, and having to steal food so that they could eat. At some point in this experience, while still in Nashville, he was robbed of a great deal of money. I did not get clarification from Dr. Du Bois whether this was his money or the choir's money. Whatever the case, it had a traumatic effect on him. The second incident was a racial incident that occurred on one of his many visits into downtown Nashville. While walking and dressed in a suit as usual, he accidentally bumped into a white woman. He immediately apologized; the woman turned, saw that he was black, slapped him, no doubt enraged at a polite gesture coming from a black man. She perceived his behavior as arrogant (Marable 1986, p. 11). Du Bois never forgot this, and despite his involvement in the community, he never went into Nashville again during his student years.

It was at Fisk that Du Bois decided to present himself in his manner and speech as very correct and proper—a model of a gentleman. This was part of a very deliberate image that he decided to convey early in his college years. He was determined to show to all others, white and black, that a black man could be refined and cultured, and could enjoy all of the high and noble things of life. So he endeavored to be just the opposite of the accepted stereotypes that black men had to be subservient, unkempt, and without good taste. For the rest of his life he was always immaculately dressed and sensitive to his public image. This attention to image pervaded everything he did.

Du Bois finally got to Harvard. His professors at Fisk recommended him and he was admitted as a junior. He was given a fellowship of $250 and deliberately lived off campus in a rooming house. This is significant because most of the white students lived on campus in a series of halls with distinct dining clubs. Du Bois intentionally limited his involvement with Harvard to his studies after his glee club application was turned down. And, as before, he found social support and encouragement in the Boston black community and wrote with several other students for the *Boston Courant*, a black weekly. I suspect that he found black women in Boston to be among the more progressive members of the community—his friendship with St. Pierre Ruffin, a national leader of the black women's club movement and editor of the *Courant* was an indication of this (Marable 1986, p. 14). Du Bois' life-long support of women's equity and political enfranchisement is a point seriously underestimated by Du Bois biographers—it was in evidence as far back as Great Barrington but it took formal expression during his Harvard years in Boston. As others have pointed out, by his Boston years Du Bois was very clear about his long-term goals for improving the political and social conditions and relative position of African Americans in the United States and of playing a leadership role in this improvement.

Despite Du Bois' reticence as to social involvement with whites at Harvard, he had very good and close relations with several faculty members who were his mentors. They were Albert Bushnell Hart in history, George Santayana, and William James in philosophy. In fact, Du Bois was very much impressed with William James, was a guest in the home of Dr. and Mrs. James, and for a while thought that he would be a philosopher. But financial considerations changed his mind. At Harvard, after his bachelor's degree and while working on his master's degree, he gave a paper at the 1891 meeting of the American Historical Association. This paper was on the "Suppression of the African Slave Trade." It was very unusual for a black person to be allowed to present a paper at this time. There were substantial written comments on Du Bois' paper from the professors present. Shortly after this presentation, he completed his master's degree.

Du Bois wanted to study abroad. This was something that he wanted to do while at Fisk, but, there, he had neither the money nor the opportunity. At Harvard it was the practice that, after completing their masters degrees, the best students went to Europe for their doctoral degrees. Former U.S. President Rutherford B. Hayes was a member of a Harvard board and was quoted as saying with regard to overseas fellowship funds that the money was always given to white students because no Negro was capable. Du Bois wrote an angry letter to Hayes. To his surprise, Hayes met with Du Bois in New York and agreed to financially support his trip to Germany from the Slater Fund for the Education of Negroes. After his meeting with Hayes, Du Bois celebrated by walking down Fifth Avenue in New York, saw an expensive shirt in a shop window, and bought it—he had to be dressed appropriately in Europe.

Berlin was important to him; he loved his studies and did very well at Friedrich Wilhelm University. Because his money was so limited, he kept very strict financial accounts, which became a life-long habit. His best male friend was a Jewish student from Poland. They took a trip together where a hotel manager agreed to give Du Bois a room but not his Jewish friend. Du Bois was amazed at this reversal of what one expected in the United States. Of course, he did not stay there. Du Bois and his friend continued to correspond after he left Germany. It was also in Germany that Du Bois met the sociologist Max Weber who, later in Du Bois' career, visited him in Atlanta.

Weber wanted to have Du Bois' *Souls of Black Folks* (1903) translated into German, but the project was never done, probably because of World War I. But despite doing well academically, Du Bois did not get his Ph.D. from Friedrich Wilhelm University. The faculty refused to give him an early oral examination and the Slater Fund refused to provide additional funds. He believed that he deserved the doctorate and was very disappointed.

Du Bois came home in debt and without a Ph.D., but he had learned a great lesson—that racism against black people in the United States was neither an innate condition nor a natural disposition among European peoples. He saw it then as a peculiar American phenomenon. He was all the more determined to devote his career to challenging racism. It was on his twenty-fifth birthday that he recorded in his diary that he pledged to make a difference in history. By then all of the necessary experiences and training were in place for him to begin his extraordinary career. At this point the only thing missing was an idea, a goal, and an alternative to the social system as he knew it. He knew about Karl Marx and had attended local meetings of the German Social Democratic party, but he was not a socialist when he came back from Germany. But more importantly, he was on his way toward defining his own sense of socialism.

Early Career and Family

After returning from Europe, Du Bois started his teaching career as an instructor of Latin and Greek at Wilberforce College in Xenia, Ohio. He wanted to teach more but they would not let him. His attire and obvious lack of religious piety were of great concern to the college's religious administration. Meanwhile, he worked on his Harvard Ph.D. dissertation, "The Suppression of the African Slave Trade, 1638–1870." He was awarded the degree in 1895, and the thesis became part of the Harvard Historical Series studies as volume one. While in Ohio, Du Bois also married. He was physically a very handsome man, and women were very attracted to him. He welcomed them, loved every bit of it, had no hang-ups with women, and had great respect for them. His first wife was Nina Gomer Du Bois. She was a student at Wilberforce, from an Iowa farm background. She was also biracial—her father was a black carpenter and her mother was German.

Du Bois' attire, abrupt marriage, and outspoken views alienated him from the Wilberforce administration; for this reason he knew that it would not be long before they terminated his appointment. The perfect opportunity came along. He was recruited to come to the University of Pennsylvania and to a settlement house in Philadelphia to do a study of the Negro community in Philadelphia. He went to Philadelphia with his young bride and baby, moved into the Seventh Ward (the study site), and lived over a cafeteria. Du Bois worked around the clock for one-and-a-half years studying everything that was available on the Seventh Ward. He personally interviewed 5,000 individuals and paid particular attention to their migration patterns from the South and how they financially managed amidst extreme poverty in Philadelphia. Meanwhile, Nina suffered.

Living in the city for the first time and taking care of their first child was an ordeal. Du Bois' salary did not put them much above the condition of others in the community. This is when Du Bois wrote his classic, *The Philadelphia Negro* (1899), which is the first urban sociological study ever done in the United States. He began urban sociology as it is known today; he had no model, no theories, and no established methodologies from which to base his work. Du Bois stated modestly, sometime in the 1950s, that, "I made this study of the Philadelphia Negro which is even recognized today as a good sort of social study and has been very widely used."

The Philadelphia Negro was an extraordinary study and was recognized as such shortly after publication. With Du Bois' training, published Harvard thesis, and now a major work, he should have been sought after by the major universities. But this was the 1890s when the plight of black people in the United States and in many other parts of the world was becoming more desperate. The only place Du Bois could get a university position was in a black college. Given his scholarly and personal interests in black people, he went after another black college appointment. This time it was at Atlanta University, which was somewhat more enlightened and tolerant of Du Bois' liberal views of God and his willingness to speak out. Atlanta University also wanted Du Bois because the university was interested in doing a series of conference studies on the plight of black people in cities—Dr. Du Bois was perfectly qualified. He was appointed as Professor of History and Economics in 1897 and was soon on his way toward producing another series of vitally important studies.

In Atlanta, tragedy struck soon after he and his family were settled. Their son and first child, Burghardt Gomer Du Bois, died of sewage pollution from Atlanta's water system a year and a half after his birth. He was buried in Great Barrington. Nina Gomer Du Bois continued to be very unhappy in Atlanta as she had been in Philadelphia, but now the loss of their son was a devastating burden. Dr. Du Bois told me that his wife never recovered from this loss and was quite depressed thereafter. The loss of his son sensitized Du Bois, and gave him a sense of the spiritual meaning that so many other blacks around him depended on. In addition, Atlanta was becoming increasingly dangerous as the iron curtain of Jim Crow descended on the South. In anticipation of a white race riot against blacks, the Du Bois' had a secret hiding place in their house for their daughter, Yolanda, in case their home was attacked. While Du Bois was away doing research in Alabama for the federal government, Mrs. Du Bois had to use it in 1906 during a major uprising. Fortunately, the rioters did not harm her, the baby, or the house on the Atlanta University campus. Du Bois caught the first train back. He sat with his shotgun on the porch for hours just in case the rioters came back. Shortly after, he moved his family to Baltimore and for years had two residences—in Baltimore and Atlanta.

What many Du Bois scholars are not aware of is the extent to which Du Bois conducted studies for the U.S. government. Besides his better-known Atlanta University conference studies, he did extensive fieldwork of sharecropping in Alabama and Virginia. This was very dangerous work. He risked his life many times interviewing sharecroppers at night in fields, at crossroads, and at informants' homes. As a result, few people knew the South as well as Du Bois. He knew its heart and soul. Since these were contracted studies, they were turned over to the government and were not published. Some years later, Dr. Du Bois came to the conclusion that they were not being used by the government to better the plight of black sharecroppers. So he went to the Labor Department to get them. What he found out was that his years of work, and what were undoubtedly the most important and extensive studies of sharecropping ever done, had been destroyed. They did not even offer to give the studies back to him or give them to a library or archive which was then the practice. The studies that survived, such as *The Negroes of Farmville, Virginia: A Social Study* (1898); *The Negro in the Black Belt: Some Social Sketches* (1899); and others were only a fraction of his work. He told me that the Labor Department analysts thought the studies were too critical, too detailed, too real, and amounted to a condemnation of the South. This was one of the most devastating events in Du Bois' professional career—for years afterwards, he did not even want to talk about it.

The Labor Department was not the only agency that found Du Bois' work threatening. In time, as at Wilberforce College, Du Bois' work and his willingness to be outspoken got him in hot water repeatedly with the Atlanta University administration. He was simply too radical; but the lack of funding did not prevent him from completing an extraordinary series of studies. He did the entire Atlanta University studies over fourteen years on less than $5,000 per year. In addition, he wrote *The Souls of Black Folks: Essays and*

Sketches (1903); *John Brown* (1909); and edited conference works, *The Negro in Business* (1899); *The College-Bred Negro* (1900); *The Negro Common School* (1901); *The Negro Artisan* (1902); *The Negro Church* (1903); *Some Notes on Negro Crime, Particularly in Georgia* (1904); and *The Health and Physique of the Negro American* (1906). Wealthy donors refused to contribute to the university because of his presence and his prominence in criticizing Booker T. Washington. He was concerned that he was an embarrassment to Atlanta University, which he loved, and was costing this struggling institution money it desperately needed.

Du Bois' experiences doing research, in the community, and in criticizing the most prominent black powerbroker and accommodationist in the early Jim Crow period, Booker T. Washington, affected Du Bois' political thinking. By 1907 he realized that there was an alternative to Jim Crow racial segregation and economic exploitation. He considered himself a socialist and said so. But Du Bois' criticism of American racism was not limited to domestic affairs; his magazine and newspaper writing while in Atlanta made this very clear. Ever since his years in Europe, Du Bois had paid particular attention to the international scope of racial oppression. By 1901 and 1902 he was aware of the atrocities committed by the U.S. Army in the Philippines. He knew of the Anti-Imperialist League in 1899, headed by Moorfield Storey, who later played a prominent role in the founding of the National Association for the Advancement of Colored People (NAACP). Du Bois showed pictures of the atrocities committed by the American troops in the Philippines in his classroom. This is also the time when Du Bois met the prominent anthropologist, Franz Boas, who came to speak in Atlanta. Boas had been working his way intellectually toward exposing the racial myth of innate white superiority, but he was not fully there yet. It was Du Bois' growing sense that the world could be changed for the better, his determination to make change for the better happen, and the increasing isolation and struggle to hold onto to his academic position that prompted Du Bois to prepare to leave Atlanta by 1909. He resigned from Atlanta University in 1910 to join the newly founded NAACP.

Early Activism

The first decade of this century was decisive in the growth of Du Bois' political perspective. A series of developments in this first decade showed a progressive radicalization of Du Bois' thoughts. In 1900 at the first Pan-African Conference, Du Bois wrote the appeal to the world. But this was not an anti-imperialist statement. Rather, it was a liberal appeal for decency towards the colonies—he argued that it was in the best interest of all concerned that the major colonial powers treat their colonial nations humanely, that colonialism be eventually ended, and that it was up to educated Africans to make plans for this transition. He was not a radical at that time. At first he was even mildly supportive of Booker T. Washington. Only as Washington became the powerbroker for powerful industrial interests and failed to use his influence to oppose Jim Crow did Du Bois become concerned. And then, Du Bois focused mainly on Washington's potentially abusive business practices. There were others who were much more critical of Washington (Marable 1986, p. 46).

Booker T. Washington's apologetic leadership and service as a powerbroker in the face of worsening racial oppression radicalized many, including Du Bois. This was the decade (1900–1910) when the iron curtain of de jure segregation and racism rose in the South in very much the same fashion that open racism is being re-institutionalized today. This was the "Bloody Decade" with close to eight hundred lynchings, when the South passed its anti-black Jim Crow legislation. Remember it was in these critical regressive years that Du Bois traveled throughout Alabama, Virginia, and Georgia interviewing sharecroppers and ordinary black folks whose lives and livelihoods were being crushed. He was in the rural countryside doing increasingly covert and dangerous interviews as the rapes, nightriding, and hangings of black men and youth intensified. By the end of the decade his field experiments had radicalized him and alienated him from the accomodationist leadership of Booker T. Washington.

As the first decade of the new century passed, what pushed an increasingly radical Du Bois into a position of national leadership was the publication of *The Souls of Black Folks* in 1903. A key chapter in this book is "On Booker T. Washington and Others." This is a slightly revised version of "The Religion of the Negro" published in *New World* magazine (Boston) in 1900. *The Souls of Black Folks* was a bestseller and pushed Du Bois' relatively mild but pointed critique of Booker T. Washington into wide circulation and prominence. So when one considers the combination of factors—increasing racism, Du Bois' emerging radicalism, his prominence after *Souls,* and his personal ambition to improve the condition of the race—having to leave Atlanta University and his future leadership in the formation of the Niagara Movement and of the NAACP could have been predicted.

The Niagara Movement was to be an alternative to Booker T. Washington's organization and agenda. Like Du Bois, its members were college-educated and professional black men who advocated civil rights for blacks, enforcement of laws against lynching, and demanded that Blacks have access to a liberal arts education as a foundation for work in the trades and the professions. But given Du Bois' academic publication, research commitments, and disposition as a scholar, leadership was not one of his strengths. Booker T. Washington's "Tuskegee machine" campaign against the movement and its smear tactics nearly destroyed the Niagara Movement. Washington's opposition was also directly responsible for taking over a number of black community newspapers that were initially sympathetic to Du Bois' critique of Washington and for the unemployment of a number of Niagara Movement members (Marable 1986, p. 70).

Beginning of the NAACP

While the Niagara Movement was struggling for its survival, a white reform group, called the Constitution League and headed by John Milholland, had fallen out with Booker T. Washington as well. They had been supporters of Washington, but their critique of the Roosevelt administration's mass dishonorable discharge of black troops after the Brownsville, Texas riot put the league at odds with both President Roosevelt and Booker T. Washington. Du Bois knew Milholland well. It was Milholland who paid for Du Bois to go to London in 1910 to challenge and debate Booker T. Washington. In addition, Milholland's daughter, Inez, was a lawyer and one of the white women who helped found the NAACP. She was very radical but died in her thirties. Du Bois and Milholland's friendship led to the joining of the black Niagara Movement and the white Constitution League and the formation of the National Association for the Advancement of Colored People in 1909.

But it took more than Du Bois and Milholland's friendship to get the NAACP started. The decisive event was the 1908 Springfield, Illinois riot where a number of black men were lynched. A white socialist who was a founder of the NAACP as well, William English Walling, later described the riot and lynchings and called for white liberals to build a new social movement. In 1909, the first NAACP convention was held in New York City with both blacks and whites in attendance. Much of the historical writing about the early founding of the NAACP portrays its white cofounders as sort of liberal reformers. Many were a lot more than that. They were, in fact, socialists and radicals in their day. George Frazier Miller, the black minister from Brooklyn, was a socialist. Also by this time Du Bois called himself a socialist, though he did not clearly define what he meant by it. Among the white NAACP founders was Mary White Ovington, a left-socialist. The most "moderate" of these white founders was Oswald Garrison Villard who was not a socialist and not nearly as radical as his grandfather, William Lloyd Garrison. He, like Milholland, was an early supporter of Booker T. Washington but had become quite critical of the Tuskegee machine's excesses as well.

Here it must be pointed out that the NAACP as its founders conceived of it is not in its philosophy, goals, potential, or strategies, the organization we know today. Then the NAACP stood for the international advancement of "colored people." This was not just for African Americans. It was to include Filipinos, Native Americans, and Puerto Ricans as well. This was stated quite explicitly at the founding of the NAACP. I am afraid the current leadership has forgotten that. They did not call themselves "colored" because it was a high-class thing to do or because they were snobbish or wanted to deny who they were. They meant just that "colored peoples." The first president of the NAACP was the white radical, Moorfield Storey. Storey was also the first president of the Anti-Imperialist League of the United States. His interest prior to the NAACP included the liberation of the Philippines from the United States and genocide committed in this country against Native Americans. Du Bois was a member of the league and, while he was in Atlanta, wrote to Storey congratulating him on his work. The pictures Du Bois showed to his classes of the atrocities of U.S. troops in the Philippines were obtained from Moorfield Storey.

If anyone has any doubts about the radical roots and persons behind the founding of the NAACP, they should read *The New York Times* article on the founding of the NAACP to see how frightened many were of the organization and its founders. A black radical group that advocated racial equity could be ignored and then would have to struggle to survive assaults from Booker T. Washington, as was the case of the Niagara Movement. A white radical group would be too distant from the problem and would lack credibility. However, black and white radicals together would be beyond Booker T. Washington's control; could potentially have access to the black rank and file; could have credibility as advocates and spokes-people on the race issue as it effected whites and blacks; and could have access to the white general public. An interracial radical organization would also be a living testimony that racism is unnecessary and not something innate for either blacks or whites. Ironically, the white establishment was not the only ones troubled with the idea and reality of a radical interracial organization. The black radical, Ida B. Wells-Barnett, quit the NAACP because she felt that there were too many white people involved. The black radical newspaper editor, Monroe Trotter, also refused to be a part of the NAACP for the same reason.

Just as many people think of Du Bois as just concerned with and a leader of only blacks, many divide his life and thinking according to their own sharp division between domestic and foreign affairs. This is not accurate for Du Bois. His outrage over events in the South and equally shocking events overseas was connected as far back as his student days in Berlin. He saw the connection between oppression here and overseas. The NAACP, as it was founded by others who were equally international in their perspective, was the perfect vehicle for Du Bois' activism. In which case, his leadership in the Pan-African movement was not something apart from his involvement in a globally defined NAACP and the British labor party. His Pan-Africanism was supported by the early NAACP radicals. Remember that it was John Milholland (an NAACP founder) who made it possible for Du Bois to attack Booker T. Washington in London in 1910—something that was beyond the resources of the Niagara Movement.

The Pan-African Meetings

Dr. Du Bois was not the only black activist who believed in the need for a Pan-African movement. This was a dream of black anti-colonial activists in the Caribbean, in Africa, and in the United States. Martin Delaney and Robert Campbell had a Pan-Africanism implied in their back-to-Africa efforts in the 1860s. Marcus Garvey and George Padmore called for a Pan-Africansm as well as did Monroe Trotter. Du Bois' importance to this dream is that he brought to the table his bridging of white and black radicals who could see the domestic "race problem" as part of a larger blueprint that included international oppression as well. It had been overlooked that visions of a Pan-African conference went from dream to reality in 1919 partly and critically because of the resources, contacts, and organization of a trans-racial and international socialist movements. Du Bois articulated, years before the Labor Party did, that domestic racism was an outcome of international capitalism. He and the early NAACP served as an early model for the party's realization of the advantages of interracial collaboration. Today, we underestimate the importance of socialism in the first two decades of this century in bringing together dispersed radicals and of the importance of the early Pan-African meetings. These conferences took place at the high point of European colonialism and imperialism, and were not easily organized.

Our point is evident when the Pan-African meetings in 1900 and 1914 are compared to the 1919 conference. In 1900 Du Bois' statement in the *Report of the Pan-African Conference,* "To The Nations of the World" is really very mild. This document did not have the kind of systematic critique that was in the 1919 statement, nor did the 1900 conference have the attendance, support, follow-up, or impact of the 1919 conference. Nothing came of this first meeting. The 1914 meeting really did not occur. In 1914 just before World War I, Duse Mohammed Ali and Du Bois attempted to organize the conference but were told that Paris was under martial law and the conference could not be held at that time. So the conference had to wait until after the first World War. But by 1914 Du Bois would not have written the same kind of protest and appeal for decency that he did in 1900. In this fourteen-year period he had come to see much more clearly the relationship between capitalism, imperialism, and racism at home and abroad—they were all interconnected; one could not be separated from another.

Virtually every issue of *The Crisis*, edited by Du Bois, comments on domestic and foreign affairs—and not just on Africa, but Europe, Asia, South America, and the Caribbean as well. When Du Bois organized the massive 1917 anti-lynching parade in New York, it was meant to be not only a protest against a domestic outrage (lynching), it was also meant to bring international pressure on the United States. This is why Du Bois marched at the front of the parade down New York City's most famous avenue, Fifth Avenue. If this had been simply a racial protest with no interest in attracting international attention, the parade could have been held more easily in Harlem. In fact, because of Du Bois' fine knowledge of how capitalism, imperialism, and racism worked at home and abroad, he was able to anticipate both world wars as logical outcomes of these processes. Another way to appreciate Du Bois' growing world perspective and how domestic affairs related to it is to compare the content and approach of *The Souls of Black Folks* (1903) with the greatly-ignored little book, *The Negro* (1915). *Souls* has a domestic focus and is introspective, while *The Negro* is international, bridges the geographic and historic divisions, and was and still is essential background work for a real post-colonial and post-neo-colonial Pan-Africanism.

Unlike the prior meetings, the 1919 Pan-African conference attracted the active opposition and concern of the President of the United States, Woodrow Wilson. Wilson was concerned not simply because Du Bois wrote to him, informed him that the meeting was going to take place, and asked for his support. The 1919 meeting was a threat precisely because it raised the specter of a domestic front of blacks, whites, and socialists united in their criticisms of capitalism and imperialism. But now this domestic threat was becoming international. As in 1914, the 1919 meeting might have not happened as well. Du Bois' movements around Paris were closely monitored by Colonel Edward House, a Wilson aide, and Major F. P. Schoonmaker of the U.S. Army.

Not surprisingly, Du Bois was having a great deal of trouble getting permission from the French to hold the conference. That the conference happened at all can be attributed to the support of Blaise Diagne, who, according to George Padmore, was the most influential colonial politician in France and a close friend of the French Premier, Georges Clemençeau (Marable 1986, pp. 100–101). It probably also helped that Du Bois' plans were viewed by the French and other observers as utopian, without revolutionary intent and had no chance of influencing the delegates at the postwar Paris Peace Conference. While the 1919 Paris Pan-African Conference did not dissuade the great powers' practice of colonialism, it did achieve a less ambitious goal. Educated Africans came together to get to know each other and to lay down plans to address the eventual emancipation of Africans.

Du Bois represented a radical and interracial NAACP at the 1919 Pan-African Conference that supported his leadership role—imagine such a leader and organization today. Unlike the 1900 Pan-African meeting, in 1919 Du Bois represented an organization which claimed three hundred branches and 88,488 members, half of which were in the South. By 1919 *The Crisis* magazine had a circulation of over 70,000 (Marable 1986, p. 97). An independent but important related development was the rise in socialist and union memberships during the decades leading up to 1919. Members of socialist and union organizations represented the core of domestic opposition to capitalism, were supportive of antiracism, and supported blacks as members in their organization. Given this fact, Woodrow Wilson had good reason to take notice and to be concerned.

Interactions with Booker T. Washington

There was no behind-the-scenes relationship between Booker T. Washington and W. E. B. Du Bois. For most of Booker T. Washington's career, those whom he could not control, he spied on by bribing people close to them. Washington also attempted to destroy their reputations and livelihoods through well-placed lies and misinformation in the press. Booker T. Washington's behind-the-scenes attempt to oppose Jim Crow and the lynchings came relatively late in his career, after he had served to compromise opposition to Jim Crow in its earliest and most vulnerable days. Washington's behind-the-scenes opposition to Jim Crow was independent of and in opposition to all the groups that opposed the political and educational disenfranchisement of blacks in the South from the start of Jim Crow. For decades, he tried to destroy Du Bois, nearly succeeded in destroying the Niagara Movement, and fought the

NAACP with published lies about black men and white women having sexually suggestive dances and dinners together.

Booker T. Washington recognized Du Bois' potential to oppose him before the publication of *The Souls of Black Folks* in 1903. Washington tried to control Du Bois by offering him a professorship at Tuskegee. Du Bois asked what he would teach, and never got a clear response from Washington. Washington later regretted not responding and saw this offer as a lost opportunity to try to gain control over Du Bois. Washington also tried to get Du Bois the position as superintendent of colored education in the District of Columbia as a way to control him and failed.

Then there was the 1903 meeting of black leaders sponsored by Andrew Carnegie in New York City. Carnegie paid for all of the leaders' expenses, except Du Bois'. At this meeting, Carnegie appeared at the beginning, welcomed everyone, and then left. Another time after an attempted reconciliation meeting between Washington and Du Bois in New York City, Du Bois spoke of a conversation he had with Booker T. Washington while they rode a trolley together. Du Bois asked Washington about Andrew Carnegie. Washington responded that Mr. Carnegie talked very little but had a great deal of money. At this meeting, they made plans to develop some kind of partnership and organization. But Du Bois would not have anything to do with it because he knew that Booker T. Washington was corrupt and could not be trusted. They published a couple of pamphlets together and that was the extent of their collaboration. Du Bois believed that Washington was very much aware that Carnegie was interested in him only because of the coal and iron mining prospects in Alabama. Carnegie wanted free access to these resources and did not want black labor agitation. Carnegie's relationship with Booker T. Washington paid off—Birmingham, Alabama, became the center of Carnegie's U.S. Steel Corporation. Booker T. Washington tried to discredit the NAACP and Du Bois right up to his death in 1915.

Du Bois and the "Harlem Renaissance"

Very few people know that Du Bois was also a father of the mistitled "Harlem Renaissance" along with Alain Locke. It was mistakenly identified only as a Harlem event when in fact the arts and letters among blacks flourished in St. Louis, Chicago, and New Orleans as well. It was a national renaissance. In the 1920s there were very few great black artists, writers, poets, or singers whose careers were not supported by Du Bois. He wrote about them in *The Crisis*, and the writers and poets were able to use *The Crisis* as a forum for their voices. They included Marian Anderson, Langston Hughes, Arna Bontemps, and especially Elizabeth Prophet. Du Bois first published Langston Hughes and Countee Cullen, and set up the *The Crisis'* group of writers and scholars, as well as the first serious live theater in Harlem, The Negro Theater. During the 1920s he was an organizer, agitator, and the father of the black intelligentsia.

By 1930 Du Bois had worked vigorously for three decades, was nearly sixty years old, and had lived apart from his first wife since 1906, after she moved to Baltimore. Du Bois never moved to Baltimore, nor did Nina and their daughter, Yolanda, move to New York. He visited them occasionally and corresponded. The letters were practical and focused on what Nina needed, and how Yolanda was doing. Clearly they had grown apart. Nina Gomer Du Bois died in 1950. At eighteen years old, Yolanda married Countee Cullen and eventually became a high school French teacher. It turned out that Cullen was a homosexual. He had his male lover with him on his and Yolanda's honeymoon. Du Bois did not know about the homosexuality, but he did find out that Cullen was not making love to his daughter and wrote a letter to Cullen on how to be gentle with her, how to make love, and to care for her. Countee Cullen eventually married another woman who was very wealthy and lived on Fifth Avenue. Yolanda died in her sixties in the late 1950s.

Du Bois' Relation with Marcus Garvey

Marcus Garvey came to the United States in 1916, originally at the invitation of Booker T. Washington. He was in charge of a school in Jamaica founded on the same philosophy of preparing students for practical work as Tuskegee's. But Booker T. Washington died in 1915 before Garvey's arrival. When Garvey finally got to New York, one of the first people he wanted to see was Du Bois. Garvey and Du Bois knew one another from one of Du Bois' earlier trips to Jamaica to lecture. Garvey had been a newspaper reporter and columnist who interviewed Du Bois and had been part of the welcoming committee. In New York Garvey went to Du Bois' office, but, as fate would have it, Du Bois was not there. Garvey left a note, and they continued to correspond. For the first five years of Garvey's career in the United States, Du Bois was favorably impressed with him; he was an outstanding and militant anti-imperialist, Pan-Africanist, and an inspired black orator and leader. You will find nothing critical in *The Crisis* about Garvey until 1923. Prior to that Du Bois only expressed concerns about Garvey's business associates. There were thousands of supporters who sent a dime a month to Garvey's United Negro Improvement Association. Du Bois wanted to know where that money was going. No one questioned Garvey's honesty, but his business associates left much to be desired.

In the early 1920s Marcus Garvey changed abruptly from a militant anti-imperialist to a Pan-African black capitalist and leader of black emigrationism. At the same time Garvey began to be very critical of Du Bois and of the NAACP. Like Booker T. Washington, he attacked the NAACP's interracial composition. Garvey was also very derogatory toward Du Bois; he compared Du Bois' lighter skin color to his own darker color, suggesting that Du Bois could not be trusted as a black man and leader because of his mixed blood. Garvey never really understood how color was viewed differently in the United States than in his native Jamaica. Du Bois tried to explain the difference to Garvey in *The Crisis,* but it was too late.

Garvey and several associates were framed and arrested by the U.S. government for mail fraud in 1924. But the others were not tried, and several of Garvey's crooked associates testified against him and were not prosecuted. Only Garvey was convicted and sent to prison. This is one of the first cases J. Edgar Hoover, the long-time Director of the Federal Bureau of Investigation, was involved in. Hoover considered Garvey's domestic and international movement to be a threat to the United States and wanted to get Garvey. Robert Hill, who is [currently] editing Garvey's works, is finding more and more about Garvey's abrupt change and is trying to understand how and why he became more and more conservative—to the point of having secret meetings with the Ku Klux Klan who supported Garvey's plan to take American Negroes back to Africa. The white supremacist U.S. Senator, Theodore Bilbo, was also very happy with Garvey's position and recommended that the U.S. Senate support it. Garvey and Bilbo formed a united front for which Du Bois blasted Garvey in the "Opinion" section of *The Crisis* by asking if Garvey was "A Lunatic or a Traitor?"

The Crisis Magazine and Du Bois' Leadership

By 1934 the NAACP lost its radical potential. It became increasingly distant from its international mission and its identity became primarily that of a black middle-class organization. All during this time, Du Bois maintained the independence of *The Crisis,* a journal he founded, which became the official organ of the NAACP. Du Bois was the organization's most visible and well-known figure. His prominence was based largely on the centrality that *The Crisis* took in shaping progressive black opinion. Du Bois, through *The Crisis,* was the most consistent and critical black voice in the nation for over two decades. Du Bois' views in *The Crisis* had survived Booker T. Washington, Marcus Garvey, and a host of others. Du Bois described *The Crisis* as "a little monthly magazine that would discuss the Negro problem and tell both Blacks and Whites what the NAACP was about and what it proposed to do." In doing so he made a lot of enemies, both inside and outside of the NAACP. But the magazine was financially self-sufficient. It paid for itself and his salary, and cost the NAACP nothing for twenty years while it provided the NAACP with national and international exposure.

In addition to editing *The Crisis,* Du Bois wrote weekly columns for the *New York Amsterdam News* and *The Chicago Defender.* He also traveled around the country in the 1930s, including the South, making militant speeches. Few people could have imagined that Dr. Du Bois spent years driving through the South, relieved himself in the woods, carried sandwiches to eat, traveled with a pistol and was prepared to use it, wore coveralls, and repaired his car himself. This is what you had to do as a black man traveling in the South—Du Bois was no exception. Besides being a genius, the man had endless energy. Du Bois was an extraordinarily talented and driven man—one in a million. He also had fantastic creativity.

Once I went to interview Norman Thomas, who knew Du Bois. Thomas said to me that the main thing about Du Bois was that he was a prophet. Du Bois kept planning calendars not only for months at a time, but he planned his work a decade in advance. In his Atlanta University studies of the Negro family, health, crime, and so on, Du Bois laid out what he hoped would be a century of studies. He had hoped that these studies would be redone periodically to see what had changed. Du Bois realized that Atlanta was a marvelous social laboratory of a suppressed people. Yes, he was a scholar, but he was also an activist who passionately wanted to see his people free in the United States and Africa.

Besides Du Bois the activist, he still produced pioneering scholarly works. The other classics Du Bois wrote during this time were *John Brown* (1904); *The Negro* (1915); *Darkwater: Voices Within the Veil* (1920); *The Gift of Black Folk: The Negro in the Making of America* (1924); and *Black Reconstruction* (1935). Between February of 1910 and May 1921 alone, Du Bois wrote 571 magazine editorials, articles, and commentaries. This is roughly about half of his lifetime's work in this category. He wrote two historical novels—*The Quest of the Silver Fleece* (1911); and *Dark Princess* (1928). This record of productivity does not include pamphlets, edited works, and chapters he wrote for others.

Du Bois did not show any tension between going back and forth between activism and scholarship. His only complaint was over being barred from using certain libraries because of his race. Despite all that he did, Du Bois was not able to do the research he would have liked to have done because of racial restrictions. Du Bois was doing precisely what he felt his purpose in life was, and there was no distinction in his mind between scholarship and activism.

Du Bois Leaves the NAACP

Tension had grown between Du Bois and the NAACP leadership because he was now much more radical than they. The NAACP had become a mildly reformist and gentlemanly organization which only worked consistently to oppose the crudest form of racism—lynchings. Du Bois wanted the organization to have a much larger mass following and to be more radical. In the 1930s, socialists through the CIO and the National Negro Congress were pushing Roosevelt during the Great Depression's New Deal toward progressive reforms. Twenty years earlier the NAACP might have played this role. Du Bois felt that the New Deal had both positive and negative aspects for black people, but the NAACP leadership was unable to make such distinctions. So Du Bois tried to change the NAACP by getting his own people on the NAACP board of directors and failed. By 1933, the socialist radicals were gone and the board was dominated by white liberals such as Joel Spingarn, whom Du Bois held in high regard. After failing to change the NAACP, Du Bois resigned and did so without criticizing the leadership. The NAACP acknowledged his historic work with them.

What Du Bois did not know was that Joel Spingarn was an Army intelligence officer in World War I, still maintained his government connections, and was directed to keep track of Du Bois. When Du Bois began to organize the 1919 Pan-African Conference, the Russian Revolution had already begun, and intelligence officers in this country were concerned that there might have been some connection between the Soviets and the Pan-African movement. No one knows to what extent Spingarn made reports to Washington, but he clearly watched Du Bois for years. Du Bois loved Spingarn and would have been very hurt to find this out.

In 1934 Du Bois was over sixty years old and became an Atlanta University professor again. In the next decade, he published *Black Folks Then and Now* (1939); *Dusk of Dawn* (1940); and *Color and Democracy: Colonies and Peace* (1945). He wrote several hundred more magazine and newspaper articles and taught and chaired the Atlanta University Department of Sociology. He continued to be radical, outspoken, critical, and still regarded by many as a national leader. But in 1944 the Atlanta University Board of Directors fired him. He was astonished.

Du Bois and the Cold War

One of the great ironies of Du Bois' long career is that he went back to the NAACP after being fired from Atlanta University. He was invited back to head their new research unit. He saw this as a renewed opportunity to turn the NAACP into a force against colonialism. This hope was made possible by World War II. It was a war against racism, against fascism, against Hitlerism, and for democracy. These were all things that Du Bois and the NAACP supported. But this period of elevated consciousness and unity ended when the war ended, and by 1947 big business and government were trying to reestablish the prewar status quo. Du Bois found himself at odds again with the NAACP leadership. He was not the only one who found the postwar years repressive. I was an officer assigned to a black artillery battalion during World War II. By 1949 President Truman took away my commission because of my views and friendships with Negroes—which just confirmed for them that I was a subversive.

The major source of difference Du Bois had with the NAACP leadership was over their support of President Truman's cold war against the Soviet bloc nations. The head of the NAACP, Walter White, believed that by supporting Truman there would be domestic civil rights concessions from the federal government. Du Bois asked what the NAACP could possibly gain from supporting Truman's policies, which were only a continuation of Western imperialism and colonialism. The tension between Du Bois and White over the position of the NAACP on U.S. foreign policy became evident when they served together with Mary McCloud Bethune on an advisory committee for the founding of the United Nations. Their committee represented black people in the United States. What did they encounter at the founding meeting in San Francisco? The United States, France, and Great Britain dominated the meeting. Nehru of India and the Soviet Union's V. M. Molotov tried to have an anti-colonial policy instituted from the beginning. They failed due to opposition from the big three. Du Bois noted the United States' support of continued colonialism, and the contradiction between the United Nations' Charter and the admission of fascist Argentina to the United Nations. Du Bois tried to convince the U.S. delegation to support the fight against colonialism. He was unsuccessful, said so, and then came out in opposition to U.S. pro-colonial cold war foreign policies. But Walter White and the NAACP board supported Truman's foreign policy. So in September of 1949 Du Bois was again dismissed from the NAACP.

Du Bois did not give up nor did he go into retirement as he approached eighty. By 1949 Du Bois joined Paul Robeson as co-chair of the Council on African Affairs. This was a small but important postwar public policy effort and the only voice of Africa in America at that time. Du Bois did a lot of public speaking for the council. They eventually published *Decision in Africa* (1957) written by Dr. W. Alphaeus Hunton—Hunton had been fired from Howard University for being too radical, was modest to a fault, and was highly regarded by Du Bois. The council kept alive the postwar protest on Africa, especially the case of South Africa as apartheid was being institutionalized. The council worked to educate the public and to influence U.S. foreign policy until McCarthyism closed the council and forced it into bankruptcy. Some of the council members went to jail. Alphaeus Hunton got six months for refusing to turn over the files and records of the council to J. Edgar Hoover's FBI.

In 1950, Du Bois was still an influential national voice who helped shape progressive public opinion in the United States. He was a candidate for the U.S. Senate and got 250,000 votes against a fairly progressive Herbert Lehman. Du Bois was an active and potential candidate for public office at eighty years old. I recommended to him that he run for governor instead—that was a race he might have won!

By 1950 Du Bois was also a leader in the United States for the fight against the continued development and deployment of the atomic bomb. He was chairman of the Peace Information Center, which was the U.S. arm for the distribution of the Stockholm Appeal. This was a worldwide effort to stop the development of the atomic bomb. In three paragraphs, the petition pleaded with the United States not to develop the bomb, to ban its deployment, and charged that the first nation to use an atomic weapon committed a criminal act against humanity. Two million people signed the appeal in the United States. Millions more signed it in the world community. The response of the U.S. government to the Stockholm Appeal came through President Truman's Secretary of State, Acheson. He accused Du Bois at the age of eighty-one, of being an unregistered foreign agent. Du Bois was indicted, arrested, and fingerprinted. This was in 1951. Du Bois got cables of support from all over the world. Ghana's Nkrumah asked Truman if the United States had gone insane in arresting Dr. Du Bois. India's Nehru asked the same question of the President.

Before the trial, the government offered Du Bois a deal. If he would plead guilty to being an unregistered foreign agent, they guaranteed that they would drop the charges. The government had no idea whom they had arrested. Du Bois wrote back saying that he had been offered many deals in his life, but that he was too old to even think of this one and before he would lie to his government, he would rot in jail. He went on to say that some jail time might do him some good. Du Bois believed that this was a matter of freedom of speech. He was a fanatical believer in the Bill of Rights from his early Massachusetts rearing. Fortunately he had good attorneys. The judge, named McGuire, had a lot of integrity—like an old-fashioned Republican. Du Bois was indicted under the McCormick Act—not the McCarran Act. The McCormick Act requires substantial proof of the charge. The McCarran Act does not have such a requirement—it is a bill of attainder. The government presented its case, which was no case. After a short time, the judge asked the prosecution if they had proof that Du Bois was a foreign agent—was there something in writing, a group of witnesses, or any substantial evidence? They had to answer that they had none. All they had was an informant, named O. John Rogge, who was used to indict Du Bois. The judge denounced the prosecution in open court, told them that they had wasted the time of the court and the taxpayer's money and acquitted Du Bois. The case never went to a jury. This was one of the great moments in recent history and in 1952 was the first victory against McCarthyism.

All during the late 1940s and the 1950s there were efforts to hang the "communist" label on Du Bois. Secretary of State Acheson continued to accuse Du Bois of being a dupe of the communists and to claim that the Stockholm Appeal was a communist plot. The NAACP leadership refused to assist in Du Bois' defense at the trial because they believed that he was "guilty" and because it would have jeopardized their relations with the government. There is something the government, the NAACP, and many others do not understand about Du Bois. He advocated his own brand of socialism independent of any ideology or sponsorship. But fundamentally, he was an anti-capitalist, anti-racist, anti-imperialist, and anti-colonialist. He believed that production for individual profit was a failure as a just way to organize society, was immoral, selfish, and wrong. What he believed he said and said so often—this is all in his writings. The overwhelming subject of his newspaper and magazine articles, public speeches, and scholarship after 1948 was the international context of race and class. He had a dual devotion to peace and to the struggle to end Western economic oppression. People who are comfortable with Du Bois as a domestic race scholar and activist either do not know about his anti-capitalism and internationalism or cannot deal with this side of Du Bois—they believe what the government said about him. In which case, these readers focus on his work prior to 1934 and have ignored his more mature work afterward. The late-career Du Bois is evident in *The World and Africa* (1947) and *In Battle for Peace: The Story of My 83rd Birthday* (1952).

How much of a threat was Du Bois' work and how convincing was the government's effort to discredit him? One measure of both was that *The New York Times* did not mention Du Bois' name after 1948 until he died and then mention was very brief. The leading association of American historians through their review journal, the *American Historical Review*, has not to this day reviewed his great history book, *Black Reconstruction*. He became unmentionable. But all during this time of exile in this country, Du Bois continued to write books and to send manuscripts to publishers who had accepted his work in the past—Viking, Harper, and Harcourt Brace. But now he either got no answer or got rejection postcards. I was on the editorial board of *Masses and Mainstream*, which published his final books, including *In Battle for Peace* (1952). He also wrote another historical novel, *The Black Flame* (1957), which I edited. This three-volume set sold thousands of copies.

Why Du Bois Opposed the Cold War

For Americans who have only known the Cold War until its end in 1989, it may come as a shock that the forty years of a massive defense build up, the development and deployment of nuclear weapons, and the isolation and separation of domestic from international affairs was totally unnecessary. The Soviet Union did not initially pose a military threat to the United States or to Western Europe. Du Bois traveled to the Soviet Union several times to see for himself and saw no evidence that the Soviet Union was doing anything other than rebuilding itself after the war and defending itself against threats from the West. He asked what country would want to be a military threat to anyone after suffering twenty-seven million dead and the destruction of all of the European USSR during World War II? What were they going to do to the United States which escaped World War II with no damage and which became the leading economic and military force in the world? In 1947, when Truman began the Cold War, the Soviets were absolutely no match for the United States.

The Cold War was manufactured by the very industrial and military elites that President Eisenhower warned us of in the 1950s. The Soviet threat and the spread of world communism were all exaggerated, and this fact is now slowly coming to light. This point has been admitted in *The New York Times*—the CIA exaggerated the Soviet threat for years. And now Robert McNamara tells us in his *In Retrospect: The Tragedy and Lessons of Vietnam* (1995) that the war in Vietnam could not be won and was unnecessary. President Harry Truman deliberately began this hysteria. Du Bois knew it, called it what it was, and opposed it.

The Cold War was necessary in order to preserve pre–World War II economic and political control over former colonies that aspired for freedom and looked to the Soviet Union rather than the Untied States for anti-colonial leadership. The purpose of the Cold War was to prevent the stirring of liberation movements throughout the world, in particular in Africa and Asia. These movements would have prevented the massive expansion of capitalism overseas into the former colonies and has very effectively choked the development of third world domestic economies. The outcome of this expansion capital, which began shortly after World War II, has been neocolonialism, where third world nations were granted political independence but continued to be economically dependent on European mother countries. In more recent years with the collapse of Soviet socialist opposition, neocolonialism has been intensified. Third world nations are now nothing more than labor and resource reservations for the modern global economy. The very world economic system we are looking at today could not have been possible without the Cold War isolation of the socialist potential and the perversion of countless national liberation movements into pro- or anti-Western Cold War factions.

We now know that the socialism of most national liberation movements was secondary to their nationalism. Vietnam is one of the many examples. The war in Indochina was conducted by the French and then the United States on the alleged premise that all socialists were alike, were united, and posed a threat to the United States wherever they were. So peasants in Vietnam who only wanted their national independence posed such a threat to the United States and France that there were serious plans to use atomic weapons to suppress the Vietnamese struggle against France (McNamara 1995). The only reason the atomic bomb was not used was because the English opposed it. All of this is in McNamara's book. This is why I went to North Vietnam in 1965, and Du Bois traveled to the Soviet Union and China in the 1950s—to get the facts to oppose this insanity.

Du Bois Anticipated the Present

Du Bois anticipated neo-colonialism. He, Alphaeus Hunton, and the Council on African Affairs saw the strategy of neo-colonialism developing. The laboratory of neocolonialism was in the United States' support of France's efforts to maintain colonies in Africa. The whole point of the council was to educate the public and, unlike the early Pan-African conferences, to raise money to support the liberation struggle in South Africa. It turned out that during this time in the 1950s, Max Yergan, a member of the council and president of the National Negro Congress, was a paid agent for the government and kept them informed on our plans.

Was there a connection between the Cold War and Jim Crow's ability to continue in the South after the Second World War? Absolutely. The Cold War gave the federal government an excuse to abandon the New Deal programs after World War II, to ignore poverty at home, and to put off the political enfranchisement of blacks to some unknown future date. The exploitation of black people is fundamental to the history of the United States back through the colonial period of enslavement and up through the period of de facto enslavement (sharecropping and Jim Crow). Exploitation is not an aberration on the part of the nation. It is fundamental to the organization and conduct of this country. Du Bois not only understood this, he articulated it better and more often than anyone else in this [the twentieth] century. The brilliance of Martin Luther King, Jr. was that he turned the Cold War's Jim Crow on its head. By unmasking and making evident the South's fascist practices for the entire world to see on television, King turned Cold War politics against Jim Crow practices and interests. The South became an embarrassment to the United Sates in the ideological struggle against socialism—how could the United States stand for freedom, democracy, and liberty in the world community when black people in the South were denied these basic rights?

Du Bois saw the connection between the intensification of urban racial ghettoes and the Cold War. As it was with Jim Crow and the Southern poor, the Cold War was an excuse for abandoning the urban poor, who reflected capitalism's abuses more directly than anyone else. The high point of the New Deal was the possibility of eliminating the scandalous poverty of white and black people in this country—the richest in the world. This is what the early socialists, the CIO, the National Negro Congress and the later civil rights movement were about. Du Bois was aware of this and was also aware of what could have been done instead of spending billions upon billions of dollars on preparation for war, and the development and deployment of atomic bombs.

This is what the Stockholm Appeal, the Council on African Affairs, and the U.S. Communist Party were about—pointing this out and opposing such madness. "To ban the bomb" meant opposing Washington's foreign policy with its consequences in neo-colonialism, world poverty, and ghettoization at home. If Du Bois were here today, he would not speak of one of these realities without showing the connections, influence, and importance of the others.

The drug trafficking and self-destruction that we are witnessing today in poor black communities is not a new development, nor is it unconnected to economic exploitation overseas. Those today who see black drug trafficking and abuse as simply a domestic race problem, or as simply black people's moral or cultural problem would not be pleased to read Du Bois' comments on ghettoization in the 1930s and 1940s. As far back as 1924 Du Bois looked at and focused on the forces that created ghettoes rather than the self-destructive behaviors that followed in the ghettoes. Nothing like drug trafficking, that is both national and international in scope, simply happens and happens independent of powerful self-interests—ruling-class actions. When I was in North Vietnam, I was told that one of the ways the French tried to prevent the Vietnamese liberation movement from developing was by pumping drugs into Vietnamese communities and encouraging gangsterism—just like what we have in the United States today. The French deliberately tried to corrupt the Vietnamese youth. Those in power in the United States today welcome the present chaos among blacks. The power interests and their families are not being impoverished, raped, drugged, and murdered on the streets. While this goes on, there are no significant challenges from blacks. Any sober people with un-bought leaders and a history such as black Americans would immediately challenge ruling-class control.

Du Bois knew that the Cold War, ghettoes, poverty, capitalism and profits, black disenfranchisement, racism, and the Bomb were all unnecessary. These horrors are not in any of our interests to produce or defend, and, if left to our own choices, we would not have created them. These monstrous developments all exist so that the few can control and benefit from the many. One does not have to be a communist or even a socialist to know this and to oppose such interests. Du Bois more than anyone in this century had the potential to get this across to black and white people alike. This is why he was hated, why those in power tried to send him to jail, and why he was exiled in his own land. Martin Luther King was quickly moving to the same place that Du Bois had been for years, namely, that all of the demons are interconnected—the real exercise of power in the United States, domestic and international racism, capitalism, the war in Vietnam, and neo-colonialism.

King was assassinated because of his potential, like Du Bois, to challenge powerful interests and the institutions that mask them.

Du Bois' Final Years

In 1953, Du Bois' celebrated his eighty-first birthday while traveling in the People's Republic of China. Chairman Mao received Du Bois and his second wife, Shirley Graham Du Bois. Dr. Du Bois was traveling as a leader of the international world peace movement. After this trip, the U.S. government forbade him to travel outside the Untied States. The rumors and campaign against him, the government effort to discredit him, and the growing belief among domestic civil rights leaders that there was no connection between domestic and foreign issues, isolated Du Bois from the influence he had exercised for decades. The U.S. government also took Paul Robeson's, Shirley Graham Du Bois', and my passport as well. Not long after the travel restriction was imposed, Du Bois joined the Communist Party as a protest. He wrote a long letter explaining why he joined and what he expected—the letter is in the Du Bois correspondence. He knew that those who wanted the Cold War as a key to advancing domestic poverty and racism could not ignore his action. He wanted this gesture to be one of defiance.

In the fall of 1961 Du Bois and Shirley Graham left for Ghana. I drove them to the airport. In June of that year the Supreme Court upheld the McCarran Act, which permanently banned Du Bois from travel. He was already in the process of preparing to go to Ghana to edit *The Encyclopedia Africana* at Nkrumah's invitation. But there was a period of sixty days between the time the McCarran Act was upheld by the Supreme Court and when the travel ban came into effect. Fay and I attended an emergency meeting at the Du Bois home to support whatever they decided to do. Shirley Graham and Dr. Du Bois decided to pack up and leave within ninety days. A note was sent to Ghana to see if they could come early. The response from Nkrumah was that Ghana and Africa would be honored whenever they came and that they could come anytime. Travel money was raised. The airline tickets were purchased. Several thousand of his books were bought by Fisk University. Dr. Du Bois asked me to take the files of his correspondence, since I had already agreed to edit his work. In the files were 100,000 documents, unsorted. Fay and I spent over a decade just sorting and organizing these materials.

At the time of Du Bois' departure he was ninety-two years old. At the airport Du Bois told Jim McManus of *The Guardian,* who came to cover his departure, that *The Encyclopedia Africana* was to be ten volumes and that it would take him about a decade to do each volume. Of course, he said this in jest. Earlier that week, while Fay was delivering the airline tickets, she and Du Bois sat in the garden of the Du Bois home in Brooklyn. He told Fay that he would be so happy if he could just stay at his home in the United States. He knew then that his health would not permit his return.

It is false to assume that Du Bois went to Africa because he gave up the struggle to end racism and to end the insanity of capitalism and the Cold War. His plans to write *The Encyclopedia Africana* dated back to 1909, and finally he had a standing invitation from Ghana's President, Kwame Nkrumah, to come to Africa to begin this great work. The reason why Du Bois had to go to Africa to start *The Encyclopedia Africana* is because he simply could not get the project funded in the United States. He had stationery for the project for decades. Franz Boas was to be part of it. The closest he came to getting this project funded was in the 1930s, when the Phelps-Stokes Fund provided money for an *Encyclopedia of the Negro* (1945), edited by W. E. B. Du Bois and Guy B. Johnson. This book was just an outline of what an encyclopedia devoted to blacks should have been, and a call for the more comprehensive work that Du Bois wanted to do. *The Encyclopedia Africana,* devoted to the whole of African people's past and present, was the project that Du Bois was most eminently qualified to do, but had eluded him for his entire career. An offer to finally begin this project simply could not be refused.

If Du Bois' health had not failed him, he would have come back to continue the struggle and fight the travel restrictions. But he was not well when he left. After a long illness and period of hospitalization in England and Ghana, Du Bois wrote *The ABC of Color* (1963), twice. The first manuscript was lost in the mail between Ghana and the United States—we suspect the hand of the government in this. So he wrote the book again and lived to see it published. He also finished *The Autobiography of W. E. B. Du Bois* (1968). This manuscript was also lost for several years and surfaced after Du Bois had died.

Du Bois died in Ghana on August 27, 1963, on the eve of "The March on Washington." He was ninety-five years old. His funeral was an enormous state event. Every country on earth, except the United States, sent representatives. Nkrumah and the world were in tears at the loss of the great doctor.

Postscript

There are some frequent questions about Du Bois' life and career that are not answered directly in this short review and reflection. I would like to answer some of them here:

Does the loss of travel rights still stand? I sued the U.S. government for denying me a passport. This challenge went all the way to the U.S. Supreme Court in *Aptheker v. Rusk*. The Supreme Court ruled six to four in 1963 that Secretary of State Rusk was wrong in denying my right to travel and declared that part of the McCarran Act unconstitutional. Now anyone should be able to get a passport, even to Cuba.

What did liberation mean to Dr. Du Bois? His concept of liberation changed as his life changed. During his early years, it was opposition to Jim Crow, to the lynchings, and to the compromises of Booker T. Washington. In the second phase, it became more global as he became more socialist in his thinking, and he saw it as freedom from domestic and foreign political and economic colonialism. Then finally, after World War II, he was clearly a socialist and saw liberation was dependent on letting the world liberation movements run their course. To do so, he had to challenge the Cold War and educate as many people as possible of the Cold War's real underlying motives and goals. Within this sense of liberation came his desire to see African peoples united and able to determine their own destiny. It was very appropriate for the father of Pan-Africanism to challenge capitalism, imperialism, and their modern sheep's clothing, the Cold War.

What was Du Bois' socialism? Du Bois was much too independent, creative, and knowledgeable to be a follower of anyone else's socialism. He had his own. He was a member of the Socialist Party for only one year, and left because he could not change the party's racism. Du Bois' socialism was more conscious of the race issue. Many of the white socialists were racists. There were many in the dominant faction of the original Socialist Party who were notoriously racist. But their vision of some kind of civilization where you did not exist to exploit someone else, or just to make money was correct. This is the only conclusion any clear-thinking and moral person can come to—how can one believe and then support a system of profit for the few at the expense of the many? It was this thinking that led Du Bois to socialism by 1910. This is why he did not stay with the NAACP in 1934 once it accommodated itself to the system and when there was a real opportunity to institutionalize socialist reforms in the United States. A person who might have influenced Du Bois and many others in this thinking was Mary White Ovington. She was significant in what we then called "the Negro question" as well as socialism. Ovington was from a very wealthy family that disowned her because of her views, work, and Negro friends. She lived alone for many years in the Hotel St. George in

Brooklyn. She was a remarkable woman for whom Du Bois had the highest regard.

What is your response to Harold Cruse's portrayal of W. E. B. Du Bois in Crisis of the Negro Intellectual *(1967)?* When it was fashionable for black intellectuals to be members of the Party in the late 1930s, Du Bois was not. He had already arrived at his views on the Party. He wrote about this in *Dusk of Dawn* (1939). He states that the Scottsboro Boys could not have been saved without the great international campaign the Party mounted. This was not an attack on the Party. Du Bois in fact admired the Party's work, but believed that much of what we did was not practical and would not be implemented. Fay Aptheker believes that Du Bois then still had some faith in the United States and the New Deal. He was also an official of the NAACP, while most other black intellectuals were not. Du Bois' position in the late 1930s was close to the moderate socialism of Norman Thomas, whom Du Bois knew.

With regard to Harold Cruse, I have a great deal of difficulty with his work and not only because of its inaccuracy. It is in fact very inaccurate. He has some other agenda than letting the facts speak for themselves and his own problems. I was once the invited guest of the Association for the Study of Negro Life and History in Washington and spoke at their breakfast meeting. Charles Wesley was then president of the association and formerly president of Wilberforce College. He presided over this meeting. When I began to speak, Harold Cruse stood up and began to berate me and to criticize the association for inviting "this Jew." The audience began to murmur against him and finally he was led out of the meeting still yelling and waving his arms. Whatever was bothering him then is certainly reflected in his work.

How was Du Bois able to be such a prolific writer? There are several reasons. First, he believed intensely in seeing an anti-racist civilization in the United States in his lifetime and the liberation of his people. He had strong hope for the society we could have become, not what we are today. His hope was for all people to have enough food, shelter, opportunity, and other basics to be decent and not be compelled to turn on one another as we are now witnessing. Once Arthur Spingarn asked Dr. Du Bois, "why don't you go live in Paris?" Du Bois responded that "you don't understand me . . . you don't know why I work." Second, he was a disciplinarian. When it was time for class, the door was closed and locked. He also had tremendous self-control. I have seen Shirley Graham Du Bois lose her temper, but never Dr. Du Bois. Third, he had precise work habits and did his own research. Fourth, whenever he traveled, he would combine it with research, and whatever he was doing he always set aside time to write. Finally, he always had an excellent secretary. His long-time secretary, Irene Diggs, eventually got her Ph.D. in Havana with Du Bois' help and became a university professor. It is ironic that the racists had his books in the library, while he, along with all other blacks, were banned from going into the same libraries. Later in his life he dictated his works to his next secretary, Elizabeth Lawson, who transcribed from his dictation.

How did you come to edit the Du Bois papers? Dr. Du Bois asked me in 1946 to edit his papers and his work, and Shirley Graham Du Bois continued to support his request after he died. I was honored that he asked me. I have devoted most of my career to his contributions. There was a book published by the Howard University Press some years ago that claimed I was paid some enormous sum of money to edit the Du Bois papers. This is absolutely false. The fact of the matter is that the University of Massachusetts gave $100,000 to Shirley Graham Du Bois for the Du Bois papers at my urging. I was present when they signed the contract. Fay and I never owned the papers. For years we were trustees of the papers, which we kept in the basement of our Brooklyn home. I urged Shirley to get the papers out of our house, especially after our basement began to flood. The University of Massachusetts bought the papers from her, not from me. I never got a penny for them. Fay and I considered those papers to be sacred. We never got paid, never asked, and never expected money for our trusteeship.

What were Dr. Du Bois' work habits and how did he deal with his emotions? Du Bois was a driven man all the time I knew him and I got no sense that he had ever not been so. Though he was driven, he had a set routine. He always had breakfast, some fruit at most for lunch, and stayed calm. He went to bed at 10:00 P.M. sharp. If he was a speaker at an event and they did not call on him by 10:00, he would leave. He was a moderate eater. He smoked three cigarettes a day after each meal—no more and no less. He watched what he ate. Du Bois was very much aware of what his purpose was in life, and therefore, it was important that he take good care of himself. He was afraid of what would happen if he was not here. He owned a pistol most of his life, took good care of it and had a permit for it. Fortunately, he never had to use it. Though he stayed calm, he was not a mild man, he had anger, but did not display it. He was able to write and speak to get out his frustrations. Also he was able to organize and see results.

Mrs. Aptheker pointed out that the only time she saw him excited and really enthusiastic was in Moscow after he had just returned from China in the 1950s. Remember that Du Bois was a loner, a genius, and, though he was a well-trained scholar and social scientist, he was at heart a poet. He was exacting in all he did. We found among his papers little scraps written by Du Bois on how one is to conduct himself in life and in different situations. They were written as little poems and are now in a book published by the University of Massachusetts Press. The poems were written for his students. Some are a line or two and others are whole pages, dated around 1910. The book has been a best-seller and does well during Christmas.

How did he live to be ninety-five years old? Like everything else in his life, this was calculated. He was very conscious of longevity, and in fact, was a life-long member of a longevity institute. He went to their retreat every year, got advice from them, and he took vacations regularly. He began this routine in the 1920s after he had a kidney removed. Finally, he explained to us that the director of the institute told him that they had nothing else to teach him—by this time Du Bois was about ninety years old. He managed to live well and to ninety-five years of age and on one kidney for forty-six years.

Did Du Bois see any error in his views? He came to believe that the gradual use of the courts as a way to make social change—NAACP's approach—could not address the broad structural abuses of capitalism, imperialism, and racism. Du Bois believed that he had overrated the moral character and integrity of those who rose up from the masses to lead and to serve. He felt that he had underrated the power of bribery in many forms, both direct and subtle, to buoy off the "Talented Tenth." He realized that talent removed from the masses can be easily corrupted. This is why real social change over the long run must have mass involvement. A country as rich as this can afford to buy off most potential troublemakers. Each successive Pan-African congress was more radical and critical than the last. For most of his life, Du Bois had enormous faith in the power of reason. He believed that the truth was so manifest that it had to prevail and that the problems in this country could be overcome with reason. He came to see that this was not true. Those who control would not hesitate to corrupt anyone if it served their best interest, and were not moved by reason.

The point at which Du Bois realized the depth and depravity of those who rule was when the U.S. government put Ethel and Julius Rosenberg to death as spies for allegedly giving to the Soviets secrets to the atomic bomb.

The government knew damned well that Ethel was innocent and that they had been framed. There was not one Jew on the jury of a trial held in New York City. Only the judge and prosecutors were Jews, and after the guilty verdict, the judge and prosecutors were all rewarded with promotions. This was a monstrous act and it was at this point that Du Bois realized that those in control and who benefited from the Cold War would do anything to get their way. This was one of the reasons why Du Bois later joined the Communist Party in protest. The Rosenbergs' execution had a devastating effect on many people. Many left the Party shortly afterward, not out of fear, but because they had lost hope. They became convinced that there was no use, the system and those in control could not be changed.

The strategic value of the socialist extremes? It is necessary to take a radical and far-out stance in order to allow more moderate views to take a more progressive stance than they normally would. We on the left did this consciously and as a service to social change. For example, Social Security would have never happened without our extreme view. When U.S. Representative Lundeen originally called for Social Security in 1935, his call was dismissed outright. Lundeen was on the far left. The Party knew that such a radical measure would not be accepted. We served as the front line in advocating Social Security and, in doing so, created the conditions for a more moderate bill to pass. But without our extreme view, the moderate proposal would have been seen as too radical. This is how liberals can be seen as a restraining and moderate influence. This was the game. They knew it. We knew that those in power were not going to give us everything. But we created the conditions where they had to give up something to benefit the masses. This is the same in labor strikes, you ask for the maximum in order to get some improvements.

What this generation of Americans does not realize is that whatever they have inherited and enjoy such as Social Security, health care, unemployment insurance, work-place health laws, minimum wages, and universal education were gained through struggle. And if they plan to keep them or improve on them, *they* will have to struggle to keep them. All of the positive developments in this country were gained by mass radical struggle. Now that there is no Soviet threat, and the left is no longer effective, look at what is happening. Those in power no longer have a reason to maintain the social gains of the past. For these reasons, what we are facing today is without strong opposition with an alternative ideological base. The time is right for opposition to emerge. There is going to have to be a new national struggle, and black Americans will be in the forefront of it. This is not a nationalist statement.

It is a simple fact. Blacks have suffered more than any other group, except Native Americans, and are being put into a position where they have no choice. Blacks are also closer than any other group to knowing how the system works and what should be done about it. Part of having this advanced realization and knowledge lies in the life and writing of W. E. B. Du Bois.

I wish to close by stressing W. E. B. Du Bois' courage, his absolute and unquestionable integrity, his profound honesty, and his personal devotion to justice. Du Bois personified virtue.

This paper is based on videotape-recorded interviews of Herbert and Fay Aptheker by Benjamin Bowser and Deborah Whittle on June 5 and August 4, 1995.

References

Marable, M., 1986, *W. E. B. Du Bois: Black Radical Democrat*
McNamara, R., 1995, *In Retrospect; The Tragedy and Lessons of Vietnam*

EPILOGUE

The Historical Scholarship of Herbert Aptheker

ERIC FONER, JESSE LEMISCH, AND MANNING MARABLE

From a discussion at the Institute for Research in African American Studies at Columbia University, October 30, 1996

ERIC FONER: This is Eric Foner, and I'm here with Professor Jesse Lemisch and Professor Manning Marable for our discussion of the historical scholarship of Herbert Aptheker. I am professor of history here at Columbia University. Jesse Lemisch is professor of history at John Jay College of Criminal Justice in the City University of New York, and Manning Marable is professor of history and director of the Institute for Research in African American Studies at Columbia University. Let me begin by simply asking if anybody would like to talk about the impact of Herbert Aptheker's work on their own scholarship. To what extent have Aptheker's writings influenced your own? Would anyone like to say anything about that?

MANNING MARABLE: For an entire generation of young African Americans, our entry into learning about our own people's experience in this country was Herbert's *Documentary History of the Negro People in the United States.* There is no way that I can describe the extraordinary impact it had for young African Americans growing up in this country in the fifties and sixties. It was a constant reference work. Far more profoundly influential than Fanon's *Wretched of the Earth,* it gave us a concrete sense of the voices of black protest throughout history. It provided a living connection with Frederick Douglass and with W. E. B. Du Bois, with Martin Delany and Henry Highland Garnet.

It also gave us a sense of political continuity and possibility. And it also gave me, as an undergraduate student in the late sixties, a sense that history could be a profession where the critical rethinking of the past might shape possibilities for the future. Herbert Aptheker's work symbolized that effort to combine a scholarly pursuit with a political vision, based on understanding how people create their own history through struggle.

JESSE LEMISCH: Preparing for today's discussion, I thought about Herbert's direct influence on my work and on the work of others as well, not only through his books, but also through his pamphlets—for example, *Laureates of Imperialism,* and his work on Gunnar Myrdal, C. Wright Mills, and others. My book, *On Active Service in War and Peace: Politics and Ideology in the American Historical Profession* (1975), was directly influenced by the example of Herbert as intellectual historian detecting and taking apart ideology in the social sciences, particularly liberal ideology. Turning to his books, in particular *American Negro Slave Revolts,* I think that, for me, Herbert was Eric Hobsbawm and George Rudé and E. P. Thompson before I got to Hobsbawm, Rudé, and Thompson. I see this influence very directly in my dissertation, "Jack Tar v. John Bull: The Role of New York's Seamen in Precipitating the Revolution" (1962; Garland Publishing, 1977). In *American Negro Slave Revolts,* Herbert talks about "individual acts of resistance," and finds in slaves an alternate moral code. Hobsbawm addresses related themes, though in a somewhat different way. But at that point, I'm at Yale as a graduate student, and nobody is telling me anything about Hobsbawm, not to mention the potentially enormous relevance of his work for American history. Hobsbawm's notions—"primitive rebels" and "pre-political rebellion"—are very clearly foreshadowed, albeit in somewhat rough form, in Aptheker. The Rudé component in Aptheker is the notion that we should take the mob seriously, that we should see the rationality in violent behavior, and should look for the politics that are being expressed through riot. Aptheker, like Rudé, writes at a time when LeBon is still the dominant lens through which others see the crowd. With Aptheker, you have the assumption of rationality and the pursuit of causality.

Aptheker tells about what Thompson would later call "agency," which is, after all, the central New Left notion. The great irony in Aptheker is that this notion emerges from a Stalinist party that believes in iron-bound determinism. And yet, popular front ideology presents ideas of struggle. There is much to be said about Aptheker's work on slavery itself, but I do want to put his influence in the broadest context: I believe that it prepared me for

Thompson and the others, and later meshed with the experience of agency in the Movement of the sixties.

ERIC FONER: Let me just say that the way I encountered Herbert's work was a little different from the two of you because I didn't have to discover Herbert Aptheker. He was there, in that his books were in my house as I was growing up. His particular portrait of history was very much just taken for granted in the kind of Old Left household that I grew up in. *The Documentary History of the Negro People* was on our shelf, as were *American Negro Slave Revolts* and some of his books of essays on the abolitionist movement. The notion of lower-class people exercising agency in history was simply taken for granted. Like Jesse, I found it quite surprising when I became a history major at Columbia and then a graduate student that his work was totally unknown. Well, not unknown, but it was not taught. People knew about the book *American Negro Slave Revolts,* but the general point of view was that it was grossly exaggerated, that he had magnified little incidents into rebellions. The only scholar who adopted a different point of view was James P. Shenton, who actually assigned the book in a seminar that I took, to my good fortune, as an undergraduate, on the Civil War period. We actually read the book and took it seriously as a work of scholarship that had to be on the agenda for any discussion of slavery. His essays on abolitionism and particularly the emphasis on the role of African Americans in the movement had a lot to do with how I thought about abolitionism as an interracial movement rather than simply whites in the North helping blacks in the South.

Of course, in all of these areas, Aptheker's insights are now widely accepted. Everybody now accepts that resistance was a major, permanent feature of slave life, and that African Americans played a major role in the struggle against slavery in the North and South. These insights were off the radar screen of mainstream history for such a long time.

Let me pose another question in relation to this: what does it tell us about the history profession that Aptheker was blacklisted for so long? Both as a person, who could not teach for many, many years and as a set of ideas, blacklisted as well as the individual. Another way of thinking about it is, at what point did Aptheker cease being a nonperson as far as the official mainstream historical world was concerned?

JESSE LEMISCH: Well, remember that I have fairly direct experience of how long-lasting the blacklist against Aptheker was, through my experience in organizing, along with Marv Gettleman, the campaign to censure Yale—the Yale–Aptheker affair of 1975–76. When I first knew of Herbert back in the fifties, he was being denied employment at institution after institution. I grew up knowing about political discrimination in academia through his experience. I recall historian Norman Pollack introducing a lecture by Aptheker at Yale in around 1961. It was an act of courage just to do this. But 1975–76 was not the forties or the fifties, yet Yale's history department—with C. Vann Woodward playing the leading role—did a contemptible thing, long after McCarthyism, by blocking Aptheker's appointment in another department at Yale—an insignificant one-semester lectureship in a program whose standards had been met by such appointees as the sportscaster Howard Cosell.

MANNING MARABLE: There is another aspect of Aptheker's professional career as it relates to the field of African American history. Aptheker, for many years, was denied a formal academic position, until I believe 1969 or thereabouts. Herbert has told me that it took about twenty-five years after the time he received his doctorate at Columbia before he received at least a continuing appointment. But in traditional black colleges and universities throughout the 1950s and '60s, Herbert Aptheker's voice was heard and was a familiar voice interpreting the African American past.

There is a hilarious story that's been told to me by Gwen Patton. Patton was the head of the student government association at the historically black college, Tuskegee Institute. In the midst of the civil rights movement in the mid-1960s, the African American student movement looked to history, to black history, to try to understand the roots of their own struggle. Some students at Tuskegee were sitting around and they said, "You know, what we need is somebody who can really present black history from an activist's perspective." And they said, "Now there's this one guy, this black guy named Herbert Aptheker—let's bring him here." So they find his address and write him. He writes back and says, "I'll come to Tuskegee." Gwen's waiting there at the bus station in Tuskegee. This is 1964 and this white guy gets off this bus. Gwen's amazed, shocked—it's Herbert Aptheker. Aptheker delivers a stirring address before the students and he's accepted as part of the black liberation struggle. So, I suppose white academia's loss was the black community's gain.

ERIC FONER: We haven't yet mentioned another major part of his scholarly contribution, which is his work on W. E. B. Du Bois. Herbert Aptheker was very close to Du Bois toward the end of Du Bois' long life, edited three volumes of the letters and put out a multivolume edition of Du Bois' voluminous writings and book reviews and many other things. He has put back into print a vast array of Du Bois writings that were very difficult to find, as well as helping with the final autobiography. Do you think Aptheker's work is partly responsible for the revival of Du Bois? Because Du Bois was also more or less written out of history, for a while at least, among mainstream academics. What do you think the cumulative impact of all this work on Du Bois has been?

MANNING MARABLE: From a personal standpoint, Aptheker shaped my own development in a very profound way and the nexus was Du Bois. In 1979 I was a twenty-eight year old assistant professor at the University of San Francisco. Back in those days I was also a member of the *Socialist Review* collective and I was living in the Bay area. Herbert was teaching at Berkeley and somehow we made contact and every Monday evening at about five o'clock during the entire semester in the winter and spring of 1979 we had dinner together and we just talked about Du Bois. He told me all these stories about Du Bois, how he met him and the evolving working relationship. He had just finished the three-volume edited letters of Du Bois and he was working on other kinds of volumes. That sparked in me an interest in doing work on Du Bois that continues to this day.

ERIC FONER: I'll bet I know where you had dinner with him, because I was teaching as a visiting professor at Berkeley that spring and I used to meet him now and then. It must have been the International House of Pancakes. Herbert seems to be a creature of habit, at least when it comes to cuisine.

JESSE LEMISCH: Let me add two things to that. First, on the Du Bois papers: of course there is a continuing story of political discrimination when we get into the question of NEH funding for this project, leading up to the parsimonious conditions under which Herbert ended up doing this. It was impossible to pry funding loose, clearly because he was a Communist. Second, if I can return to *American Negro Slave Revolts,* the economism of the thing really gets to me. That is, he says at one point that you can graph rebellion against figures for economic depression. If anything, this is like Rudé (Thompson once said that if Rudé had been present at the Crucifixion, he would have counted the nails), but not at all like Thompson's "The Moral Economy of the English Crowd in the Eighteenth Century" (*Past and Present* 50 [February 1971]).

ERIC FONER: Although he does put in other factors. It is true that there is always a material base, as it were, for the incidents in *Slave Revolts.* He talks about demographic differences between different regions of the South in terms of ratio of the black and white populations. As a book written in the Marxism of the late thirties, it's very much grounded in a base-superstructure model.

JESSE LEMISCH: In his little piece about the British Communist Party Historian's Group, Hobsbawm talks about how they stayed away from C. L. R. James because he was a Trotskyist, and I think that Herbert's work, though influential on mine in a positive way, had a similar downside. Coming from that historiographical background, I was cut off from other influences, in particular James and the people around him. I did finally make contact with George Rawick and his important work, but I came late to the important notion of self-activity which emerged from these circles. Self-activity is not the same as agency, but they are connected concepts.

ERIC FONER: Let me ask you to be precise on that, because I'm not quite sure what the notion of self-activity actually means. I thought you said before, one of Aptheker's emphases was agency.

MANNING MARABLE: I suppose the way James would put it is that agency implics a form of intervention on the part of intellectuals, where activists construct a vehicle, an instrument of change. Self-actualizing activity from below is where the role of the radical intellectual is not an organizer from above, but as a catalyst, as a person who provides information or resources. But the masses themselves, through their own self-activity, create new structures, new possibilities. And that is how James saw the process of revolution unfolding. He and George Padmore, in writing about the Convention People's Party or intervening in Trinidad in the 1950s and the development of the people's national movement, attempted to think about political struggle as being generated by the activism from below of everyday working people. And the task of the social historian is to find that voice and to capture the expressions of people constructing their own history.

ERIC FONER: But wouldn't you say that elements, at least, are in *American Negro Slave Revolts?* Particularly regarding what we now call day-to-day resistance to slavery?

MANNING MARABLE: Yes.

ERIC FONER: In other words, how outright rebellion grows out of daily struggles. There are these daily struggles against slavery, which involve things that might not be considered resistance by some people—shirking work or breaking tools or making believe you're ill.

JESSE LEMISCH: But I think that's too easy a way out of the James–Aptheker conflict. As I said, there was indeed a form of agency in Aptheker's work, and it was important. But it would have been fruitful for my work to have been exposed to the Trotskyist alternative; here was an alternate Left, a whole other group of people and a different intellectual tradition utilizing other notions.

ERIC FONER: I'm sure that's right. As an active member of the Communist Party one would not expect Aptheker to be influenced by Trotskyist history. Although one thing I think we have to say about Aptheker and my uncle Philip Foner, another Old Left historian, is that one of their great strengths lay in the gathering of material. They were indefatigable researchers. Aptheker's *Documentary History,* my uncle's documentary collection of four volumes on Frederick Douglass, the documentary history of black labor which my uncle did—without funding from anybody, they dug up documents incessantly. Thanks to them, the material is there for people to use in whatever way they want. You can go through it from a different perspective. So, part of their contribution was unearthing this vast array of material, which was largely ignored by other historians. And, as all of us know, that takes a lot of work. It's not easy to do.

Let's move to one or two other issues. Jesse, you mentioned the pamphlet literature that Aptheker produced, some of which has been rediscovered of late. I see his critique of Myrdal cited very frequently now that we have just gone through the fiftieth anniversary of Myrdals' *American Dilemma.* What would you say is the contribution of his historical scholarship in that form?

JESSE LEMISCH: Aptheker, you know, wrote an extraordinary essay, or maybe it was a pamphlet, on Bridgeman, the physicist who questioned reality and causality. And much the same debate is taking place now, some forty years later, around postmodern antiscientism and denials of reality. Aptheker's piece on Bridgeman had a deep impact on me and helped to lay the foundations of my critical feelings about post-structuralism today. There is, in Aptheker, this older tradition of Marxist engagement with science. There was also Herbert's essay on Myrdal, his writings on C. Wright Mills, and a wonderful pamphlet called *Laureates of Imperialism,* which looked at N. S. B. Gras, the business historian at Harvard. He also criticized Allan Nevins; I use some of this in my *On Active Service in War and Peace.* Aptheker went through Nevins' 1940 book on Rockefeller and found interpretations that reflected the liberalism of the time, and noted that when Nevins put out a new edition in 1953, the sentences had been rewritten so that what in 1940 looked to Nevins like evidence of dissatisfaction by employees now become converted into a feat of industrial statesmanship by Rockefeller.

ERIC FONER: Perhaps this work ought to be gathered and published by somebody because it is pretty hard to get hold of right now.

MANNING MARABLE: The American Left between the early 1930s and the mid-1960s did not develop like the Left in Europe. Because of anti-Communism in the United States, the Left's intellectuals never found a home in the traditional academy. And so they were connected with trade-union movements, with political organizations. I'm thinking about black intellectuals; a good example would be Oliver Cromwell Cox. They found employment at historically black institutions, but they were always marginal to the liberal discourse which defined social analysis. So Myrdal could receive a great deal of money to carry out a social science study but somebody like Cox was never funded. But Cox, an unaffiliated black progressive, could at least get employment; people who were affiliated with the Communist Party could not. In a way we have never overcome that thirty years, that absence. In some respects, Aptheker's intellectual biography reflects the pervasiveness of anti-Communism in the sense that he felt the need to respond to all the ideological issues of his time. And so, if you look at the contours of his work in the 1950s and 1960s, you see polemics against Mills and conservative intellectuals and writings about the war in Vietnam and other kinds of concerns. It seems to lack focus, but the real issue for Herbert was practical engagement with both corporate liberalism and the Right. There were so few intellectual voices on the Left that he felt compelled to carry a great burden and respond to everything.

ERIC FONER: Here's an amazing fact of which I was unaware until I reviewed the third volume of the Du Bois letters edited by Aptheker for the *New York Times Book Review*. This was in the early 1980s, I believe. Aptheker told me that this was the first time any publication of his had been reviewed in the *Times*. As you pointed out, it took a long, long time for McCarthyism to die. Now it is true that in the 1980s, and I wonder if anyone wants to speculate on whether this has any broader significance, Aptheker finally began to get some recognition. There have been sessions at the Organization of American Historians convention devoted to his work. A book of historical essays assessing the impact of *Slave Revolts* has appeared. He has been on panels, commenting on the work of others. In other words, by the 1980s his work is being recognized and indeed celebrated. Does this mean that we have now put this unhappy episode behind us? Are we now able to pat ourselves on the back and say, "Okay, academe is no longer guilty of this kind of discrimination"?

MANNING MARABLE: I think that the academy became more comfortable with left history when the prospect, or perhaps specter, of a left alternative receded from the present. By 1989, as the Berlin Wall fell, some conservatives could openly embrace Aptheker because the real "danger" to civilization had passed.

ERIC FONER: But of course it's also true—and this raises another issue—that many people who were active in the New Left now hold academic positions and the obsessive anti-Communism of a previous generation of scholars was not part of their own politics. They had already in the New Left period rejected making anti-Communism a major hallmark of their point of view. And so, as they came to be an influential group in the historical profession, perhaps it's natural that they not consider Aptheker beyond the pale.

MANNING MARABLE: I think that is absolutely correct. By the time I was in graduate school at Wisconsin in the early 1970s, Herbert Aptheker's work was not assigned by traditional American historians. In fact, Genovese's work was sneered at and criticized. But there were younger liberal historians in the department who did assign Aptheker and Genovese, and the culture of the graduate students at the time was actively engaged in critical reflections on their work. It had a tremendous impact upon the work we did. As these people came into professional maturity within a decade or two, they greatly changed the shape of the curriculum, and Aptheker's voice was then heard.

ERIC FONER: Let me raise a question related to this. Do you think that it might be the case that work of Aptheker's variety is easier to accept if it is in the realm of African-American history, where there is a tradition of emphasizing struggle? He has other work which I don't think has really been assimilated. Work which makes class struggle the central point when it is not related to African Americans is harder to accept. Herbert has written books on the American Revolution, on the Civil War, which try to emphasize the class dimensions of these conflicts, and I don't think those works are assigned or cited nearly as often as those works on African American history. Take my uncle Philip Foner's work on labor history. It's known, of course, but much of the new labor history was based on criticizing the work of people like Philip Foner. It wasn't assimilated into new history the way that Herbert Aptheker's work was assimilated into a new generation of African American scholarship.

JESSE LEMISCH: There's another way of looking at that. Maybe a little less grim than what Manning has just said about the defanging of radical ideas.

When reality forced its way into academe with the black liberation movement, academics had to say, "Well we really have to take a second look at these things."

ERIC FONER: One thing I must say about Herbert Aptheker: when I was an undergraduate in 1960–61, when the blacklist was still very, very powerful, Herbert was extremely generous and also quite insightful and helpful. When I was doing an undergraduate senior thesis, here at Columbia, on the Free Soil Party—not the most central point in American history, perhaps—and he was at the New York office of the American Institute for Marxist Studies, I went down to talk to him about my work and get his advice. I found no bitterness. After all, I'm coming from Columbia, a place that would never allow him to teach. No, he wasn't a bitter person who was obsessed with the injustices that had been meted out to him. He was very open and generous. He told me, "Don't neglect the black component of the antislavery movement even though you are studying its racism. Don't neglect the way that some of these antislavery people are able to overcome prejudice, or at least compare their views to the degree of racism elsewhere in the society. Don't judge it by the standards of 1960." This was good shrewd advice from a historian to a student. It would have been very easy for him to retreat into a bitter sentiment that the academic world has not dealt the cards straight to him.

JESSE LEMISCH: I had a similar experience. With Aptheker, you see intense Communist political commitment and the strength that came from that tradition. I come from the New Left, which was (choose one): a) more in touch with its feelings, or b) self-indulgent. When I was blacklisted after being fired from the University of Chicago in 1966, and then from Northwestern in 1969, I looked at Herbert's experience, and I thought, "Jesus, how does this guy take it? You know they portray him as a monster, don't cite him except to attack him, revile him, don't give him a job, etc., etc." And my memory is that I went to visit him at the same place that Eric went, the American Institute of Marxist Studies in New York. Herbert is there, sitting in what can only be described as a bomb shelter, and necessarily so, given the threats against him. So I said to him (this is a classic moment of dialogue between New Left and Old Left—there ought to be a Currier & Ives print of this), "Herbert, how do you take it?" and he answers, "You redouble your efforts." I was impressed by his courage, but also struck by the evasion of the emotional reality. There must have been a lot of anguish around that kind of career. I do think, for instance, that Herbert was hurt by Woodward's attacks during the Yale–Aptheker affair in 1975 and 1976; he really thought that this alleged "gentleman scholar" would treat him as a gentleman.

MANNING MARABLE: But that's what strikes me about Herbert. His predominant characteristic is a great kind of peace. His willingness to engage in conversation with students, to listen to the concerns that they have, to think through problems of a senior's paper. The story you tell, Eric, I've seen happen when I taught at Colgate. I've seen it here at Columbia with one of my doctoral students, Tim McCarthy, who has maintained a steady flow of communication with Aptheker, and how Herbert has taken time to go over his essays and to talk to him about this or that issue in his dissertation. Herbert doesn't have to do that but that's who he is. That's a part of how he sees his commitment to the profession of history. I think it's the old small "c" communist where you really try to work with young people, those young people who have something to say that speaks to the history of struggle and the history of resistance. He has a remarkable history of being a constructive supporter of a whole series of generations of young people.

ERIC FONER: I don't think we should make Aptheker into a saint. This would be unfair to any person. I also remember talking to him after my first book was published and he complained, as many people might under similar circumstances, that I had not cited a particular work of his on the American Civil War. I didn't quite understand at the time that not citing Herbert Aptheker carries more meaning than not citing other people because it is, even inadvertently, joining in the conspiracy to ignore his work. I said, "Herbert that may be true, but I did cite your work on abolitionism here." And he replied, "Well nobody could write about your subject and not cite that." So, he has a healthy pride in his accomplishments.

Let me ask before we stop if there's any other aspect of his scholarship or career that anybody wants to put on the table . . . ?

JESSE LEMISCH: In 1969, which was the glory year of the radical caucus in the American Historical Association, two thousand people came to the business meeting. Somewhat inflated ideas of what the radical caucus planned had gotten around, and it seemed that everybody had advice for me. I had lunches, as the convention got started, separately with Herbert and with Gerda Lerner. From both, I got essentially the same advice. From Gerda: "Don't go too far too fast." I will always remember those words. Herbert lectured me against "adventurism." I think both of them, viewing the impending confrontation through Old Left lenses, underestimated the strengths of the New Left's approach. The Old Left was in many ways not a very radical place. I think we were right, but who knows?

Department of History, Columbia University (Eric Foner)
Department of History, John Jay College of Criminal Justice, City University of New York (Jesse Lemisch)
Institute for Research in African American Studies, Columbia University (Manning Marable)

Sources

These essays first appeared in a number of sources and formats.

Chapter 1: *Negro History: Its Lessons for Our Time* (New York: New Century), 1956.

Chapter 2: "Maroons within the Present Limits of the United States" was originally published as article of the same title in the *Journal of Negro History* 24:2 (Apr. 1939): 167–84.

Chapter 3: "The Negro in the Abolitionist Movement" first appeared in *Science & Society*, vol. 1, no. 1 (Winter 1941): 22–23; and vol. 1, no. 2 (Spring 1941): 148–72. Used by permission of *Science & Society*.

Chapter 4: "Militant Abolitionism" first appeared in *The Journal of Negro History*, 26, no. 4 (Oct. 1941): 438–84. Republished in *To Be Free: Studies in American Negro History* (New York: International Publishers), 1948. Used by permission of International Publishers.

Chapter 5: "Class Conflicts in the South" appeared in *The Unfolding Drama: Studies in U.S. History by Herbert Aptheker*, ed. Bettina Aptheker. (New York: International), 1978. Reprinted by permission of International Publishers.

Chapter 6: "Notes from Negro History: The Struggle Inside the Ranks" appeared in *Masses and Mainstream*.

Chapter 7: "The Negro Woman" first appeared in *Masses and Mainstream* 2 (Feb. 1949): 10–17.

Chapter 8: "The American Civil War: A Centenary Article" was first published as *The American Civil War* (New York: International), 1961.

Chapter 9: "Black-White Unity" from *Racism, Imperialism and Peace: Selected Essays by Herbert Aptheker*, ed. Marvin J. Berlowitz and Carol E. Morgan (Minneapolis: MEP Publications), 1987. By permission of MEP Publications.

Chapter 10: "Mississippi Reconstruction and the Negro Leader, Charles Caldwell,"

1937. In *To Be Free: Studies in American Negro History* (New York: International), 1948. Used by permission of International Publishers.

Chapter 11: "Literacy, The Negro and World War II" first appeared in the *Journal of Negro Education* 15 (1946): 595–602.

Chapter 12: *The Negro People in America: A Critique of Gunnar Myrdal's "An American Dilemma"* was published as a pamphlet. (New York: International), 1946. Used by permission of International Publishers.

Chapter 13: Introduction to *The Suppression of the African Slave Trade* (Millwood, N.Y.: Kraus-Thompson Organization), 1973.

Chapter 14: "Personal Reflections on W. E. B. Du Bois: The Person, Scholar, and Activist," interview by Benjamin Bowser and Deborah Whittle, appeared in *W. E. B. Du Bois: The Scholar as Activist,* ed. Rutledge Dennis (Greenwich, Conn.: JAI), 1996.

"Anti-Racism in U.S. History: The First Two Hundred Years," *Nature, Society, and Thought,* 2, no. 4 (1991): 463–81. By permission of MEP Publications, Minneapolis.

Index

HERBERT APTHEKER (1915–2003) was a Marxist historian who pioneered in the field of African American history and edited the letters and collected works of W. E. B. Du Bois. Aptheker wrote more than forty books and pamphlets on a wide range of political and intellectual issues. He was a member of the U.S. Communist Party from 1939 to 1961.

ERIC FONER is De Witt Clinton Professor of History at Columbia University.

MANNING MARABLE is Professor of History, Political Science, and International and Public Affairs at Columbia University.

BETTINA APTHEKER is a professor in the department of Feminist Studies at the University of California, Santa Cruz.

The University of Illinois Press
is a founding member of the
Association of American University Presses.

Composed in 10.5/13 Adobe Minion
with Meta display
by Celia Shapland
for the University of Illinois Press
Manufactured by Thomson-Shore, Inc.

University of Illinois Press
1325 South Oak Street
Champaign, IL 61820-6903
www.press.uillinois.edu